Unbelievable

The Gospel Texts in Narrative Tradition and Historical Context.

Unbelievable

The Gospel Texts in Narrative Tradition and Historical Context.

Willie Van Peer

IFF
BOOKS

Winchester, UK
Washington, USA

JOHN HUNT PUBLISHING

First published by iff Books, 2023
iff Books is an imprint of John Hunt Publishing Ltd., No. 3 East Street, Alresford,
Hampshire SO24 9EE, UK
office@jhpbooks.com
www.johnhuntpublishing.com
www.iff-books.com

For distributor details and how to order please visit the 'Ordering' section on our website.

ISBN: 978 1 80341 204 7
978 1 80341 205 4 (ebook)
Library of Congress Control Number: 2022934411

A CIP catalogue record for this book is available from the British Library.

Design: Matthew Greenfield

UK: Printed and bound by CPI Group (UK) Ltd, Croydon, CR0 4YY
Printed in North America by CPI GPS partners

We operate a distinctive and ethical publishing philosophy in
all areas of our business, from our global network of authors to
production and worldwide distribution.

Contents

Contents

Previous books

Stylistics and Psychology. Investigations of Foregrounding
London: Routledge, 2020 (reprint). ISBN 978-0367672461.

The Taming of the Text. Explorations in
Language, Literature and Culture
London: Routledge, 2017 (reprint). ISBN 978-1-138-68338-9.

(With Frank Hakemulder and Sonia Zyngier): *Scientific*
Methods for the Humanities
Amsterdam/Philadelphia: John Benjamins, 2012. ISBN 978-90-
272 3348-6.

The Quality of Literature. Linguistic Studies in Literary Evaluation
Amsterdam/Philadelphia: Benjamins, 2008. ISBN 978-90-272-
3336-3.

(With Max Louwerse): *Interdisciplinary Studies in Thematics*
Amsterdam/Philadelphia: John Benjamins, 2002. ISBN 978-90-
272-3888-7.

(With Seymour Chatman): *New Perspectives on*
Narrative Perspective
Albany, NY: SUNY Press, 2001. ISBN 0-7914-4788-X.

Preface

What do we know about Jesus of Nazareth? Not a great deal—but still enough to form an image of him and his followers, based mainly on the four Gospels. This book examines the historical origins of the Gospels: where and when they originated, how they differ and how they influenced each other, who the authors were, what is known about their intentions, and which precursors of those texts are known. In short, this book presents a cultural history of the book that so deeply influenced and still influences Western societies. The systematic study of the original texts of Christianity also provides answers to a number of pressing questions: Who was Jesus anyway? What did he undeniably say and teach, and what not? Who were his disciples? How did they deal with his ideas? Were there other prophets who were considered "competitors"? And how did his ideas enter or not enter into Christianity as we know it today?

Research into the historical sources of the Gospels is now some two hundred years old. But in the last few decades, new discoveries have been made that shed a remarkable light on Jesus and the genesis of early Christianity. It is not surprising that these insights are sometimes at odds with what most Christians believe. Therefore, it is the time to discover the true roots of the religion that shaped Western society.

One might think that in our highly secularized society these texts no longer play a role. But nothing could be further from the truth. With unfailing regularity there are reports in the media about Jesus and the Gospels. Then there are all kinds of "revelations" about the origins of Christianity. Or just google "Jesus" ... to see more than a billion hits. In short, despite massive secularization, the figure of Jesus and the texts of the Gospels continue to fascinate. But what is true about those stories? In most of them, the traditional image of Jesus with his apostles can be found. There is very little concerning the historical facts that permeates the perception of the general public. What, for example, are the authentic words of Jesus, and what are not? The famous statement "He that is without sin among you, let him first cast a stone at her" (John 8:7) was certainly not spoken by Jesus, because the whole story, beautiful as it is, did not actually happen.

Perhaps as a reader you are wondering how and why, in the twenty-first century, anyone would bother to find out where two-thousand-year-old texts come from. Maybe because of an overdose of curiosity? For me, it all started in 1993, when I was on sabbatical at Stanford University in California. During one of my many visits to the university bookstore, my eye fell on an intriguing title: *The Lost Gospel: The Book of Q and Christian Origins* by Burton L. Mack. I bought it, took it home, read it overnight and was so fascinated that I started reading just about everything on this topic that I could lay my hands on. Ever since then, I have been going through life with a perhaps curious pursuit: reading up on the true origins of Christianity.

I myself am no specialist in the field—except that I've been trained as a philologist, have a Ph.D. in linguistics, and have been deeply involved with the placement of literary texts in cultural contexts. In this book I base myself mainly on secondary literature in English, and some in German. At first sight this seems odd, because research into the historical roots of the New Testament originated largely in Germany. But an independent secular study of the texts has developed much further in the English-speaking world. And that is exactly the purpose of this book: to submit a nonpartisan account of this history. The book does not judge faith or religion; I cherish the freedom we all have in matters of faith. Instead, this is about the history of texts, about critically examining them without literally believing them.

So, what is the New Testament about? It contains 27 "books":

the four Gospels (Matthew, Mark, Luke, John),
the Acts of the Apostles,
the letters of Paul (14 in all),
the letters of James, Peter (two), John (three), Judas, and the book of Revelation.

The question of whether all of these books are authentic will be discussed in more detail later (some of them are not). Please keep in mind that no original texts exist. Everything printed in your copy of the New Testament is based on copies of copies of copies—and no one knows how many copies lead back to the original. And anyhow, what would an original be? All kinds of texts circulated after the death of Jesus, and most of them were based on oral tradition, on stories passed on by word of mouth (see in more detail in chapters 7 and 8). So the New Testament is largely based on stories that were told and later written down, always with adjustments and adaptations. For this reason, we need to travel back from the written texts we possess to what happened originally. It promises to be an interesting journey!

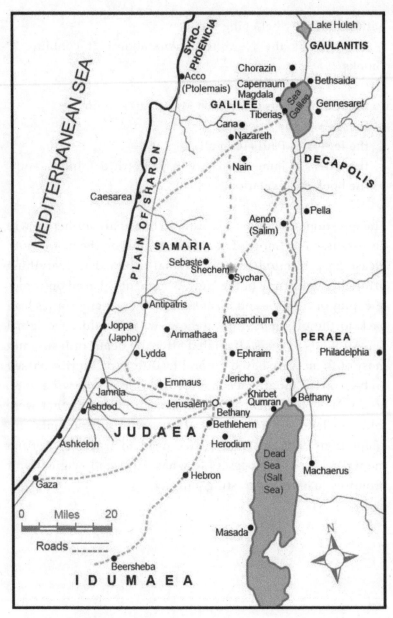

Map of Palestine at the time of the New Testament

Introduction

In the Beginning Was the Word

This is a book about the origins of a book known as the New Testament. The title, *Unbelievable*, is intended to make readers think. I once asked both believers and nonbelievers if they knew where the real New Testament lay. It soon turned out that no one could really answer this simple question. They made a wide variety of suggestions, ranging from "certainly somewhere in Rome," or "in the Vatican, presumably," to "maybe in a locker in the Pope's bedroom?" But most people admitted not knowing the answer—to never having considered the question at all. In order to provide a meaningful and differentiated answer to that question, this book has been written.

Why is the New Testament so important?

Why is it so important to know how the New Testament came into being? You probably don't walk around every day with the New Testament in your pocket. But it's a text that has had a profound and lasting influence on society and culture. My respect for religion is grounded in it. I would not want to miss the cathedrals, the paintings by Rogier van der Weyden, or the medieval Madonna statues. Even less would I want to miss Bach's *St. Matthew Passion*, or the mystical poems of Meister Eckhart or Hadewych. These are undoubtedly "peaks of depth" in European culture. Even if one is unfamiliar with the text of the New Testament, its ideas form the basis of Western culture. It lies beneath some of the most important principles on which society is based: the principle of reciprocity, the intimate connection between freedom and truth, the principle of individual responsibility, and the practice of consensual marriage.

The principle of reciprocity

In Western cultures, the principle of reciprocity is the primary basis for relationships between people. Traditionally, it is also called the "Golden Rule" and can be found in the New Testament: "Therefore all things whatsoever ye would that men should do to you, do ye even so to them" (Matt. 7:12) and "As ye would that men should do to you, do ye also to them likewise" (Luke 6:31).

In the eighteenth century, this principle led Immanuel Kant to his famous "categorical imperative." But his formulation goes one step further. Ultimately, according to the Golden Rule, a criminal could persuade a judge that he should be acquitted ... "After all, Your Honor, do not do to others what you would not want to be done to yourself." In other words, the Golden Rule still allows for an egocentric interpretation. But this is no longer the case with the categorical imperative, which states: "Always act in such a way that your own behavior becomes a general rule, which everyone has to act upon."

A second formulation of Kant's is that one should always treat people as an end, never as a means to an end. According to Kant, the two formulations amount to the same thing: the general principle takes precedence over one's own preference. In his 1785 work, *Grundlegung zur Metaphysik der Sitten* (Groundwork for the Metaphysics of Morals), Kant illustrates how (and why) the categorical imperative works, with the following example. Suppose a man is compelled to borrow money by necessity. He knows that he cannot pay the money back, but also realizes that he will not be lent any money unless he firmly promises to pay it back at a certain time. He intends to make this promise, but is still conscientious enough to ask himself, "Is it not contrary to law and duty for me to help myself out of trouble in this way?" If he chooses to do so after all, his maxim would be: If I believe I am in need of money, I will borrow money and promise to repay it, even though I know that this will never happen. This principle of self-benefit may well be compatible with my future well-being, but the question now is whether it is justified. So I turn the claim of self-benefit into a general law and question what the situation would be if my maxim became a general law. Then it dawns on me that my maxim could never count as a general law of nature and agree to itself, because it would then necessarily contradict itself. For the generality of a law by virtue of which anyone who thinks they are in need can make a promise without the intention of keeping that promise would make it impossible to promise anything at all. No one would believe that anything had been promised, and would regard any statement to that effect as meaningless.

What is to be made of this principle of reciprocity? In Western legal systems, one's rights are limited to those which are also given to others. One cannot claim a right that would in principle be denied someone else, such as the right to divorce your spouse and at the same time deny your spouse that right. This probably seems self-evident. But that's precisely why it is important to realize that it's not evident at all. There is no compelling reason to assume it is. One has only to read a newspaper to see that there are enough societies where this principle does not apply. For instance, in the country with the most inhabitants on earth, one group, the Communist Party, arrogates to itself rights that it systematically denies the rest of the population. The principle of reciprocity does not apply in today's China. This is all the more astonishing because the classic work that defined Chinese norms and values asserted this very principle of reciprocity. The *Analecta* of Confucius (number 15.24) literally reads: "Zigong asked: 'Is there any one word that can serve to live a person's whole life?' The Master answered, 'Should it not be reciprocity? What you do not want for yourself, do not do to others.'"

The principle of reciprocity in Confucius is further disregarded in this book, because there has been too little interaction between Confucian and Christian doctrines over the past millennia. But what about the other religions with which there has indeed been much interaction, namely Judaism and Islam?

To begin with Judaism, at first glance there seems to be such a principle in force. As it says in Leviticus, "Thou shalt not defraud, neither rob him" (Lev. 19:13), and "Thou shalt not defraud ... stand against the blood of thy neighbor" (Lev. 19:16). From this, one might conclude that the principle occupies an important place in Jewish religion. But, as always, one must pay attention to the context. The situation becomes clear in the previous verse: "Thou shalt not hate thy brother. ... Thou shalt not avenge, nor bear any grudge against the children of thy people, but thou shalt love thy neighbor as thyself: I am the Lord" (Lev. 19:17-18). It is clear that the word "neighbor" is meant here in an ethnocentric sense, in that you must love your Jewish neighbor as yourself. Maybe Jesus also meant the word in this sense. But in later Christianity its scope was generalized. In any case, in Christianity "neighbor" means *all* people, regardless of their ancestry, descent, or the group they belong to. I know of only one passage in the Old Testament in which there is a clear reciprocity with Gentile people: "But the stranger that dwelleth with you shall be unto you as one born among you, and thou shalt love him as thyself; for ye were strangers in the land of Egypt" (Lev. 19:34). Here it is unmistakable that non-Jews are referred to. One could still argue, however, that it involves a quid pro quo; they are "paying back" the hospitality they have enjoyed. But this is a long way from the universal principle of reciprocity as expressed in Christianity.

What about the Golden Rule in Islam? This question has a relatively simple answer: neither in the *Qur'an* nor in the *Hadith* is the Golden Rule found in an explicit form. Of course there are verses where the text admonishes believers to be kind to each other. For instance, in Sura 4, verse 36 it says:

> be virtuous toward parents and kinsfolk, toward orphans and the indigent, toward the neighbor who is of kin and the neighbor who is not of kin, toward the companion at your

8

side and the traveler, and toward those whom your right hand possess.

(All quotations from the *Qur'an* are from *The Study Quran*, ed. Seyyed Hossein Nasr. New York: HarperOne, 2017.)

But obviously this is far from the universalistic ethics that prevailed in early Christianity.

So here is the seriousness of the situation: neither of the other two religions of the book proclaims, let alone recognizes the principle of universal reciprocity. Given the political constellation of nations built on these religions, it can only be concluded that we are dealing with fundamentally different cultures. This is not to say that bridges between these different cultures cannot be built, but it is good to realize how different the foundations of these cultures are.

In short, it seems that it was Christianity that promulgated the principle of the Golden Rule. Over time, this passed seamlessly into the legal traditions of the West (at least in theory; in practice it often left much to be desired). Judaism and Islam, however, do not subscribe to the principle of reciprocity even to that extent. But there is more.

The principle of truthfulness

Another foundation developed by Christianity concerns the intimate link between freedom and truth. Voltaire wrote in 1769, in his *Histoire du Parlement de Paris* (History of the Paris Parliament), that knowing and speaking truth is tied to freedom. Anyone who is prevented from thinking freely cannot proclaim the truth. In Hitler's Nazi Germany one could not speak the truth without risk to one's own life and that of one's family. This close connection between truth and freedom is explicitly stated in the New Testament in the Gospel according to John: "And ye shall know the truth, and the truth shall make you free" (John 8:32). Here, the way to truth was paved. The insight was restated at the time of the enlightenment by John Stuart Mill in 1859 in his book *On Liberty*. There, Mill explains that a search for truth is impossible if complete and unconditional freedom of speech is not guaranteed: "Complete liberty of contradicting and disproving our opinion is the very condition which justifies us in assuming its truth for the purpose of action" (Penguin edition 1981, p. 79).

Early Christianity focuses on the notion of truth: there is only *one* god; there is only *one* faith, and therefore only *one* truth. Everything else is error and lies. Perhaps this pursuit of truth already carried the germ of later scientific development, which in fact took place only in the Christian West. In contrast to the other religions of the book, it is in Christianity's worldview that the notion of truthfulness is central.

A number of texts in the Jewish religion advise against lying. For instance, in Leviticus: "Ye shall not steal, neither deal falsely, neither lie one to another" (Lev. 19:11). But given the tribal nature of this religion, the question arises whether this commandment also applies with regard to Gentiles.

If one goes searching in the sacred texts of Islam for a statement in which lying is disapproved of, one will return empty-handed because there is no such verse in the *Qur'an*. One of the few verses in which the word "true" turns up is Sura 9, verse 119: "You, who believe! Reverence your Lord, and be among the truthful." However, the previous verse clarifies that the statement concerns three loyal servants to the prophet who did not give in to the enemy. So "true" here means something closer to "loyal." The *Qur'an* does not praise truthfulness, nor does it specifically place a prohibition on lying.

The principle of truthfulness, like that of reciprocity, owes its existence largely to the New Testament. There is no other book that has so fundamentally influenced Western dealings with truth. Certainly other important books have been written, and much could be said about each of them, but none has left as deep a mark as the New Testament. Admittedly, Jewish and Arab cultures have indirectly influenced Western culture, and its legal system is indebted to Roman law and the Code Napoléon. And then there are the countless movements for social justice, some Christian in inspiration, but also many secular ones, culminating in socialism. In short, Christianity is one of the undeniable foundations of our society.

The principle of individual responsibility

Individualism is another consequence of Christianity, in that each person is responsible for their own actions. The work of Geert Hofstede, one of the most frequently cited social scientists, is significant in this respect. His groundbreaking research in 1971 for IBM across 70 countries, with more than 100,000 participants, established a framework of the profound differences between national cultures which he termed "cultural dimensions." One of these dimensions is the difference between individualistic and collectivistic cultures. In the list below, a sample of countries (nationalities) are ranked according to the extent to which individualism is a central value in that culture. The index ranges from 0 (purely collectivist) to 100 (purely individualistic):

91 United States
90 Australia
89 Great Britain
80 Canada
80 Netherlands
80 New Zealand
78 Belgium
46 Morocco
41 Iran
38 Arab countries
27 East Africa
20 West Africa
14 Pakistan

As can be seen, Christian countries are at the top of the list, while non-Christian countries score lowest. It is true that there are some conflicting scores here and there, especially in South America, but in general it is clear that individualism ranks high in cultures that underwent the influence of Christianity.

The principle of consensual marriage

In addition, Christianity has revolutionized marriage mores. This relationship in cultures formed by Christianity differs greatly from marriage in most other cultures. For example, already from the sixth century onward, the Catholic Church emphasized consensual marriage. By elevating marriage to a sacrament, its voluntariness became central. James Q. Wilson sums up the historical roots of this attitude as follows:

> Throughout the Middle Ages, the church increasingly emphasized its view of the marriage as the voluntary "union of two hearts" acting in response to affection. The consent of the betrothed, initially advanced as an addition to parental consent, in time came to take the place of it. In this, the church set itself against lay opinion, clan power, and feudal practice and, perhaps unintentionally, against the long-term prospects for male dominance of the conjugal pair.
> (1993, p. 203)

Of course this is a somewhat flattering picture that does not mention the fact that often parents forced their daughters to marry particular men of status. But all in all, there was a reasonable freedom of choice of partner in Christian cultures, certainly when compared with other cultures.

This view of marriage became further reinforced by the worship of Mary in Catholic countries. As far as I know, hardly any other cultures have so abundantly depicted the relationship between mother and child as those shaped by Christianity. The countless images of the Madonna show the affection a mother feels for her child. In my opinion, this also explains why Christian societies hardly have any arranged marriages. In these societies partners choose each other in principle on the basis of mutual attraction, and they do so as free individuals. William Goode (1963) concluded, in his monumental study of family structures in different cultures, that "for the past thousand years the Western family systems have been very different from those in China, Japan and the Arab countries" (quoted in Wilson, p. 207).

Overall, the New Testament grounds and feeds one's sense of identity. Without it, I would not be myself. The principle of reciprocity, the bond between truth and freedom, the centrality of the individual, and marriage as a voluntary union between adults who choose each other out of affection, are all thanks to the New Testament—as are the thousands of beautiful works of art, literature and music, inspired by its stories and its spirituality. However, a problem remains.

The problem of church authorities

A hierarchy arose early on in Christianity. Initially, after the death of Jesus, it consisted only of James, his brother, and the first followers. But gradually the need arose for an overview of which groups of followers existed, where they were based, and what they believed. As the number of groups of Christians grew rapidly, the need for some form of systematic control increased, sometimes urgently, because great differences in theology arose between various Christian groups, for instance on the question of the extent to which Jesus was man and/or god. So bishops (literally "overseers") were appointed, to make sure that all Christians shared the same faith. In this way, the church hierarchy was born.

The task of these church authorities was to protect the faith from "errors," based on the principle of truthfulness. The history of these ecclesiastical authorities is complex, and characterized by both positive and negative aspects. On the one hand, the four principles just mentioned were guaranteed by church leadership. On the other hand, religious authorities have been responsible for terrible atrocities, such as the extermination of the Cathars, the persecution of witches, and the gruesome religious wars. The Catholic Church condemned the use of torture only with the encyclical of Pope Pius VII in 1816. It admitted the inhumanity of slavery when, under the pressure of social developments, it no longer dared to do otherwise. Pope Pius XII never condemned the atrocities of the Nazis. He could have excommunicated the Nazi leaders, as he did so many who dared to express a dissenting opinion toward the Vatican. But no Nazi, not even Hitler, was ever excommunicated for crimes against humanity. The recent opening up of the Pius XII archives leaves no doubt that the Catholic Church knowingly refused to support the Allies in their condemnation of Nazi barbarity. It is important to keep all of these facts in mind.

An ecclesiastical leadership is, of course, conservative by its very nature, for its task is to preserve what is considered to be the true faith, and to keep out whatever contradicts it. Throughout history, this conservatism has led to a hardening of positions, and a resulting rigidity in church leadership—with disastrous consequences for its credibility. The appendix to this book gives a brief overview of one such debilitating conflict, the Galileo case, in which church leadership could have averted a loss of face, but seriously damaged its own image by extreme adherence to literal interpretations of biblical texts. The fact that this was about a scientific matter is irrelevant. The loss of face was caused by ill-perceived and stubborn adherence to dogma. In the course of this book I will show how, on other points too, church authorities are often at odds with scholarship.

However, this book is not intended to be a reckoning with the mistakes and cruelties of the Christian church. For that, one can consult the monumental works of Karlheinz Deschner, *Christianity's Criminal History* (10 volumes, 1986-2013). But neither is this intended to encourage the reader to live a pious life. No doubt the texts of the New Testament may induce a moral or religious lifestyle. Commendable as that may be, it is not what this book is about. My purpose is exclusively to present the results of sound scholarly research, even if they run counter to the current views of religious opinion makers.

One thing is asked of you, in reading this book, and that is to put aside the view proclaimed by many religious opinion makers that the texts of the New Testament were written or inspired by God. The reason for this is simple: those in scholarship do not consider supernatural explanations. If there is a solar eclipse ring, it is not explained as a divine decision. Research does not look for supernatural explanations; it searches for the most convincing, most probable natural causes, which can be controlled by anyone wishing to do so. The New Testament from this perspective is the work of humans. And all human work is imperfect and not without error. However, the leadership of the Catholic Church (and to a lesser extent that of Protestant denominations) declares that it is infallible in matters of faith. In doing so, it repeats the mistake it made with Galileo Galilei four hundred years ago.

How did the New Testament come into being? For the vast majority of people, this question is still answered by tradition—which has, however, been largely debunked by recent research. It is precisely these distorted representations that this book aims to expose. Why? Because a cultural asset derives its value from the way it was created. It is important to know that there was a Holocaust, that women were oppressed in the past, that people were sold and exploited as slaves. If one doesn't know about the past, it is difficult to judge the present, and one will be ill-prepared for the future. Enlightenment is needed. If we want to understand how the

New Testament came into being and laid the basis for our social structure, we will have to confront its history head-on.

Faith versus research?

It is exactly here that a paradox arises. Despite the central place of the New Testament in society, there is much confusion, not to say ignorance, about its origins. The bibliography at the end of this book lists several publications on the subject, all state-of-the-art research from a non-theological perspective.

Two remarks need to be made here. The first concerns the aim of studying the Bible. It is possible to treat the New Testament as a guide to one's life; groups who study the Bible usually start from this premise. Such groups consist mostly of believers who read the texts in a spiritual sense. They want to learn from the reading for their own lives, for a deepening of their faith, for a higher spirituality. There is nothing to say against this, but it is not the purpose of the present book. Although this book also studies the Bible, its express intention is to illuminate the *history* of the New Testament from a scholarly perspective. To this end I draw on various disciplines: history, archaeology, linguistics, anthropology, cultural studies, and also on medical science, when discussing the execution of Jesus. A number of things that are said in the New Testament about the suffering of Jesus, for example, are medically speaking, virtually impossible. All these disciplines together inform one about the background of the texts contained in the New Testament. Providing this information is the very first and most important purpose of this book.

The second remark I wish to make concerns the neutrality of this endeavor. In no way does the book attempt to open up a polemic of any kind. The material contained in this book is completely self-evident to professionals in the field. Where there are ongoing discussions about specific things, this will be explicitly stated in the text. Nevertheless, as a reader, you may still be shocked by what you read. This is probably because the relevant research results have not penetrated broad layers of society. Here is yet another reason for distributing this knowledge: it is largely lacking (or has been hidden) from public discourse. Again, this is mostly because of church politics. As Robert Funk and his collaborators of the *Jesus Seminar* aptly note: "The church appears to smother the historical Jesus by superimposing this heavenly figure on him in the creed: Jesus is displaced by the Christ" (Funk 1993, p. 7).

A completely different question you may ask yourself, as the reader, is whether there is a danger that this research may cause you to lose your faith, or that you can no longer believe the texts of the New Testament. The short answer is "no." If one gains a better understanding of the origin and background of these texts, one's awareness of its value will grow. One can compare it to other studies. Does my appreciation of Shakespeare diminish when I study his texts attentively? Probably not. Does a student of art history find Michelangelo's sculptures less beautiful? Does a musicologist love Mozart's music less? Does a doctor have less admiration for the human body? Is the universe less interesting when you have insight into the structure of matter? We can go on like this for a while. But the core of the argument is clear. A deeper insight into a subject usually increases one's admiration for it. So it is with the history of the New Testament. The more one understands how it came into being, the more one may appreciate it.

This insight, however, can be at odds with the dogmas that ecclesiastical authorities impose on their faithful. Apparently church institutions like to keep the results of research secret, or try to disprove such results. The deeper reason for this lies in the mystification these authorities often associate with biblical texts. It is not the task of church authorities to disseminate academic information, for sure. But at least they should be expected not to cover up research results — which they do. A good example is the so-called virgin birth of Jesus. As will be seen in Chapter 8, the oldest texts in the New Testament blatantly contradict the virginity of Jesus' mother. Several such distortions presented to believers are disproved not only by research, but often also by the "holy" texts themselves.

One could argue, though, that a scholarly study of the New Testament involves a certain disenchantment, leading to a more sober view of the matter. This may make the New Testament less mysterious, less euphoric, less unique. It may also make the New Testament stories less like fairy tales. This disenchantment of the world has been going on for some time now (ever since the scientific revolution of the seventeenth century). Ultimately, everyone has to choose whether to believe in an enchanted or a disenchanted world ... I myself believe that disenchantment actually reveals the deeper sense of things.

But there is yet another reason why this book need not undermine one's religious faith. After all, "faith" can also mean a conviction that inspires action, something one may call a "commitment" such as to a more compassionate world, to a reduction of poverty—or, a typical New Testament attitude—to work toward greater human compassion. Such a commitment does not disappear when one finds that the official church line denies or obfuscates scholarly knowledge. This finding sheds light on how the church functions, not on one's own convictions.

At this point the reader may wonder if such a thing as "research" on the New Testament exists. Yes, it does, and it is in fact quite old. Some five hundred years ago, Erasmus of Rotterdam undertook the task of first publishing the complete text of the New Testament in the original language (in 1516). That publication was the beginning of a gradual but profound reflection on and research into the origins of that text. About a hundred years later, as a young man, Spinoza raised questions about the many "miracles" in the Hebrew Bible. And from that moment on, a steady stream of careful investigation leads to the present. But one should not forget that knowledge is constantly evolving, so that in the future, current findings will be replaced by better ones. For instance, through new texts being discovered, a whole new light is being shed on the genesis of the New Testament. Such discoveries cannot be foreseen. And they are in the nature of scholarly research.

Why is this research important? Because it brings to light discoveries that go against one's everyday views on the New Testament. In order to form some idea about the content of the texts for yourself, here is a short quiz that allows you to familiarize yourself with some basic facts.

A small quiz

Here are 12 questions, if you like, because according to tradition, Jesus had 12 followers. The intention is not to give yourself marks, but to sharpen your attention to particular facts, which will be discussed later. You will find the list of answers shortly after the quiz. You can, of course, start by looking up the answers right away. But then you are robbing yourself of the opportunity to explore your own thoughts. So I encourage you to challenge your own knowledge against that of the experts. Here are the questions:

1. In what language was the New Testament written?
2. How many brothers did Jesus have?
3. What was Jesus' last name?
4. Which New Testament text(s) is/are the oldest?
5. How many manuscripts of the New Testament exist? (A manuscript is a handwritten text, written before the invention of printing in about 1450 by Johannes Gutenberg.)
6. When does the oldest manuscript of the complete New Testament date from?
7. And when does the oldest manuscript of the Old

Testament date from?

8. Did Jesus say of himself in public that he was King of the Jews?
9. Did Pontius Pilate really live?
10. Who provided the current world position of Christianity?
11. Was Jesus ever in Egypt?
12. When does the English version of the New Testament date from?

Numbers are used to refer to a specific piece of Gospel text. The first digit is the chapter; the numbers after the colon refer to the verse lines. So a reference like "Mark 1:2" means the second verse line of the first chapter of the Gospel of Mark. In English, the King James Version (KJV), also called the King James Bible, is the best known, and it can be consulted online at https://kjvonline. org/new-testament. Some editions also have explanations of text passages here and there. But if you really want to study the text, you should consult the critical edition of Nestle-Aland (2012).

But now to the answers to the quiz questions:

1. In what language was the New Testament written?
I will elaborate on the reasons for this later in the book, but the fact is that the whole of the original text of the New Testament is in Greek. It is not the Greek that is spoken in Greece today, nor of Homer and Plato, but that of Greek antiquity. By the time Christianity emerged, the Greek language had changed somewhat, so that this variant of the language is now referred to as "New Testament Greek."

2. How many brothers did Jesus have?
It is not known exactly how many, but he had at least four (James, Joseph, Simon, Judas). He also had sisters, but their names are not recorded. If you are surprised by the answer,

refer to the text of the New Testament itself (see Mark 6:3 and Matt. 13:55-56).

3. What was Jesus' last name?

Ordinary people had no surnames at the time. Other indications were used, for example, someone's profession, like Joseph "the carpenter" or John "the Baptist." This is not so strange when one realizes that many contemporary surnames are also derived from professions such as "Smith" or "Baker." Place names were also used, so reference is made to Jesus "of Nazareth." Christ was by no means his surname! The word "Christ" originated in texts written after his death.

4. Which New Testament text(s) is/are the oldest?

The Gospel according to Mark is the oldest of the Gospels, but the authentic letters of Paul were written some twenty years before Mark's Gospel. In fact, a number of Paul's letters were not written by him, but by someone else who usurped his name. So they are forgeries. I will come back to that later. In any case, the real letters of Paul are the very oldest texts in the New Testament. They were written before the Gospels even existed.

5. How many manuscripts of the New Testament exist?

It's not known exactly how many there are. At the moment there are some 27,000, to which new manuscripts are regularly added! For an overview of the study of these manuscripts, consult Nongbri (2018).

6. When does the oldest manuscript of the complete New Testament date from?

The first complete text of the New Testament as we know it today dates from the middle of the fourth century (later included in the *Codex Sinaiticus*). More about this later.

7. And when does the oldest manuscript of the Old

Testament date from?

Until recently, the Old Testament was dated from around the year 1000, namely as the *Aleppo Codex* (c. 920) and the *Leningrad Codex* (c. 1008). The discovery of the Qumran (or Dead Sea) Scrolls throws a new light on this, because about a quarter of those texts come from the Old Testament, so the Hebrew Bible, and therefore antedate the previous dating by almost a thousand years.

8. Did Jesus say of himself in public that he was King of the Jews?

Certainly not—nowhere in the New Testament. This is important for understanding the role of Judas; see Chapter 9.

9. Did Pontius Pilate really live?

Definitely. I will provide convincing proof of this in Chapter 2.

10. Who provided the current world position of Christianity?

Paul, who was neither an apostle nor did he ever meet Jesus. But without him, Christianity as we know it today would not have come into being.

11. Was Jesus ever in Egypt?

Never—despite the story of the flight to Egypt. This story (as told in Matt. 2:13-23) is a fabrication, and had the function of embedding Jesus in Jewish history. In the Gospel of Luke, instead of fleeing to Egypt, Mary and Joseph travel to the temple in Jerusalem.

12. When does the English version of the New Testament date from?

It dates from 1611. This is the famous King James Version (KJV), also called the Authorized Version (AV), translated as commissioned by King James. An earlier translation, by William Tyndale in 1525, was the ultimate basis for subsequent editions; see Chapter 4. So, the first English translation of the New Testament originated more than one and a half millennia after the facts.

In summary, there are good reasons to be informed about the roots of your culture, and in the West, these lie to a considerable extent in the Christian traditions of Europe. This chapter has exposed a number of guiding principles that have emerged from Christianity: reciprocity, the importance of the relationship between freedom and truth, the right of the individual, and consensual marriage. I now leave these bases of Christianity behind, to concentrate on what studying the New Testament can reveal about its origins and development. For this, methodical research is required.

Try it out yourself!

But you are probably wondering what this means. Perhaps the best way to gain insight into methodical research is to try it out yourself. For that purpose, here is an "assignment." It is similar to a real problem in the study of the New Testament, one that kept scholars searching for a solution for a long time. The solution is a mere hundred years old. So you can trace the path from the problem to the solution yourself, by doing the assignment. Sure, it takes some time—and creativity! Of course, you can skip doing it and read up on the solution in the next chapter. But if you do that, you'll miss out on an important experience, namely to feel how such a search develops, how you first find a problem and articulate the concept, how you then look for ways to find an explanation, and how this ultimately leads to a clear insight. That experience can't be replaced by the reading of a chapter. Carrying out the search also gives a sense of commitment, because research is not for the privileged few, but is accessible to anyone who takes the trouble. So, here is the task at hand:

1. Look up these passages in the Gospel of Luke: 3:3-6, 3:7-9, 3:21-22, 6:20-22, 6:31, and 6:36-38. Then look for the passages in the Gospels of Mark and Matthew which correspond in content to what is said in these Luke texts.
2. What do you find?
3. What is the problem?
4. Do you see a structure in the problem?
5. Can you think of a solution to the problem?

See if you can find a solution yourself. In the next chapter, I will discuss an extremely important insight into the origins of the New Testament that arose from this problem.

Chapter 1

The Look of the Scholar

At the end of the previous chapter I asked you to complete an assignment. Of course, you would like to know the solution now. You'll get that in a moment; but in the run-up we need to explain a few more terms.

Evidence

The wildest theories circulate about the New Testament. Some of these theories can also be read in book form, but most of the authors are only interested in sensation, not in enlightenment. Many of the views of these sensational books can be refuted with common sense. One of the most important elements here is that scholarship is based on actual evidence, which means proof. Pure speculation, without any evidence, is not research because it is not evidence-based.

Dan Brown's bestseller *The Da Vinci Code* shows how common sense combined with analytic methods can be used to refute its sensationalist message. It is certainly a bestseller; some 100 million copies have been sold. (Strange, one could say, for a book that is so poorly written. In a *New York Times* review, renowned author Stephen King ironically judged it as "How not to write an English sentence.") The book is a combination thriller, detective story and mystery novel. Its central theme is that Jesus and Mary Magdalene had a relationship which resulted in a daughter. Brown bases this on the painting *The Last Supper* by Leonardo da Vinci, which can be seen in the Monastery of Santa Maria delle Grazie in Milan.

Leonardo da Vinci, *The Last Supper* (1495-1498),
fresco, Santa Maria delle Grazie, Milan (detail).

In the painting, Jesus is seated at the center. Seen from our point
of view, John is sitting to his left, whispering something in his
ear. According to tradition, John was the youngest apostle. He
is mentioned a few times in the gospels as the apostle loved
by Jesus. (The word "apostle" traditionally refers to the 12 first
followers of Jesus. The term itself is derived from the Greek
ἀπόστολος (apóstolos), meaning "envoy.")

According to Dan Brown, however, the figure to the left of
Jesus is not the apostle John, but Mary Magdalene. The name
"John" is said to be a code for her. As proof of this, Brown
refers to the V-shaped gap between the left arm of John/Mary
Magdalene and the right arm of Jesus. This V is supposed to be
a symbol of the "sacred feminine."

This sounds like a serious theory, but of course none of it is
believable. First of all, there is no indication anywhere that the
letter V stood or stands for femininity. It does stand for victory
(Winston Churchill in 1943) or more recently for vegan. Besides,
how and why would Leonardo da Vinci, who lived about 1,450
years after Jesus, have known about such a relationship? And
why would he have invented the V-shape as a code? In short,

the authoritative idea behind this book is not based on provable facts and is therefore not evidence-based. But, amazingly, there are scores of readers who believe it all to be true, not recognizing the lack of evidence as well as the lack of historical background.

The first important method in science involves avoiding contradictions as far as possible. According to logic, contradictions are always untrue. However, it cannot be denied that there are several contradictions in the New Testament. Incidentally, the New Testament is full of contradictions. An example: Paul's letter to the Romans says, "For whosoever shall call upon the name of the Lord shall be saved" (Rom. 10:13). But this is diametrically opposed to what Jesus himself says: "Not all who say to me, Lord, Lord! will enter the kingdom of heaven" (Matt. 7:21). These two statements cannot both be true at the same time. Therefore, a solution must be found. There are only a few possibilities:

1. One of the two statements is untrue.
2. Both statements are untrue.
3. There are two views in Christianity which coexist.

To judge whether one of the statements is untrue, their historical context needs to be examined. It is possible, for example, that one of the two statements did not occur historically as such in the text, but was added or changed by a later copyist. The third option listed above is that the contradiction exists, but is present in Christianity itself (or in its texts). However, if this is the case, it imports a fundamental contradiction into religion.

In Matthew (10:34) we read: "You shall not think that I have come to bring peace on earth, but a sword." But in the same Gospel we also read: "Put your sword in its place! For whoever takes the sword will perish by the sword" (Matt. 26:52). What is the real message? And what is a believer to do with such contradictions? By the way, this is not only a problem for Christianity. The *Qur'an*, the holy book of the Muslims, contains similar contradictions. There are passages that promote peaceful behavior, such as: "O you who believe! Be steadfast for God, bearing witness to justice, and let not hatred for a people lead you to be unjust. Be just; that is nearer to reverence" (Sura 5:8), and "Truly god loves the virtuous" (Sura 5:13). But in other places the opposite is proclaimed, for example, "O you who believe! Fight those disbelievers who are near you, and let them find harshness in you" (Sura 9:123), while other passages call for a holy war: "Let them fight in the way of God, those who would sell the life of this world for the Hereafter. And whoever fights in the way of God—whether he is slain or victorious—We shall grant him a great reward" (Sura 4:74).

Similar contradictions are also found in the Jewish Torah. On the one hand, the text calls for tolerance. In Leviticus is the well-known rule: "You shall love your neighbor as yourself" (Lev. 19:18). But in other passages, the Torah calls for the extermination of all enemies. For instance,

> If thou hearest say of any city which the LORD thy God hath given thee to dwell therein, There are some unholy men come up out of the midst of thee, and have deceived the citizens of their city, saying, Let us go and serve other gods, which ye know not; then thou shalt search, inquire, and enquire thoroughly. And if it be found that it is certain that such an abomination is done among you, then thou shalt smite the citizens of that city with the edge of the sword, and execute upon it the curse, upon all that is therein, even upon their cattle, with the edge of the sword.
> (Deut. 13:13-16)

It seems that these holy books typically contain internal contradictions. As a result, rulers and religious leaders were known to interpret or use text excerpts as they saw fit. And they still do.

The upsurge of scholarly research

In the case of the New Testament, scholarly research gained momentum toward the end of the Reformation. Erasmus of Rotterdam was the first to reconstruct a reliable text of the New Testament in Greek, complete with his own Latin translation. In attempting this, he had to deal with differences between the manuscripts available to him. By carefully comparing the extant versions, he arrived at the publication of the *Novum Instrumentum omne*. This is, in fact, the first scholarly edition of the New Testament. After careful examination of all the variants, this work was the most reliable edition at the time, based on what was then known in 1516. Erasmus had also laid the foundation for philology (linguistics and literary studies, including textual criticism).

What is explosive here, and again a revealing example of the problem with the church authorities, is that this work of Erasmus, i.e., the first scholarly approach to the texts of the New Testament, was put on the *Index* at the Council of Trent in the 16th century, in other words: forbidden for the faithful to read. Accordingly, the Catholic Church declared the Bible forbidden reading!

But this was only the beginning. In his *Tractatus Theologico-Politicus* (1670, printed anonymously for his own protection), the philosopher Spinoza was the first to discuss the inconsistencies in the Old Testament, and more specifically the miraculous events it described. His argument was that miracles were an insult to the traditional view of God, because they meant that God had apparently created a world so flawed that he had to constantly repair it, using miracles to make things work the way he wanted. Even more important is Spinoza's insight that mysterious passages in biblical texts need to be understood based on the situation and intent of the author in his time. In other words, the Bible is not a textbook on physics, but a work on moral principles. As Gadamer puts it,

No one would have thought to interpret the work of Euclid as incorporating the life, studies, morals, and customs of the writer, and the same is true of the spirit of the Bible in moral matters (…). It is only because there are incomprehensible things in the stories of the Bible that their understanding depends on whether we can see from its writings as a whole what the author intended.

(Gadamer 2014, p. 177; transl. W. Van Peer)

Spinoza was therefore the first to develop a historical interpretation of the texts. He thereby became the founder of the later development of the systematic study of the Bible.

Since the New Testament was written some two thousand years ago, its study involves a great deal of history, but also archaeology, and of course philology, the close study of ancient texts alongside knowledge of ancient and often extinct languages. This means that it is not easy to live up to the claim of "scientificity." A simple label of "this is scientific" cannot be applied, because scientific research is always incomplete and error-prone. Research findings must therefore be evaluated first in their entirety, and second over a longer period.

The same, of course, applies to the study of the New Testament. For a long time, the prevailing opinion was that the Gospel according to Matthew was the oldest. Nowadays, however, the totality of the data shows that Mark's must be the oldest Gospel. But how does one arrive at this conclusion? Here another aspect comes into play. Research is often not carried out individually. Typically, researchers are involved in frequent communication, interaction, cooperation, and critical review of each other's findings and data. There are several journals, associations, and organizations devoted to the study of the New Testament. BibleGateway.com (https://byustudies. byu.edu/article/bible-gateway-and-the-new-testament-gateway-two-biblical-websites) is a good example of this.

There, the reader will find an overview of what is happening in this area of scholarship.

Your assignment

You remember the earlier exercise? It was to find corresponding passages in Luke's Gospel in the Gospels of Mark and Matthew. You probably soon noticed that there are many similarities between Matthew and Luke on the one hand, and Matthew and Mark on the other. Perhaps you had the idea of arranging that data in some kind of overview or table, so that it looked like this:

Mark	Matt.	Luke
1:1-8	3:1-6	3:3-6
0	3:7-9	3:7-9
1:9-11	3:13-17	3:21-22
0	5:3-12	6:20-22
0	7:12	6:31
0	7:1-5	6:36-38

The table shows that there are many similarities between these three Gospels. That is why they are called the synoptic Gospels, while the Gospel according to John is very different from them. But there are also differences between the synoptic Gospels, and it is these that have attracted early attention and interest in the study of the New Testament. Scholars have gone looking for even more of these differences. The table above can be completed with the following:

Mark	Matt.	Luke
4:24	5:39-48	6:27-38
0	7:3-5	6:39-42
0	7:16-20	6:43-45
0	7:24-27	6:46-49
0	8:5-13	7:1-10

0	6:1-4	0
0	0	10:38-41
0	5:1-12	6:20-26
(11:25-26)	6:9-15	11:2-4
0	6:16-18	0
0	7:7-11	11:9-12
0	0	12:13-21
0	6:25-33	12:22-34
2:18-22	9:14-17	5:33-39
0	13:36-43	0
0	13:44-52	0

By using such tables, a pattern can be detected. In a way, this is remarkable, because one would assume that the more observations one makes, the more difficult it becomes to see the forest for the trees. But the researcher assumes the opposite, namely that the more observations one makes, and the better one structures the results (as in these tables) the greater the chance of discovering a pattern. This method is often used in historical text research.

Usually, believers read the New Testament *vertically*. They read (or hear) something about the life of Jesus from one Gospel, and something else from another Gospel, and so on. The end result is that readers select the common denominators from the whole New Testament. The various parts of the story are forged into a new "vertical" story in which there is no distinction between what is mentioned in each of the individual Gospels.

Scholars also read these texts *horizontally*. Individual passages are systematically compared with one another. And if one compares many passages with many others, it leads to creating the kind of tables shown above. But then, how can the tables be evaluated or interpreted? Well, the following conclusions can be drawn from the information tabled above:

1. Not all of the texts of one Gospel appear in each of the other three Gospels.
2. Almost every text in Mark has a corresponding passage in Matthew and Luke.
3. However, the opposite is not the case!
4. Matthew and Luke contain almost identical passages, but they are not mentioned in Mark.

    These are important conclusions in themselves. So there is a great deal of agreement between Matthew and Luke. Did you notice anything special about the identical passages? In fact, they are all in *direct speech*, i.e. what is quoted verbatim. Therefore, the final conclusion is:

5. The identical passages in Matthew and Luke that do not appear in Mark are generally written in direct speech. For the most part, they are the words that Jesus is said to have spoken personally.

For instance, compare the passage "Blessed are the spiritually poor, for theirs is the kingdom of heaven" (Matt. 5:3) with "Blessed are you poor, for the kingdom of God is yours" (Luke 6:20). In fact, they are not literally the same, but the contents are very close, and they are always assumed to be literal statements by Jesus.

With this in mind, conclusions 2 and 3 (as noted above) can be explained together if one assumes that the Gospels of Matthew and Luke were written after Mark's, and that Matthew and Luke used the text by Mark. Only in this way can one understand that the Gospels of Matthew and Luke have parallel passages to the text of Mark. However, it does not explain the fact that the Gospels of Matthew and Luke have so many similarities in passages that have no counterpart in the text of Mark. (Matthew and Luke probably did not know of each other's writing of a Gospel.) It would be explained, however, if one assumes that Matthew and Luke drew from another text besides Mark's for their own Gospels. But which text? German scholars suggest that there must have been a text that both Matthew and Luke made use of, but that Mark did not have, or did not use. Scholars refer to this as "*Q*," standing for the German word *Quelle*, meaning "source."

Did the authors of later Gospels then copy from earlier texts? This must be considered as very probable. But do not forget that each author also had his own point of view, and accordingly adapted the other texts which he borrowed or made use of. Were there other texts from which they borrowed things? Most certainly. Where then is the "divine" Holy Spirit who dictated or whispered the words into their ears and minds? In 1893, according to the traditional view of the Church, Pope Leo XIII published the encyclical *Providentissimus Deus* with the following explanation of the "inerrancy of the Holy Scriptures" (cited in George 1995, p. 211):

> For the books all and complete, which the Church recognizes as sacred and canonical, with all their parts, are written under inspiration of the Holy Spirit. But far from admitting that an error can occur in the divine inspiration, it already in and of itself not merely excludes any error, but excludes it as reprehensible as necessarily as it is necessary that God, the Supreme Truth, is not at all as the author of an error.

Here, too, one can see how averse the church leadership was to a serious inquiry, and de facto forbade a rational investigation of the texts. The believer must believe, not think! The very conception of religion developed over a long period and constructed by humans contradicts the dogmatic view propagated by the church authorities.

This traditional picture—that the New Testament was written by four men simultaneously under the inspiration of the Holy Spirit—is completely fabricated and contradicts all historical evidence. The texts of the Gospels were written at different times and in different places. They influenced each other and they also used earlier texts and traditions. What is needed is a differentiated historical origin of these texts.

Schematically the findings of the assignment can be rendered as follows:

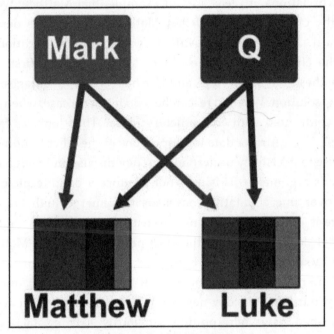

The two-source hypothesis

This figure shows that both Matthew and Luke used Mark's text (the grey parts on the left), although Matthew used more of Mark than Luke did. Luke used a higher proportion of *Q* (the black portion) than Matthew did. Finally, the light grey section to the right shows the "own" material of each author, where it is clear that Luke invented more of his own material than Matthew, especially about the birth and childhood of Jesus. In short, each author composed his own text in a very personal way. One comes to such an insight only when one reads the text horizontally.

But here is a crucial issue to bear in mind: the model that Matthew and Luke both used the text of Mark and additionally Q is a *hypothesis*. It is a very serious hypothesis, accepted by the vast majority of scholars. But so far, Q has not been found. Moreover, this is not the only hypothesis on the subject. Other interpretations or ideas are, for example, that Matthew would be the oldest Gospel and that Mark and Luke were derived from it. This is usually justified by the fact that traditionally in the New Testament the text of Matthew occurs first. This hypothesis has supporters, and also has certain advantages over the Q solution. What do researchers do in such a case, when they are confronted with contradictory ideas? They look, as far as possible, for further data to support one or the other hypothesis, or else to decisively undermine it. They discuss and weigh each other's arguments. This may not produce a definite picture— but over time, a tentative consensus may emerge. In this regard, there is currently a certain consensus among experts that the model sketched above is the most probable, and that Matthew and Luke therefore used both Mark's text and Q. But no one can guarantee that this model will hold forever. It cannot be ruled out that someday new manuscripts might be discovered that shed new light on the previously existing facts, and require a revision of the current hypotheses. After all, science is constantly changing—which sometimes makes it difficult for an outsider to follow and can give the impression of arbitrariness. But this is basically the model of scientific inquiry: formulate hypotheses (with a high degree of probability and conforming to other known facts) and then collect independent data that allow one to estimate the likelihood of the hypothesis. Nearly all information contained in the following chapters is based on research that applied this model. The independent nature of the data is of crucial importance in this respect.

History as a "science"?

So is the study of history "scientific"? Yes, it certainly can be, if one follows the model sketched above together with certain rules for interpreting data. An example that comes close to studying the New Testament is the following.

In Bach's *St. Matthew Passion*, there is a recitative that begins with the words: "My Jesus is silent to false lies." The piece consists of 10 measures and has 39 chords. Now, strangely enough, musicologists find that verse 10 of Psalm 39 (in the Old Testament) reads: "I will be silent, and will not open my mouth; for you have done it." Is the similarity of these numbers (39 and 10) a coincidence, or is this a matter of number symbolism? To answer this question, it is necessary to research it historically to establish whether such number symbolism was used in Bach's time. If you could not find any sources on this, then you would have to devote more time to explaining the coincidence. But don't worry, there is plenty of evidence that such numerical symbolism was in fact practiced during the Baroque period; see for example Tatlow (1991), or Van Houten (1985). One may conclude that historical research has its own methods, but in essence the testing of hypotheses is fundamentally the same as in the sciences. The "assignment" earlier discussed and analyzed was an example of this.

Miracles

This leads inevitably to the question of what can be said scientifically about the innumerable miracles in the New Testament. Of the more than 7 billion people on earth today, not a single one can walk on liquid water. However, could anyone do so 2,000 years ago? How does one deal with such questions objectively? The best answer I know comes from Bart Ehrman, of the University of North Carolina, one of the great current specialists in the field of New Testament studies. His argumentation relates to the core of what historiography is.

Historians look for explanations of historical facts, for example, why the French Revolution happened, or how the Romans won the war against Carthage, or why Hitler had such a great success for a limited time. These questions are difficult to answer because the events are in the past, so historians have to rely on sources. And sources always raise the question of whether they are authentic—because they can be falsified. With ruins, commemorative stones, and coins, it's more difficult, but with texts, it's very easy. Paper is patient.

The essence of Ehrman's argument goes like this: historians look for the *most probable* explanation of historical events. The Gospel according to John is traditionally attributed—by name—to Jesus' favorite apostle, who was called John. But this is hardly possible. Let's assume that Jesus' disciple would have been 20 years old in the year 30, when Jesus died. According to the best information available, the Gospel of John was written around the years 100 to 120. Then John, who was young in the time that Jesus lived, would have written this Gospel when he was at least 90 years old. This is highly unlikely in a time when the average life expectancy might not have even been 40 years. It is not impossible, but it is not very probable. It is much more likely that the author of this Gospel was another John (it is important to remember that there were no surnames). Moreover, the disciple John in the Gospels most probably could not write at all, let alone write in an elegant Greek. So we need to choose between the two explanations (the man who wrote the Gospel was the disciple of Jesus, or someone else who was also called John). And since the second explanation, that of a later author, is the most probable, it is preferred in historiography.

But miracles do not fit so easily into the search for probable events. They do fit well into the apocalyptic context in which Jesus and other prophets proclaimed their message. These miracles marked the end of time and, of course, the special gifts available to these prophets. But what does the precise study of the texts tell us about these miracles? The answer to this question is quite simple: nothing at all.

This is not an exceptional situation that applies only to research into the New Testament. It is, on the contrary, the typical situation of all historical research. Historians must constantly choose between several possibilities. Did the poverty of large segments of the population cause the French Revolution, as claimed by Christopher Hibbert (1980)? Or was it corruption and moral decay at court, as suggested by Robert Darnton (1996)? Were there other causes? Or were they all at play? But how did they fit together? Historians look for the most likely explanation. That is the real work of the historian, to give the most probable explanation for something that happened in the past. But miracles, by definition, are precisely the most improbable events.

Of the billions of people who have lived on this earth, no one has ever succeeded, with sufficient evidence, in returning to life after death. A miracle is therefore highly improbable and therefore not suitable for a historical explanation. Of course, one can and may believe such a thing. One may believe the most improbable things (as long as one does not harm anyone else in the process). But in a research context, this kind of belief is not accepted, or at least not accepted as a credible explanation. The métier of the historical scholar is to look for what is most likely to explain why something happened in the past. And a miracle is exactly the most improbable event imaginable. So historians can't prove it. Ergo, if someone believes in miracles, this is not compatible with objective explanations for historical events.

Chapter 2

Back To the Sources

Before I begin this chapter, an important comment is in order: there are *no* truly contemporary sources about Jesus in existence. By "sources," I mean verifiable, reliable and neutral texts such as inscriptions or official documents, which were written about Jesus during his lifetime. Trustworthy sources are available regarding, for example, the person of Pilate, as will be described in more detail below. But for the figure of Jesus and what he did, there is no such reliable evidence outside the New Testament. It simply does not exist anywhere. In this chapter, therefore, I will discuss a number of texts that refer to Jesus, but without exception they come from a (sometimes considerably) later date, and they are never direct "sources." But they are all we have. Therefore, we must critically examine them for their content.

Did Jesus really exist?

Some people—even including a movement called the "Christ Myth Theory"—deny the historical existence of Jesus. Well-known proponents of this view include Carrier (2012), Doherty (2009), and Price (2003). However, the general conclusion regarding this movement is absolutely negative. Grant (2004) summarizes the situation as follows: "In recent years no serious scholar has dared to postulate the non-historicity of Jesus, or at least very few have, and they have failed to refute the much stronger, indeed very abundant, evidence to the contrary" (p. 200).

So how does one get a reliable or credible answer to the question of Jesus' existence? Quite clearly, by critically examining the historical sources. What sources are these? The answer to this question is complicated by the fact that there were no surnames in Palestine at the beginning of the Christian era. Therefore, Jesus was not the only Jesus; there may have been hundreds of them and there were also dozens of itinerant preachers and prophets like Jesus.

In this chapter I will discuss the sources that can illuminate something about the historical person of Jesus. All in all, this leads to a rather meager harvest. But when all the sources are taken together, it seems almost inevitable that there was once a Jesus of Nazareth. According to these sources, he was a Jewish man, an apocalyptic preacher and teacher; see Meier (1991). The meaning of the word "apocalyptic" will be discussed shortly. At this moment it is enough to know that he proclaimed that a new kingdom was coming. Also, everything indicates that he was crucified in Jerusalem during the reign of the Roman Emperor Tiberius, when Pontius Pilate was governor of the Roman province of Judea, in the years 26 to 36. These are the most important dates (for now).

What sources *do* we have?

Jesus is not mentioned by any Roman or Greek author from the first century. But millions of other people from that time are not mentioned either. We also have no textual source about the reign of Pontius Pilate outside of the Gospels. However, there are some archaeological findings: some coins with his name and image, and part of an inscription (in Caesarea Maritima, a city on the coast) stating that he was Roman prefect, the fifth prefect of the Roman province of Judea, from 26 to 36. This inscription is on the so-called "Stone of Pilate." Some of the inscribed letters are no longer easy to read.

The "Stone of Pilate" from Caesarea Maritima, 26-37,
Israel Museum, Jerusalem.

Presumably the original full text was:

(DIS AUGUSTI)S TIBERIÉUM(PO)NTIUS PILATUS(PRAEF)
ECTUS IUDA(EA)E(FECIT D)E(DICAVIT).

An English translation would be something like, "Pontius Pilate, prefect of Judea, built and dedicated this Tiberieum to the divine Tiberius." Roman emperors were often worshipped as gods. According to archaeologists, the stone is authentic and confirms the existence of Pontius Pilate as Roman prefect in the province of Judea. This, of course, does not prove Pilate's role as described in the New Testament.

We also have three Roman sources, namely Pliny the Younger (61/62-113/114), Suetonius (70-130) and Tacitus (56-after 118). Then there are Coptic sources (the Nag Hammadi codices) and finally Jewish sources, namely the rabbinic texts, the Dead Sea Scrolls and the writings of Flavius Josephus (37-100). I now discuss these sources one by one.

Roman sources

So, first, there is *Pliny the Younger*, "the Younger" to separate him from his much more famous uncle, who was mainly a natural scientist. Pliny the Younger was governor of a Roman province in what is now Turkey. He was, in fact, still young when he wrote a series of letters seeking advice from Emperor Trajan in Rome. His tenth letter, written in the year 112, is of particular interest. Earlier, he had passed a law in his province forbidding assemblies. The reason for this is unknown; probably it was for fear of riots. But this law created a problem, because even firemen (or whatever they were called at the time) were not allowed to "assemble." Pliny mentions this problem in his letter. But he also writes about another group that was illegally assembling: the "Christians." From Pliny's description of this group, three important things about these early Christians are made clear. First, the group was made up of people of different (mainly lower) socioeconomic levels. His letter also states that they ate meals together and that they sang hymns to Christ as to a god. The letter says nothing about the historical Jesus, but it does say something about groups of Christians.

Suetonius (70-130) was a Roman writer from the early empire, mainly an author of biographies. For us, his important work is *De vita caesarum* (The Lives of the Emperors), published around the year 115. It consists of 12 biographies of Roman emperors, including that of Emperor Claudius who reigned from 41 to 54, and who issued an edict that all Jews had to leave Rome because of disturbances of the peace. The letter mentions that these disturbances were *impulsore Chresto* (at the hands of Chrestus). That is all he says. Was this Jesus of Nazareth? We do not know. However, there is a clear parallel with a New Testament passage, though in Acts 18:2 which reads: "because Emperor Claudius had commanded all Jews to leave Rome." The debate continues among scholars as to whether Christians are involved in this passage. But there is good evidence that it may be true.

Tacitus (56-120) was one of the most important historians of the Roman period. He was also one of the greatest linguistic stylists of his time. The compact style with which he expresses himself is unprecedented in Latin. He is also an unparalleled critic of the Roman state. His *Ab excessu divi Augusti* (Annals of Imperial Rome) in 16 volumes, c. 116, is one of the most important sources for the study of the Roman empire. One passage of particular importance concerns the great fire in Rome in 64 (Book XV 44). According to Tacitus, the then emperor Nero himself had set fire to Rome, but falsely accused those whom *vulgus Chrestianos appellabat* (the people called Chrestians). Here is what Tacitus writes:

> *Auctor nominis eius Christus Tiberio imperitante per procuratorem Pontium Pilatum supplicio adfectus erat; repressaque in praesens exitiabilis superstitio rursum erumpebat, non modo per Iudaeam, originem eius mali, sed per urbem etiam.*
>
> (The man from whom this name derives, Christ, had been executed under the reign of Tiberius at the instigation of the procurator Pontius Pilate, and suppressed for the moment,

however, the sinister superstition broke out again, not only in Judea, the country of origin of this evil, but also in the city = Rome.)

Here is some information in brief that independently confirms that there was a Christ who was executed by Pontius Pilate at the time of Emperor Tiberius and had followers even as far as Rome in the year 64. Tacitus is generally considered to be an extremely reliable historical author. It is clear that he has considerable contempt for Christians, and considers their movement a danger to the state, which makes the source credible.

The records of these three Roman sources outside of the New Testament are sparse, to say the least, with consensus that Tacitus' account is highly trustworthy. But together, Pliny the Younger, Suetonius, and Tacitus show that there was a movement of followers of Jesus at the end of the first and beginning of the second centuries, of Christians or "Chrests" who worshipped a Christ and were apparently distrusted by the Roman authorities. This does not offer much as a proof of Jesus' authenticity, but at least it gives a clear indication of the existence of his followers not long after his death, even in the capital of Rome. Apart from these, there are also non-Roman sources.

Coptic sources

The Coptic sources are mainly the codices of Nag Hammadi, in Upper Egypt (on the Nile, about some fifty miles northwest of Luxor). In 1945, local farmers discovered a clay jar in a cave. It contained 13 leather-bound codices made of papyrus and one more book.

A "codex" (plural "codices") was the precursor of a modern book. In ancient times, most writing was done on papyrus made from a papyrus plant, which was the precursor of what is now known as paper. This was already used in ancient Egypt during the time of Pharaoh Khufu (known by the name "Cheops") around 2500 BC. The sheets of papyrus were usually rolled up in scrolls. Nowadays, we also scroll down a menu on a computer screen, in a way reminiscent of the people of antiquity unrolling a scroll to read it. The advantage of ancient scrolls was that they were light and very easy to carry, but the disadvantage was that one had to "scroll" all the time, which made it difficult to search for a passage of text. There were two ways to write on such a scroll: from top to bottom, which meant unrolling it vertically — or from left to right or vice versa, which required unrolling it horizontally. However, one did not write across the entire width or length of the scroll, but in columns of a certain width (which were to become pages). At some stage, someone came up with the idea of folding these columns, to create a kind of accordion (squeezebox) instead of a roll, which sped up the search considerably. Then it quickly became clear that one could also cut the "accordion" columns into pieces and connect the individual columns together. This is what is known as a codex.

Although some texts in the 13 codices of Nag Hammadi clearly date from early times, the manuscripts themselves are from the third to fourth centuries. They contain various religious writings in the ancient Coptic language, but most likely they are translations from Greek. The Greek originals (which we do not have) probably date from the second to third centuries, but even then the Coptic translations are particularly valuable for the study of the New Testament. One of the Nag Hammadi texts is the only complete copy of the Gospel of Thomas in existence, and of several others, such as the Gospel of Philip. The codices contain statements of Jesus, details of the apostles, liturgical texts, apocalyptic texts (about the end of the world) and the like.

It is also important to know that these are largely so-called Gnostic texts. The term is derived from the Greek γνῶσις (gnosis), which means knowledge, insight, understanding. In this case, relating to early Christianity, Gnosticism refers to "secret" knowledge of a religious, spiritual, or mystical nature, knowledge that seeks to gain deeper insight into the coherence and meaning of everything. It claims to be the basis for the unfathomable mysteries of the world, especially the relationship between man, matter and divine origin, and also promises the initiated enlightenment and liberation from this world (see Chapter 9 on the apocryphal texts).

Coptic was spoken in the last stage of development of ancient Egyptian until the 17th century and is still used in the Christian liturgy of the Coptic Church of Alexandria in Egypt. However, no one speaks the language anymore; it is similar to Latin worship in the Catholic Church or the use of Church Slavonic in the Orthodox Church. The Coptic language at the time of Jesus was written using the Greek alphabet, with seven characters from the Demotic (the last stage of development of the Egyptian writing system, after the hieroglyphics and their simplified version, the Hieratic).

In the media, one occasionally hears about the difficulties of the Coptic Church in Egypt. The Copts make up about ten percent of the Egyptian population. So, after all, about nine million Egyptians are Christians. The Coptic Church is one of the oldest Christian communities. According to tradition, it was founded in 42, but this is probably more legend than fact. In any case, the discovery of the Coptic writings in Nag Hammadi represents an enormous enrichment of our knowledge about the early Christian communities. Again, these texts do not establish direct proof of Jesus' life, but they certainly attest to the lively culture of Christian communities.

Jewish sources
Finally, there are also some Jewish sources. Of particular importance in the rabbinic texts is the Jewish Talmud, a collection of loose commentaries, anecdotes, proverbs, commandments, descriptions of customs, written from the beginning of the

third century. But the oldest existing manuscript of the Talmud dates from 1395. This is the so-called Babylonian Talmud, the Codex Hebr. 95 (to be found online at: https://www.loc.gov/item/2021667743).

The Talmud was written about two hundred years after the death of Jesus. It does not mention Jesus, other than in a later commentary, the *Gemara* (from the Aramaic *gamar*, "to study"), a version of which was written in the fifth century by scholars in Babylon. The Gemara does not mention Jesus by name, but scholars agree that there are two references to Jesus in the (later) Gemara.

First, he is mentioned as Ben Panthera, son of Panthera, a Roman soldier who had seduced Mary. This may appear strange from a Western perspective, but that is what it says. This news comes from the Jewish writer Celsus from the second century. In his book Ἀληθὴς λόγος (*Alethes logos*, The True Doctrine), Celsus claims that Mary was impregnated by a Roman archer named Abdes Panthera. (It's maybe a little ticklish in this context that the name "Panthera" is similar to the Greek *Parthenos*, meaning virgin.)

The second reference to Jesus is that he had been a practitioner of black magic in Egypt (see the story of the flight to Egypt in the Gospel of Matthew). According to the Gemara, he had five apprentices and was hanged for a charge of sorcery at Easter in Jerusalem.

And then there are the *Dead Sea Scrolls*, also known as the Qumran texts, 981 of them in all. In the winter of 1946, two Bedouin shepherds, Mohammed ed-Dib and Ahmed Mohammed, discovered a series of text scrolls in the caves of Qumran, near the Dead Sea. (These were scrolls, not codices.) Perhaps they were written by the Essenes, a religious Jewish sect next to but smaller than the Pharisees and Sadducees, who lived in a kind of monastic community of celibacy, poverty and charity. They practiced a religion that focused on the end of all things worldly. However, there is much debate among experts about the Essenes. There are even scholars who, based on recent research, doubt both the existence of the sect and whether the Qumran texts were written or preserved by its members. Sources for the existence of the Essenes, however, are found in Pliny the Elder and in the work of Flavius Josephus.

The Dead Sea Scrolls are written largely on parchment, with some on papyrus and some on bronze, in Hebrew, Aramaic, and Nabataean. But there is almost nothing in these texts concerning the New Testament. They relate primarily to Old Testament content (about forty percent), to apocryphal texts from the Jewish religion (about thirty percent), and finally, to previously unknown texts about the commandments of a Jewish religious community (thirty percent).

Despite what is sometimes claimed in sensational messages, the texts have no bearing on Christianity. The name of Jesus is not mentioned anywhere in the texts. And nowhere is reference made to what he did. Nor are there any references to John the Baptist or to Paul. So there is nothing. Can I say it any more clearly? When dealing with people who claim that the Dead Sea Scrolls confirm the authenticity of the New Testament, one is dealing with fools or frauds. An example of one such clear-cut case is Robert Eisenman (1997) of California State University, Long Beach. He claims, against the consensus of his colleagues, that the Dead Sea Scrolls were written by an early Christian group. Interestingly, in this context, the Gospels themselves warn against this kind of deception (see Matt. 24:3-5, 11:24; Mark 13:5-6; Luke 21:7-8).

Since the Dead Sea Scrolls mention nothing about Jesus or Christians, I will not discuss them here, despite the sensational nature of their discovery. It was sensational, no doubt, because they advance the textual history of large portions of the Jewish Bible (i.e., the Old Testament) by a thousand years. But for the study of the New Testament, the scrolls are negligible in content.

They do, however, offer an informative picture of how such religious communities lived at that time. They are therefore of great socio-historical value.

The final Jewish source mentioned here is *Flavius Josephus* (37-100), who was the only Jewish writer of his time to say anything about Jesus (around the year 94). He was born Joseph ben Matityahu in Jerusalem and was a complex figure, whose historical writings from the first century are significant. His two most important works are Ἱστορία Ἰουδαϊκοῦ πολέμου πρὸς Ῥωμαίους (*Bellum Judaicum* or *De Bello Judaico*, "A History of the Jewish War") from 75 to 79, and Ἰουδαϊκὴ Ἀρχαιολογία (*Antiquitates Judaicae*, "A History of the Jewish People"). The latter book contains the following passage, which in English translation reads:

Ananus, the high priest, assembled the sanhedrin of judges, and brought before them the brother of Jesus, who was called Christ, whose name was James, and some others; and when he had formed an accusation against them as breakers of the law, he delivered them to be stoned.
(*Antiquitates Judaicae*, 20.9.1)

This is one of the very few direct references to Jesus (through his brother, James) outside of the New Testament, and so it is of great historical value. There is a second passage in this work by Flavius Josephus that specifically refers to Jesus:

Now there was about this time Jesus, a wise man, if it be lawful to call him a man; for he was a doer of wonderful works, a teacher of such men as receive the truth with pleasure. He drew over to him both many of the Jews and many of the Gentiles. He was the Christ. And when Pilate, at the suggestion of the principal men amongst us, had condemned him to the cross, 9) those that loved him at the first did not forsake him; for he appeared to them alive again the third day; 10) as the divine prophets had foretold these and ten thousand other wonderful things concerning him. And the tribe of Christians, so named from him, are not extinct at this day.

(Book 8, Chapter 3, 3)

At first glance, this seems to confirm the content of the New Testament. However, there is a snag; all manuscripts of the text of Flavius Josephus are of Christian origin. The oldest one dates back to the 11th century! It is extremely likely that copyists "adapted" the text in the Christian sense. For example, it is extremely unlikely that Flavius Josephus, who had a strong antipathy to Christianity, would have written that Jesus was the "Christ." The phrase "if he may be called a man" likewise represents a later addition by Christian copyists. The reference to the Old Testament predictions, the resurrection, and the "tens of thousands of signs" are almost certainly Christian additions that Flavius Josephus did not write himself. Nevertheless, there is a broad consensus among scholars that the core of these two passages in *Antiquitates Judaicae* is historically reliable and that Jesus existed and had followers.

More history

The question of the historical Jesus returns us to the quiz questions from the Introduction, one of which was: how many brothers did Jesus have?

Did Jesus have brothers?

That Jesus had brothers, if we believe the texts of the Gospels, is certain—despite the Catholic teaching that Mary always remained a virgin. This is probably still the official view of the Catholic Church. In paragraph 449 of the *Catechism*, the book that teaches the fundamental aspects of the Catholic faith, she is even called ἀειπάρθενος ("always virgin").

However, there is no reason to doubt that Jesus came from a large Jewish family. Four of Jesus' brothers are mentioned in the Gospels themselves, namely James, Joseph, Simon, and Judas. See Mark 6:3 and Matt. 13:55-56, where the text literally states that these were Jesus' brothers and Mary's sons. It also says that he had sisters, but they are not mentioned by name. In some of his letters, Paul also refers explicitly to the brothers of Jesus.

Nonetheless, in church circles, this is often denied or covered up. It is then argued that these were not in fact brothers, but cousins or other relatives, because "brother" is often a much broader concept in Semitic cultures than in Western languages. Moreover, the word "brothers" is always used loosely in Paul's letters when referring to fellow Christians as "brothers and sisters in Christ."

A reasonable person would then naturally wonder why it says "brothers" in the Gospels after all. But more importantly, Mediterranean culture or not, in *Greek* there is a clear difference between the words "brother" (ἀδελφός, *adelfos*, literally *a-delfos*, "from the same womb") and "nephew" (ξαδελφός, *ksadelfos*, in the sense of "child of an uncle or aunt"). When both words are available in a language, it means that people consciously or purposefully distinguish between these types of relationships. Of course, one can argue that there are hidden messages in the Gospels, and that the word *adelfos* is one of them. Dan Brown (whom we mentioned in Chapter 1) uses this kind of invention and builds a success story on it. That may be good for his story and his wallet, but it's completely unfounded from a historical point of view.

The glossary in the critical edition of Nestle-Aland (2012) defines "brother" as the only translation of *adelfos*. And the lexicon of Thayer and Strong, one of the most important standard works for New Testament Greek, explicitly points out that *adelfos* here does not mean "cousin." Jesus' brothers, it literally says, "are neither sons of Joseph with another woman to whom he was married before Mary as sometimes claimed (...), nor cousins." It could not be clearer. Indeed, would authors whose native language was Greek get it wrong and use an incorrect word? An even more vital point is made by Thayer and Strong: "See Luke 2:7—where, if Mary bore no children other than Jesus, the expression υἱόν μονογενῆ would have been used instead of υἱόν πρωτότοκον." What this means is that Luke 2:7 literally says, "She gave birth to her first son." In Greek, "firstborn" expressly means that other children followed, otherwise the expression "firstborn" would not have been used, but replaced by μονογενῆ (*monogené*, literally, "only child"). And this word is used elsewhere, for example in Luke 8:42 and 9:38, where in each case it concerns an only child, presumably a single surviving child, because birth control was (and is) forbidden by Jewish religion. But this word *monogené* is never used for Jesus. Again, why would native speakers systematically make mistakes in word choice? The answer, of course, is clear—because otherwise the dogma of Mary's virginity would not be tenable (more on this in Chapter 4).

The birth of Jesus

There is consensus among proponents of traditional teachings that Jesus was born in Bethlehem. A detailed account of this can be found in Luke. The second chapter of his Gospel tells that there was a census in the time of Emperor Augustus in which Mary and Joseph were required to participate. However, there are two problems with this story. The text states: "And this taxing was first made, when Cyrenius was governor in Syria. And all went to be taxed, every one into his own city. And Joseph also went up from Galilee, out of the city of Nazareth, into Judaea, unto the city of David, because he was of the house and lineage of David." (Luke 2:2-4)

Now, according to biblical sources, King David must have

lived about a thousand years before the birth of Jesus. Imagine there is a census taking place in your country in the foreseeable future. You would have to report to a town where your ancestors had lived a thousand years ago. The absurdity of this story may be clear, but the text also deals with a linguistic problem inherent in many cultural narratives. The "city of David" is a so-called *epitheton ornans,* a decorative term for Bethlehem, and the point here is that Jesus is to be "placed" in the history of Israel by means of King David.

But who ordered them to go to Bethlehem? Quirinius or the Emperor Augustus? Why would the Roman authorities care where anyone's ancestors came from? The Romans were only interested in how many people lived in a particular city, not where they came from a thousand years ago. The Romans were practical people. The reason for such a census was to know how many taxes a place had to pay.

But here comes the second, much bigger problem with the census. Emperor Augustus was probably the most powerful man on earth at that time, with a huge administration in his empire. The documents of all his decrees exist, but there is nothing about a general census. Simply put, there was no census in Palestine under Augustus. As mentioned in Augustus' *Index rerum gestarum,* four censuses of the *cives Romani* (Roman citizens) took place during his reign. But there is no trace of a census of foreign citizens during the reign of Emperor Augustus.

Luke is the only evangelist who refers to a ruler who organized a census in Palestine, in AD 7. But this date does not correspond to the year in which Jesus was born according to ancient tradition. Moreover, Luke contradicts Matthew here. The latter claims that Jesus was born in the time of Herod the Great. Herod was king of Palestine, but he died in the year 4 BC and there is no doubt about that. According to the very reliable Tacitus, the census in year 7 BC was organized not by Quirinius, but by the governor, Saturninus — while Quirinius acted as *legatus Caesarius pro praetore*, military leader. He was appointed city governor of Syria, which included the province of Judea. However, Mary and Joseph did not live in Judea, but in Galilee, another province, and so they could not have been summoned for this census. Consequently, the New Testament does not provide a faithful record of the census story, and is in stark contradiction to the historical facts.

According to Luke, after the birth, Mary and Joseph go to the temple with their firstborn to dedicate him to God. But in another Gospel, in Matthew, the family is said to have fled to Egypt after the birth (Matt. 2:13-15) and there is no reference to a temple at all in this text. So what was it? A public visit to the temple or a secret flight to Egypt? Of course, there could not have been both.

In Matthew's Gospel (2:16) there is another spectacular story, that of the infanticide. Herod (c. 73 BC-4 BC), the Jewish king of Judea, had ordered his men to kill all boys younger than two years old. Such a decree is certainly consistent with Herod's character, and some information about the atrocities he committed is available. Flavius Josephus is particularly specific about this in his *Antiquitates Judaicae*, so one might reasonably expect infanticide to appear on this list of atrocities. But no, Flavius Josephus says not a word about it, even though he is clearly intent on portraying Herod as unfavorably as possible. Conclusion? Historically, there was never any such infanticide.

There is another striking detail in this Gospel that should not be overlooked, which is the visit of the wise men (Matt. 2) from the east, presumably from Mesopotamia. Where exactly they came from is not stated. So these wise men arrive in Jerusalem after following a star that they saw. They ask in the city where the newborn king of the Jews is. Herod gets upset. A new king of the Jews? Then his own position will be threatened, so he sends the wise men on a journey to find out where this child was born. "And lo, the star, which they saw in the east, went before them, till it came and stood over where the young child was" (Matt. 2:9). How can a star "go before" someone? One can use stars to orient oneself, with the Pole Star, for example, to find the north. But to suggest that a star would move in such a way as to lead people somewhere is simply implausible and at odds with everyday experience as well as astronomical knowledge.

That is what any sober person would think. But lo and behold, reality always provides surprises. On Thursday, October 23, 2014, the University of Groningen in the Netherlands hosted a two-day conference titled "The Star of Bethlehem." The aim was to celebrate both the 400th anniversary of the university and the 400th anniversary of Johannes Kepler's book *De vero Anno* (*The True Year*, 1614). The starting point for the conference was the book *The Star of Bethlehem: The Legacy of the Magi* (Rutgers University Press, 1999) by American astronomer, Michael Molnar, who claims to have found the star, or rather, the planet. Peter Barthel, astronomer at the University of Groningen, says he is a fan of this theory. According to him, Matthew's Gospel story is not a fairy tale; where there is smoke, there is fire! So the star must be explained, and Molnar believes he has found the solution: it is the planet Jupiter. And immediately there are headlines in the newspapers and media. The planet Jupiter was dominated by Aries in the year 6 BC, and according to Molnar, Aries was the symbol of Judea, among other things. However, according to Stephan Heilen, a classical philologist at the University of Osnabrück, there is only one single reference to the ram as the symbol of Judea in all of the literature, so the theoretical underpinning of Molnar's claim is a bit thin. So Jesus was born—most probably not in Bethlehem, but in Nazareth, where his parents lived. Why should Joseph and Mary (heavily pregnant) have walked about 90 miles? Because of this census, of course—which did not occur.

Still other attempts have been made to explain the "star," for example that it was Halley's comet in 12 BC. (But comets were seen as a sign of doom in ancient times.) Or it was a supernova, according to Chinese astronomers, in 5 BC, or the conjunction of Jupiter and Venus in 2 BC. But all of these events would have been difficult to observe with the naked eye, apart from a supernova which is a spectacular event with the luminosity of about a billion suns. And a supernova does not move in our perception either. So how could it have given direction to the wise men? And by the way, if this star was such a spectacular sign, why is it recorded only in Matthew?

Such "revelations" appear with the regularity of a clock. Another astronomer, David Hughes of the University of Sheffield, also wrote a book about the star: *The Star of Bethlehem Mystery* (1981). According to him, the star was not Jupiter, but a conjunction of the planets Jupiter and Saturn in 7 BC. Astronomers seem to disagree with each other's discoveries. And by the way, plenty of money can be earned from such "revelations." In an article in the Dutch newspaper *De Volkskrant*, Hughes himself reveals that his advance on the book was about half a year's salary. This article subtly states that the supporters of the search for the true star are almost all active in church circles, including the initiator of the two-day conference, Peter Barthel, who exclaims triumphantly, "Beautiful, isn't it? Everything is right."

But I don't think one can get very far in astrophysical circles with this kind of reasoning. What is "right" here? The Gospels don't even agree on what year Jesus was born; according to Matthew it was before the year 4 BC, but according to Luke it was in the year 6. Fortunately, there are astronomers who keep a clear head and argue factually, like Aaron Adair. His 2013 book, *The Star of Bethlehem: A Skeptical View* dismantles the theories of his colleagues. I consider this recommended reading!

But there are more questions. Why would three wise men have come from Mesopotamia or Baghdad to Palestine? Jesus was a baby like any other baby. There is no reference at all to his "divinity" before the Gospel of John (c. 100-120). In Matthew, Jesus is sometimes referred to as the king of the Jews, but of course he is not at that moment. Jesus becomes important shortly before and after his death, but during his life he is just one of the itinerant preachers. At his birth there is no indication of his future importance, so there is no reason for the Magi to come and look for him. It is a beautiful story invented *a posteriori*. It always comes down to the same problem: some people consider the New Testament to be a historical record of events. But it is not, because no text in the New Testament was written by eyewitnesses. Again, it's a wonderful story, and I would not have missed it as a child. But it is a symbolic story, to bring people together spiritually. It is not a record of historical facts.

Were the Gospels dictated by God?

This is the traditional view, still adhered to by many believers, and propagated by church authorities. What can one make of it?

We have no authentic texts from God. Would an omnipotent and omniscient God not have easily provided humankind with a reliable text? But we have only copies of copies, with thousands of differences (sometimes particularly significant) between the copies. Nevertheless, the view that the Bible is a record of historical events is widespread, especially, of course, among devout Christians. But if the New Testament has something valuable to convey, is it some facts from 2,000 years ago? Or is it the spiritual message of humility and charity? Again, for the sake of clarity, I repeat: the Gospels bring a spiritual message; they are *not* a record of actual events. Scholarly research shows this very clearly. None of the Gospels contain a reliable account of the events of that time. Indeed, the force of the evidence against this kind of reading is overwhelming. They are stories that seek to convey a deeper message, without a historically accurate account. None of the authors claim to be witnesses, either. The clearest in this regard is Luke. He says of his predecessors that they tried to give an accurate account of events, but that he (Luke 1:1-2) did his best to investigate everything thoroughly. In other words, he says that I, Luke, investigated the accurate descriptions in the sources because I myself was not present at the events. Believers find themselves in a curious situation. On the one hand, they accept the text literally as the word of God, but at the same time they do not believe the text when it states that it was not written by a witness.

That the Bible is not an accurate record of historical events can be proven by impressive evidence: there are historical and geographical inaccuracies, cultural anomalies, as well as episodes in the stories that were added later. In the remainder of this book, I will discuss the various kinds of problems that the texts present. This leads to a conclusion far beyond the observation of inaccuracies, namely that the different stories in the New Testament have fundamentally different intentions. It is an amalgam in which different interpretations of the "good news" have been thrown together in the course of its history. First, I take a look at inaccuracies that inevitably cast doubt on the reliability of the texts, beginning with the geography of Palestine.

Geographical Inaccuracies

For us, geography does not hold many great secrets: We have maps and satellites that give us accurate information about the land, the mountains, the rivers and the cities. 2,000 years ago it was very different: there was not even a simple map of Palestine. You had to know which city was where, from descriptions by others, or by asking along the way. People probably had a very different approach to geographical positioning than we do today. In this sense, we can also expect geographical inaccuracies in the New Testament: without a compass, map (not to mention a GPS), such inaccuracies are almost inevitable.

Nevertheless, some of these inaccuracies are so serious that it is contrary to expectation and leads to the conclusion that the author was hardly familiar with the geography of the land. Jesus was a wandering preacher, so the Gospels often refer to places where he preached or passed by. Let's look at an example: Mark says, "And again, departing from the coast of Tyre and Sidon, he came unto the Sea of Galilee, through the midst of the coasts of Decapolis." (Mark 7:31) Oh, this could take a long time! Tyre is on the Mediterranean Sea, about thirty-five miles northwest of the Sea of Galilee. But Jesus wants to go to the lake. Then he must go southeast. But according to Mark, he went via Sidon—which is about twenty miles north of Tyre. This is absurd: You don't go from Oxford to Portsmouth via London, just as you don't go from Rochester to Buffalo via New York. But also the reference to the so-called "Decapolis" (the "ten cities") is completely wrong, because it was a group of ten cities with predominantly Greek-speaking inhabitants, which lay south of the lake!

But this is not the only incongruity. Elsewhere, Jesus is told to cast a devil out of a possessed man. The text reads, "And they came over to the other side of the sea, into the country of the Gadarenes. And when he was come out of the ship, immediately there met him out of the tombs a man with an unclean spirit" (Mark 5:1-2). Nothing to worry about, the unsuspecting reader thinks. Except that Gerasa, the city in question, is about 35 miles southeast of the Sea of Galilee. Mark is clearly not at home in Palestine. Matthew (who uses Mark's text) tries to correct the error by mentioning the city of Gadara instead of Gerasa. But Gadara is not on the lake either, a little closer, but still seven miles from it!

Such geographical inaccuracies and contradictions give information about the reliability of the authors. But they do not necessarily have far-reaching consequences for the foundation of the Christian faith. It is easy to call these errors inaccuracies. The fact that the authors did not live in Palestine itself also explains geographical inaccuracies: They did not know the country well. One can try to minimize these errors, but in any case, the fact remains that the authors who wrote these stories were clearly not sufficiently familiar with the country. Anyone who wants people to believe that the Gospels were written by direct followers of Jesus—who traveled with him through the land—should pick up a map of Palestine.

Historical errors

I have already indicated several times that the New Testament mentions events that did not take place. There was no infanticide ordered by Herod, no Star of Bethlehem, no birth in Bethlehem, no flight to Egypt. But these are not the only inaccuracies. And some of them are quite crucial.

For example, why would a heavily pregnant young woman about to give birth walk 90 miles, from Nazareth to Bethlehem, without good reason? Note also that she then walks another 90 miles after giving birth, this time through the desert (from Bethlehem to Egypt), with her baby and her betrothed. Mary seems to be very sporty—a marathon runner! Or did she have a donkey to sit on? That was a luxury at that time. Even so, the journey took five days. Five days before the birth, all day on a donkey, and then another five days on a donkey to Egypt, for a total of ten days ...

This is the moment to revisit Chapter 1 regarding the probabilities of events. Is this story of 180 miles before and after the birth probable? No, it is highly improbable. Once again, it is a beautiful story, which can have deep symbolic meaning. But of course it did not really happen, based on very clear proof of the historical inaccuracies of the narrative.

Cultural Flaws

In Luke (1:39-56) we read that Mary, the mother of Jesus, is visited by an angel who tells her that she is pregnant with a divine child. She is still a young woman, and this is her first pregnancy; girls were (and still are) traditionally married young in this culture, usually in an arranged marriage. But not in the case of Mary—which leads one to wonder why her parents are not looking for a suitable husband for her. Now, I assume that Mary was 15 or 16 years old at the time. But immediately after the angel's visit, she sets out to visit her cousin. The latter lives in Judea, Mary in Nazareth. In such a traditional society, is it conceivable that a very young girl could set out alone? It is not even possible in the 21st century for a young woman in Palestine to go out on her own, let alone over a distance of 90 miles! The roads were much more dangerous then than they are today. I lived for several years in such traditional cultures (Algeria, Mali) and often for longer periods in more modern countries (Egypt, Tunisia). Even today, young women in these societies are subject to severe restrictions when it comes to traveling. The suggestion that a young girl would just go out alone like that 2,000 years ago is simply not credible.

However, cultural inaccuracies are not always so innocuous. In his second letter to the Corinthians, Paul explains how he was cornered in Damascus: "In Damascus the governor under Ar'-e-tas the king kept the city of the Damascenes with a garrison, desirous to apprehend me: and through a window in a basket I was let down by the wall, and escaped his hands" (2 Cor. 11:32-33). But in Acts, written later, instead of the Syrian governor, there are suddenly the Jews—although they had nothing to say in Damascus. Acts 9:23-25 reads:

But after that many days were fulfilled, the Jews took council to kill him: But their laying await was known of Saul (Paul). And they watched the gates day and night to kill him. Then the disciples took him by night, and let him down by the wall in a basket.

Here, of course, one wonders how could the Jews guard the gates of a city in another country? Perhaps another mistake, one might say, but what transpires here is a deliberate strategy to cast the Jews in a bad light. The seeds of 2,000 years of anti-Judaism are being sown. And is God himself supposed to have inspired this hatred of Jews? That raises the question why Paul and Luke did this, they themselves being Jews. The cause lies in the ongoing conflict between nascent Christianity and traditional Judaism.

These geographic and historical inaccuracies could be described as sloppiness, errors, omissions, or laxity. But in the case of cultural inaccuracies, such explanations are much more serious. It cannot be due to carelessness that the story has the young mother Mary walking alone. Or did she have a companion? If so, who was he, and why is he not mentioned? And it would seem that the anti-Jewish mockery in the stories was no slip of the tongue, but seems to have been the result of a well-considered decision.

Conclusions

Summing up everything so far, a few conclusions are possible. The first is that very little is known about the man who so profoundly shaped the history of the West. But the sources also suggest another conclusion: in all likelihood he actually lived, promulgated ideas, gathered followers around him, and was executed by the Romans. But neither the birth in Bethlehem, nor the infanticide, nor the star the wise men followed, nor the flight into Egypt can be accepted in historical context.

Furthermore, shortly after Jesus' death, there were already groups of followers spreading in urban centers. Their interaction with other groups in the Roman Empire was not without friction. Finally, a detailed study of the sources shows that some religious dogmas are based on trivial errors, such as the idea that Jesus was born of a virgin.

Chapter 3

Babylonian Confusion of Tongues

From the beginning of this scholarly journey, we are in for a surprise: the New Testament is written entirely in Greek. This New Testament Greek, however, is not the Greek of Homer or Sophocles, but is the so-called *Koiné*, a unified form of Greek based on the Attic dialect spoken in Attica, where Athens is also located. It is a simple Greek that originated around the fourth century BC. It had to be simple because everyone, including ordinary people who had not studied, needed to be able to understand the New Testament without problems. The text was subsequently translated into all kinds of other languages; about 1,700 years later it was also translated into English. And new translations keep being added. The latest so far is probably *Di Jamiekan Nyuu Testiment*, in Creole English of Jamaica, published by the Bible Society of the West Indies in 2012 (several fragments of which can be heard on the Internet).

The fact that the New Testament was originally written in Greek surprises many people. The present chapter attempts to clarify this complex linguistic situation. In any case, there is no doubt among experts; they agree that the four Gospels were written directly in Greek. Therefore, they are not translations from another language, not even from the language that Jesus spoke as his mother tongue. This means that readers have no access to what Jesus originally said.

To explore the reasons why these texts were written in Greek, one must travel back in history. More than 2,000 years ago, the world had no electricity, tap water, telephones or air conditioning, no cars, bicycles or trains. The average life expectancy was low, probably around 30 to 40 years. There was no question of equality between men and women. The daily diet was monotonous, and most people lived in abject poverty. Relationships were characterized by brutal injustice. In short, it was a completely different world. For example, military power entirely determined who was in charge. Not that military power has no meaning at all nowadays, but in today's world it is hard to imagine that, for example, the French army would invade Italy or the Netherlands. Comparable things have happened in the past, but some time ago. In New Testament times, whoever had military superiority had the power, and took advantage of it to the full. Power could be in the form of roving bands of armed people, but also regular armies. Jerusalem was later literally razed to the ground. Slavery, bloodshed and terrible torture were part of everyday reality.

It is necessary to deal with the subject of the military, because in 63 BC, Palestine was conquered by the Romans. From then on, it was a province of the Roman Empire covering a huge area: all of Italy, France and the Iberian Peninsula, a large part of Germany and all of Italy, the Balkans, a wide strip along the North African coast, a large part of Egypt, three-quarters of present-day Turkey and, a little later, a considerable part of the Middle East. In short, it was a gigantic territory centrally administered from Rome, although there were also forms of local administration with some quasi-independence. As long as the interests of the Roman Empire were not violated, local rulers could do whatever suited them.

Why Greek?

The Romans spoke Latin. This was the official language of administration, the army, and legislation. Since the New Testament was written around the figure of Jesus, who lived in a province of this Roman Empire, one would expect the New Testament to be written in Latin. Moreover, Latin was also (until recently) the language used in Catholic worship for more than a thousand years. So why are these New Testament texts not written in Latin? The reason is that the Romans did not consider their own language as a cultural language. It was more the language of daily life, a language for practical matters. But why Greek? To answer this, one must go back even further into history, some three centuries before Jesus. This part of the story is a short but necessary detour from the New Testament, to understand why the Gospels were written in Greek. From the third century BC onward, Greek was the cultured language used by the educated.

Let's start at the beginning. If you studied Greek at school, you may have read texts by Demosthenes (384-324 BC). Some of these have been given the name "philippics." A philippic today means something like a diatribe against something or someone. These speeches by Demosthenes were directed specifically against Philip II of Macedonia, king of the country north of Greece who was intent on conquering (among other things) the Greek city-states. Demosthenes was a tireless and fierce advocate of self-defense against Philip, and of taking measures to arm oneself against the dangers Philip posed. But despite his world-renowned rhetorical gifts, Demosthenes lost this battle. At the Battle of Chaeronea in 338 BC, the Greeks were finally defeated by Philip. And this brought an end to Greek democracy.

Philip's son, Alexander, was appropriately known as "Alexander the Great" because he created a gigantic empire. From his small Macedonia, he and his armies conquered a territory stretching across India and Pakistan to the foot of the Himalayas and present-day Tibet, all in just a few years. However, in 323 BC at the age of 33, Alexander died unexpectedly in Babylon, today's Iraq. There is still speculation about the cause of his death as well as the location of his tomb. In any case, Alexander's sudden death meant that this gigantic empire was divided among his generals. This created the so-called Diadochian kingdom (διάδοχοι), in which Greek remained the official language. The Greco-Bactrian kingdom, for example, in Central Asia, lasted until AD 125, and the Indo-Greek kingdom, in what is now Pakistan, existed from 180 to 10 BC. Eventually these kingdoms collapsed as the Greeks intermarried with the local population—something Alexander had encouraged (and practiced himself).

With Alexander's conquests, Greek culture—and with it, the Greek language—spread widely. Greek was the language used throughout the Mediterranean, the Middle East and far beyond, and was cultivated by local elites. This period in history is called Hellenism, the time from Alexander to Cleopatra, when Greek culture was at its peak and left deep traces still to be found today. When speaking of a *colossal* blunder, or of *stoically* enduring life's adversities, we use words that have their roots in Hellenistic culture, just as with *museum, hydraulic,* or *eureka* (Chaniotis 2018, p. 2). This Hellenistic age owes its name to the "Hellenizers," a Jewish group who adopted Greek customs (p. 1).

And so we return to Jewish culture in the Roman Empire, for it so happens that the New Testament was originally written entirely in Greek. Anyone who wanted to have any influence at that time was expected to do so in Greek. However, the direct followers of Jesus did not know Greek; therefore, it is almost impossible that the Gospels were written by them. This brings one directly to crucial questions of the reliability of statements in the New Testament. For if these texts were not written by the direct followers of Jesus, who then were their authors?

In this regard, it is important to know that the Greeks (or I should say the Hellenes) occupied an important place in Palestine 2,000 years ago. The city of Sepphoris, for example, was a thoroughly Hellenistic city based exclusively on Greek culture, which happened to be a good hour's walk from Nazareth. Is it conceivable that Jesus was ever there? Quite possibly; he was a wandering preacher, always on the move, although he actually had no business there—precisely because Greek was the language of this city. Is it conceivable that Jesus could also speak and write Greek well? We do not know, but it is extremely unlikely. Greek was the language of the social upper class, the elite, and Jesus, the son of a carpenter, certainly did not belong to this group. Perhaps "carpenter" is not quite the correct term, though. The word used for him in Greek is τέκτων (*tekton*), meaning worker or craftsman, perhaps skilled, but perhaps not. It is quite unlikely that such a worker could speak Greek at that time, let alone write it.

The language Jesus spoke

So Jesus probably didn't speak Greek, but then what? Because he was Jewish, many think he spoke Hebrew. But no: his mother tongue was a language spoken in the Middle East at the time, namely Aramaic (not to be confused with Armenian), a Semitic language related to Hebrew and Arabic. And he probably spoke it in a dialect of Galilee that differed slightly from the dialect of Jerusalem. These Aramaic dialects were quite different, but they were mutually intelligible, as always, with a little bit of good will. Aramaic has had its own script since the ninth century BC and was used as a "lingua franca" (vernacular) in the Middle East for about three thousand years, since it is still spoken today by about half a million people, spread over various countries in the Middle East, especially in Iraq, Iran, Lebanon, and Syria. The language belongs to the Eastern group of Semitic languages, and is also related to Akkadian, which was used in Mesopotamia (in Assyria and Babylon, between the Euphrates and Tigris rivers) for about two thousand years until the eighth century BC. I am not talking about a few small language communities, but rather about a widespread and respected language which was also spoken by the Jews in Palestine at that time. By the way, the Hebrew, Syriac and Nabataean scripts developed, in part, from the Aramaic script, which later led to development of the Arabic script. Even some Indian scripts originated from Aramaic. Modern Arabic is also heavily influenced by Aramaic. Here is an example, from the text of the *Lord's Prayer* as found in Matt. 6:5-13 and Luke 11:1-4, reconstructed from Aramaic (which can also be heard on the Internet):

Avvon d-bish-maiya,
nith-qaddash shim-mukh.
Tih-teh mal-chootukh.
Nih-weh çiw-yanukh:
ei-chana d'bish-maiya: ap b'ar-ah.
O'shwooq lan kho-bein:
ei-chana d'ap kh'nan shwiq-qan l'khaya-ween. Oo'la te-
ellan l'niss-yoona:
il la paç-çan min beesha.
Mid-til di-luhluh hai mal-choota
oo khai-la oo tush-bookh-ta l'alam al-mein. Aameen.

Anyone who listens to a spoken version will hear that the sound of Aramaic is similar to that of Hebrew or Arabic. Strangely, the text of the *Lord's Prayer* is not found in the Gospels of Mark or John. If this prayer is so important to Christians, surely one would expect it to appear in all the Gospels? The fact that it does not is related to how these separate Gospels came to be. (More about that later.)

No witnesses

Another aspect of the linguistic situation concerns literacy. Who could read at the time when the New Testament was written? The most thorough research on this question has been done by Catherine Hezser (2001). Her conclusion is that no more than three percent of the people in Palestine could read at that time, let alone write. However, the Gospels were not written in Aramaic, but, as we have seen, in good (albeit simple) Greek, in the *Koiné*. Their authors, therefore, must have been particularly well educated Greek speakers. In other words, the texts in the New Testament do not come from the direct followers of Jesus, and so they are not eyewitness accounts by Jesus' followers. Indeed, none of the evangelists claim to have been eyewitnesses to the events.

Moreover, even if they had been, solid research determines that eyewitness accounts are not particularly accurate. For instance, a recent U.S. government report (*Identifying the Culprit: Assessing Eyewitness Identification*, National Academies Press 2014) shows that, based on DNA research, 75% of recent convictions (some including the death penalty), for which DNA samples were available from the crime scene, were based on witness *mis*-identifications. Therefore, even if there had been witnesses in Jesus' time, not everything they said would have necessarily been true. In any case, there are no direct witness accounts of Jesus. That sounds like a pretty disturbing conclusion. There is not one single piece of writing in existence by anyone who knew Jesus personally. Not a single one. All the texts in the New Testament were written by people who had never met Jesus, without exception. This means no direct witnesses to anything Jesus ever said or did, neither in apocryphal texts (see Chapter 9), nor in the Nag Hammadi texts, nor as we have already seen, in the Dead Sea Scrolls.

This does not mean that Jesus did not live; only that there are no direct witnesses of his life. But the entire Christian religion is not based on eyewitness accounts. (Probably the same is true for other religions, but that is beyond our interest here. But these book religions are at least partly based on oral traditions that were written down later.) This brings me to something modern readers will doubtless wonder about: How should the many miraculous stories told in the New Testament be understood? I refer, of course, to the miracles. Are all of these stories considered true events? A historical approach is also needed to deal with this question linguistically.

Strange miracles

I have already explained in Chapter 1 how historians deal with so-called miracles in the New Testament. In this chapter, I look at such miracles from a linguistic point of view. Sometimes, in fact, these miracles have a very simple explanation—one that has to do with language. Take the famous miracle of Jesus walking on water, as described in John 6:19. In brief, Jesus has earlier performed the miracle of the multiplication of the loaves. Then he retires to the hills, and his followers want to go home and get into their boat. However, in the middle of the water there is a storm and they are in danger. Suddenly Jesus appears and walks on the water. The original text, according to Nestle-Aland (2012, p. 312), is:

θεωροῦσιν τὸν Ἰησοῦν περιπατοῦντα ἐπὶ τῆς θαλάσσης
(theorousin ton Iesoun peripatounta epi tes thalasses)

What does this mean? To better understand these words, one should first know something about the structure of the Greek language. If you did not learn Greek in school, don't let this scare you off! One important thing to know is that Greek (like Russian, or—indeed—English from before the year 1000) is a language with *declensions*. That means that words change their shape depending on their grammatical function, i.e. whether they are the subject or the object in a sentence. The English word "peripatetics"—describing philosophers or teachers who taught while walking around—comes from the Greek περιπατῶν (peripatoon), so it has something to do with "walking." The word τῆς (tes) comes closest to "the" in English. I will come back to ἐπὶ (epi) in a moment, but what is θαλάσσης (thalasses)?

Thalassa in Xenophon

Some of you may have heard this word, *thalassa*, in a completely different context: the *Anabasis*, a story in seven books written by Xenophon, a Greek professional soldier, philosopher and historian. It is the account of the journey of ten thousand young men in which Xenophon himself participated, beginning in 401 BC. They were Greek mercenaries commanded by the Persian Cyrus the Younger, who wanted to use them to push his brother Artaxerxes from the throne. They left Sardis, on the west coast of what is now Turkey (then called Ionia), where there were many Greek settlements. Deeper and deeper they moved into the country, into Persia. In Kunaxa, on the banks of the Euphrates, a decisive battle with the army of King Artaxerxes took place. In this battle the Greeks were not defeated — quite the opposite — but Cyrus, their leader, was killed. Their generals were then invited to consult with the Persian king, who promptly (and in a cowardly manner) had them all assassinated. The Greek troops now stood in the midst of a totally unknown and hostile territory with no leader, no money, no protector, with their lives in great danger and with only one desire, to return home as soon as possible. But how to get back to Greece from Persia on foot? Xenophon was elected by the soldiers as their new leader. He suggested that they go north through the interior of the country to the Black Sea, because there were some Greek settlements there. One can imagine the fear, hardship and dangers of the young men on such a journey, about seven hundred miles on foot in all kinds of weather, with heavy armor, very little food, and surrounded by hostile tribes. At some point, after months, they actually reached the Black Sea. At the sight of the sea, a cry of joy rang out through the ranks of the ten thousand: "Thalassa! Thalassa! The sea! The sea!" This cry was remembered as the salvation of the Greek army (although their troubles were not over, for they were no longer welcome in their own country).

But what is the connection between θάλασσα (thalassa) and θαλάσσης (thalasses) in John's Gospel? I will discuss this for a moment, because it allows one to provide a possible explanation for the miracle.

Greek is a "synthetic" language. This means that it uses declensions, also called "cases." English has lost most of its declensions—but it used to have them until a thousand years ago. It still has a few of them in pronouns. For instance, the pronoun "he" which acts as the subject in a sentence, changes to "him" when it is an object, as in "I saw *him*," NOT "I saw *he*." Such declensions (cases) have names. The one for the subject "he" is called the *nominative*, the one for the object "him" is *accusative*. Or, when we talk of someone possessing something, "he" changes to "his," like in "*his* book." This case is called the *genitive*. Similarly, "she" changes to "her" and "I" to "me" or "my." Then there is also the *dative*, which is when there is talk of a recipient, as in "I gave *him* his book." These are declensions: the words change their shape according to their grammatical functions in a sentence. And as the examples make clear, the changes can be rather radical.

In the sentence from the story in which Jesus walks on the water (*theorousin ton Iesoun peripatounta epi tes thalasses*), the word *epi* is a preposition that can be used with different cases (the genitive, dative or accusative). There is certainly no dative here, because that would be Θαλάσση (*thalassē*). The form Θαλάσσης (*thalassēs*) here is genitive. Then, according to the glossary in Nestle-Aland's critical edition (2012, p. 70), in such a case (with the genitive), *epi* means on, over, to, after, before, at, under. But this is not very helpful. Take a look at the last word in the quotation above. Might Jesus have gone "under water"? Quite possibly, based on grammar. So we have recourse to a Greek grammar, and then the solution to the apparent miracle of walking on water reveals itself, because my grammar book states that *epi* with genitive case means *on*, *at*, *by*. An example of this would be (again from Xenophon, the Greek historian mentioned above) ἐπὶ τοῦ ποταμοῦ (epi tou potamou): *by* the river. Its similarity to the phrase in the New Testament is striking. In both cases, it refers to a location near a body of water (river, lake). In this way, a linguistic analysis shows that Jesus walked *by* the sea, not *on* it.

This seems to make sense of the miracle. The most appropriate or simplest translation is not "on," but "by" or "along" the water. However, I will return to this miracle later. Of course not all miracles can be explained so easily by a linguistic analysis. But the passage in which Jesus walks on water is a good example of the clarity a linguistic approach can bring. The issue, however, becomes more complicated.

That Lazarus, who had died, was brought back to life by Jesus (Luke 7:12-17) cannot be explained by linguistic analysis. In the first place, this story, like all miracles, is meant to illustrate Jesus' special powers. However, there is a problem here. Let us assume that Jesus actually performed these kinds of spectacular miracles, turning water into wine, multiplying bread and fish a thousandfold, raising the dead, and so on. Now suppose for an instant that he really could and did do so; would it not be logical to expect the Roman authorities to immediately recruit such a person to serve the emperor in Rome with his miraculous powers?

Cognitive dissonance

Of course, tradition also plays a role. Once such an understanding of Jesus' extraordinary powers took root in a Christian community, it began to take on a life of its own. This may be expressed in the complex term, "ideological inertia." There is extensive and thorough research in psychology on this topic. People do not easily abandon their beliefs, even when there is good evidence to the contrary. The theory that demonstrates this is the theory of cognitive dissonance, first developed by Leon Festinger in 1956. Because this theory offers guidance in understanding any religious (and more generally, any ideological) movement, I dwell on it for a moment.

Out of the daily bombardment with information of all kinds, we distill our own beliefs and convictions. But now and then, we are confronted with conflicts between particular beliefs. Smokers, for instance, are torn between, on the one hand, the awareness that smoking is bad for their health, and on the other, their intense desire to light a cigarette. (One can easily replace smoking in this context with fast food, sugar, alcohol, drugs, late nights and more.) When circumstances confront one with an explicit opposition between two such contrasting alternatives, this is *cognitive dissonance*: the two elements "clash" as in musical dissonance. Someone in this situation will then try to acquire as much reliable information as possible, to "eliminate" one of the two beliefs, in order to be relieved of the dissonance. That is what one would expect. However—and here lies the relevant contribution of Festinger—that is *not* what happens. Continuing with the example of smoking, people will rather construct reasons to stay with their unhealthy habit, as opposed to living a healthy life. They will then come up with justifications such as "There is no scientific proof that smoking causes cancer," or "My grandfather was a chain smoker and lived to be 90 years old," or "By smoking I can concentrate better," and so on. This is a strategy to avoid the unpleasant feelings of dissonance while adhering to one belief in opposition to the other, which has much more evidence in its favor.

An extreme form of this behavior was observed by Festinger. In his book *When Prophecy Fails* (1956), he describes a religious sect in which the members believed that the world was going to be destroyed—with the exception of themselves, of course. In order to study the social mechanisms of such beliefs, Festinger and some of his coworkers registered as sect members of the group. The leader of the sect, a Marian Keech (Dorothy Martin was her real name, an inhabitant of Chicago), had received an "extraterrestrial letter," saying that her followers would be rescued because they adhered to the purity of the doctrine, while the rest of humanity would perish in a deluge. The letter mentioned a date on which this would happen. The sect members who sternly believed this, assembled on that specific day, waiting for the spacecraft that would save them from annihilation. They waited and waited, in vain. No spacecraft arrived.

This confronted the members with an extreme form of cognitive dissonance between their hopes and the failure of the prediction. But, to the utter amazement of Festinger and his coworkers, instead of concluding that their belief was mistaken, they now believed more strongly than ever before that their belief was justified, some even fanatically so. Then they came up with rationalizations of the kind provided by the smokers, mentioned above: "There must have been a mistake in the calculation of the day," or "God had answered their prayers and was willing to spare the world, thanks to their efforts," or "The creatures in the spacecraft were prepared to give the world another chance." Ultimately, most members remained true followers of Marian Keech until her death.

Between their religious belief and the failed prophecy, the followers faced a choice between two alternatives: to change their original belief, or to change the beliefs of the rest of the world. In fact, they had but one possible choice, which was the latter. They had invested too much of their lives in this belief; therefore, the world had to change!

The example illustrates precisely the kind of processes people undergo when they are confronted with contradictions (dissonance) between separate views, one of which is privileged by their very attachment to it. People then often try to resolve this dissonance by interpreting one or both of the views differently.

Everyone knows that no one can walk on liquid water. But if you are a believer and you read the story of Jesus walking on water, you are faced with a cognitive dissonance. One knows that this cannot be true. So there is a search for reconciliation between dissonant views. For most believers, this leads to the declaration that Jesus is divine and therefore can accomplish anything. This new interpretation also has the advantage of showing what special powers Jesus has, which in turn is an important element in the drive for mission and conversion. If Jesus can do these extraordinary things, you had better believe in him.

It is clear that such attempts to reconcile dissonant views can bring peace of mind, but do not really solve the problem. In Western culture, it is more common to try to dig deeper into the problem to see if either view is wrong, or whether they both are. And the most reliable method to use is a critical and rational one. Returning to the story of Jesus on the water, the result of rational analysis is an erroneous translation, which is much more plausible than explaining the dissonance away by appealing to Jesus' supernatural powers. This is precisely the classic refutation of miracles as elaborated by David Hume as early as 1748. The argument boils down to a probability assessment: Which is more likely—that the witness is mistaken or that a violation of the laws of nature actually took place? In his famous formulation: "No testimony is sufficient to establish a miracle, unless the testimony be of such a kind, that its falsehood would be more miraculous, than the fact, which it endeavors to establish" (Hume 2008, p. 83).

Worth telling

There is another more important reason to analyze the miracle more deeply, namely that the story becomes even more exciting and compelling when Jesus walks *on* the water and not *by* it. The events then become "worth telling." Suppose you come home and tell your partner that you saw someone walking along the water. The response will be, in all probability, "Yes, and?" It's clear that the thing is hardly worth mentioning. But if I come home and tell my partner that I saw someone walking *on* the water, well, that's something! I may be assured now of immediate attention, followed by questions of: What? Where? How? What do you mean? The example shows that good stories try to tell unexpected or strange things. In fairy tales or novels about the future, or in the Harry Potter books, there are things that are not possible in everyday life. Readers know this, and yet they are captivated by these texts. They know, of course, that Emma and Anna never existed, but they still experience *Madame Bovary* and *Anna Karenina* as deeply moving novels.

This view of stories is at least as old as the *Poetics* of the Greek philosopher Aristotle (c. 335 BC), who said, "For the purposes of poetry a convincing impossibility is preferable to an unconvincing possibility" (Poetics 1461b). Volumes have been written about this sentence. Aristotle makes it clear that a good storyteller must talk about impossible things. But they must nonetheless be probable. He discourages discussion of improbable things that are possible. It should be remembered that the *Poetics* was intended as a manual for writers. The original title is Περὶ ποιητικῆς (*Peri poietikês*), which roughly means, "On the making (of literary texts)." In this case, it means: How do I write a good story, or tragedy?

Currently, this view is most systematically represented in the theory of "foregrounding" (see, among others, Van Peer 1986 and Van Peer 2007). This notion of drawing things into the foreground is also called *alienation, defamiliarization, de-automatization,* and even *making strange*. The notion—which is widely used in literary theory—derives especially from the Russian Formalists, who coined the term *ostranenie* for it in Russian, which literally means "making strange"; see also Berlina (2017). What good writers, storytellers, poets, and playwrights do is to "alienate" one's perceptions in their texts, so that the world no longer resembles one's everyday reality in many ways. The result is usually mild shock. As a reader, you are surprised by what you read—which may set you thinking. Most of the time, the confrontation with this somewhat strange world is also permeated with emotion, which is of course the intention because authors want to stir, to touch one's feelings.

With this in mind, I must now take a large step back. Linguistic analyses like the previous one are extremely useful, but they have their limitations; their value must be related to the context. I have disregarded context in the previous sections, for didactic reasons. But now I return to the same fragment in John's Gospel. It turns out that the earlier analysis does not apply, for it is clear that in this version of the story, Jesus' disciples are *in* the boat on the lake. John 6:19 says: "So when they had rowed about five and twenty or thirty furlongs, they see Jesus walking on the sea, and drawing nigh unto the ship; and they were afraid."

All of this is supported by the same story in two other Gospels (Matt. 14.22 ff. and Mark 6.45 ff.). There, however, the narrative is much more complex. In Matthew, the disciples see Jesus coming and get scared because they think he is a ghost. Jesus, however, speaks to them and invites Peter to come to him. Peter gets out of the boat and walks toward Jesus—also *on* the water. Here, of course, my previous analysis of the Greek preposition *epi* is no longer valid, since they are all in the middle of the lake. But then Peter hesitates and immediately sinks into the water. He calls out to Jesus to save him, because he cannot swim. Jesus gives him his hand and together they calmly walk across the water and step into the boat. This story is much more successful "as a story" than in John, because Matthew uses more foregrounding (alienation) than John by having the action take place in the middle of the lake, and by having Peter almost drown. The story accordingly becomes more "tellworthy." Moreover, this version of the story contains an additional lesson. Jesus asks Peter why he doubted him. The lesson, naturally, is that followers should not doubt Jesus' special powers. In Mark, however, the episode with Peter is missing, which means there is less foregrounding. All of this explains why, of the three versions of this episode, the one in Matthew is almost always chosen rather than the other two. It is likely that the less spectacular versions in John and Mark are closer to the original narrative, and that Matthew has made the story more "worth telling."

Up to this point, I have been working quite intensively with the Greek text of the New Testament, which proved very useful in helping to clarify things. While a historian cannot explain why someone would walk on water, because it does not fit the methods of historiography, a Greek dictionary and a Greek grammar can work wonders in this regard. However, the linguistic situation surrounding the New Testament is even more complex.

Two important translations

Long before the English translation of the Bible, two other extremely important translations existed that shaped Christianity for more than a thousand years. The first of these is the *Septuagint*. This is the oldest translation of the Hebrew Bible (the Old Testament) in Greek, the *Koiné*, but with many Hebrew and Aramaic elements, created in 250-100 BC, in Alexandria (Egypt), then the largest center of learning. According to legend, this translation was made by 70 scholars, hence the Latin word *septuaginta* for the number 70.

That they spoke Greek in the Egyptian town of Alexandria is not unexpected, as we have already seen. Greek was spoken there until the twentieth century. Between 1957 and 1960, the English author Lawrence Durrell published four novels under the title *The Alexandra Quartet*, beautifully evocative of the city and its culture, with psychological portraits and analyses to be savored. The events take place before and during WWII. And the language of communication in the city? Greek! It is said in passing of Aboiut Mnemjian, the barber: "His Greek is defective but adventurous and vivid (...)" (Durrell 1962, p. 36). In fact, French, English, Hebrew, Armenian, Italian, and Arabic, and probably several other languages were spoken, in addition to Greek. This was abruptly ended by the Arab nationalist policies of President Nasser in 1956, who issued a decree requiring foreigners to leave the country. The result of this short-sighted policy was a huge economic and intellectual loss for Egypt. The fact that the *Septuagint* was written in Alexandria is no accident; the city has always been multicultural, home to the world's largest library of antiquity. Today it is a largely monocultural city.

No less important is a second text, the *Vulgate* (Biblia Vulgata), but this time the New Testament was translated from Greek into Latin. Jerome of Stridon made this translation of the Bible between 390 and 405 in Bethlehem, where he was able to use the *Hexapla*, a voluminous work containing a word-for-word comparison of the Greek *Septuagint* with the original Hebrew scriptures. This translation of the New Testament into Latin was based on the best Greek manuscripts available at the time. Large portions of the Old Testament were translated from Hebrew into Latin by Jerome himself. This *Vulgate* was the official version of the Bible for the Catholic Church for more than a thousand years. I now look at a dramatic issue from these two translations, concerning the virginity of the mother of Jesus.

The virgin Mary

The importance of analyzing the linguistic situation for a correct understanding of the New Testament is demonstrated in an even more forceful way in relation to the dogma of the virgin birth of Jesus. According to tradition, Mary, the mother of Jesus, did not have sexual intercourse with her husband, but gave birth to a child. The conception had taken place through the Holy Spirit, in other words, through God himself. Therefore, it is a huge problem for the Church that the brothers and sisters of Jesus are mentioned in the Gospels, because then Mary would not have remained a virgin, would she?

But why do the churches cling so tenaciously to the virginity of Jesus' mother? I cannot suggest a good explanation, except that it has hardened into a premise they want to defend at all costs, so again it is a case of "ideological inertia." The churches will inevitably lose the argument with historical reality, because this story about the virgin birth is extremely easy to explain. Just like walking on water, we are again dealing with a language problem. It is now time to clear up this mystery once and for all. I must mention expressly that what follows here is not a personal conviction of mine, but the undisputed opinion of almost all secular specialists in this field. Everyone agrees on this point: The so-called virginity of Mary is based on a *translation error*. How did it come about?

I begin with Matthew 1:18-25 and Luke 1:26-38, which are the only passages in the New Testament where the virgin birth is mentioned. Nothing is said about it in the Gospel of Mark, nor in the Gospel of John. Paul's letters, the oldest documents in the New Testament, also say nothing about the virginity of Jesus' mother. Let's look at the texts, first Matthew, who says:

> Now the birth of Jesus was on this wise. When as his mother was espoused to Joseph, before they came together, she was found with child of the Holy Ghost. Then Joseph, her husband, being a just man, and not willing to make her a public example, was minded to put her away privily. But while he thought on these things, behold, the angel of the Lord appeared unto him in a dream, saying, Joseph, thou son of David, fear not to take unto thee Mary, thy wife: for that which is conceived in her is of the Holy Ghost. And she shall bring forth a son, and thou shalt call his name Jesus: for he shall save his people from their sins. Now all this was done, that it might be fulfilled which was spoken of the

Lord by the prophet, saying, "Behold, a virgin shall be with child, and shall bring forth a son, and they shall call his name Immanuel, which being interpreted is: God with us." Then Joseph being raised from sleep did as the angel of the Lord had bidden him and took unto him his wife: And knew her not till she had brought forth her firstborn son; and he called his name Jesus.

(Matt. 1:18-25)

In the case of Luke's Gospel, the wording is somewhat different, but the tenor is the same:

And in the sixth month the angel Gabriel was sent from God unto a city of Galilee named Nazareth, to a virgin espoused to a man whose name was Joseph, of the house of David; and the virgin's name was Mary. And the angel came in unto her and said, "Hail, thou that art highly favored, the Lord is with thee!: Blessed art thou among women." And when she saw him, she was troubled at his saying and cast in her mind, what manner of salutation this should be. And the angel said unto her, "Fear not, Mary: for thou hast found favor with God. And behold, thou shalt in thy womb, and bring forth a son, and shalt call his name Jesus." (...) Then said Mary unto the angel, "How shall this, seeing I know not a man?" And the angel answered and said unto her, "The Holy Ghost shall come upon thee, and the power of the Highest shall overshadow thee (...)."

(Luke 1:26-35)

It is clear. In both fragments it is literally said that Mary is (or will become) pregnant without having had sexual relations with a man. In Luke it is not so clear, but in Matthew reference is made to a text from the Old Testament. The evangelist used the text to make it clear that the virgin birth of Jesus was foretold by a prophecy in the Old Testament of the Jews. One must not forget that Matthew was a Greek-speaking Jew and was therefore very familiar with the ancient prophecies. The text in question that Matthew refers to is Isaiah 7:14. But what does the text of this prophecy say in the original Hebrew?

לֹא וּגְמַע וֹמֶשׁ תאָרְקוּ גֵּב תְדָלִיו הֹרָה הָמְלַעָה תָנָה תוֹא בָכָל אוֹגְ וְתִי נַכְלֹדִי:
(Therefore the LORD himself will give you a sign: Behold, a young woman is with child and will bear a son, and she will name him Immanuel.)

The Hebrew word that is of interest here is: הָמְלַעָה (almah). Its translation is "a young woman"; it does not mean that she would be a virgin, but simply means a young woman of childbearing age, married or unmarried. Under no circumstances does it mean "virgin." The word for virgin in Hebrew is בתולה (betulah).

The problem that arises here is that in the *Septuagint* translation, the person who translated the Hebrew word *almah* apparently did not understand it and mistranslated it as παρθένος (*parthenos*), virgin. Since then, Christians face a two-thousand-year-old problem, namely how a virgin can give birth to a child. Of course, if one invokes divine omnipotence or supernatural powers, the cognitive dissonance is easily solved. However, the book you are reading is about the historical study of the New Testament, and magical explanations have no place here. In any case, there is no need for magic, because the incredibly straightforward explanation is that it is a simple translation error. The *Encyclopedia Judaica* describes it as "a two-thousand-year-old misunderstanding of Isaiah 7:14 (...) that gives no indication of the chastity of the woman in question" (Skolnik 2006, p. 540).

Again, one observes the same phenomenon: Church authorities refer to texts they want to understand literally, which forces them into insurmountable problems. Such an attitude also has a name: fundamentalism. There is much going on in the media today about fundamentalism in Islam, but Christianity has it also. The idea that Jesus' mother was a virgin is an expression of this fundamentalism, and a historical-linguistic analysis makes it clear how people came to this strange view. When one includes the historical context, many things are revealed. So is the figure of Jesus in the midst of the Hellenistic culture of Palestine.

Jesus as a cynic philosopher

There is yet another reason why Greek is so important. Not only the Greek language itself, but also Greek philosophy was significant in the creation of the New Testament. Several specialists have suggested that Jesus actually fits very well into the Greek philosophy of *Cynicism*. The word as used here means something quite different from its usually understood meaning in everyday English. The name for Cynic philosophy, κυνισμός (*kynismos*), derives from the genitive form *kynos* of the Greek word κύων (*kyon*) for "dog," and originated in Athens in the fifth century BC. Its core consists of the view that a simple and virtuous life leads to happiness. The Cynic philosophers were characterized by their strong aversion to social convention and their preference for a natural life of utter poverty. The best known of them is probably Diogenes of Sinope, a disciple of Socrates. As he walked from one statue to another, each time extending his begging hand, onlookers asked why he begged at statues, to which Diogenes replied, "To practice getting nothing." One can imagine such an attitude in figures such as John the Baptist or Jesus of Nazareth. Compare, for example, "Behold the fowls of the air: they sow not, neither do they reap, nor gather into barns" (Matt. 6:26). Another anecdote about Diogenes concerns Alexander the Great, who asked Diogenes if he could do something for him, fulfill any wish of his. To this, Diogenes replied, "Yes, get out of my sun for a moment." (A wealth of information about Diogenes can be found in the voluminous work of another Diogenes, namely Diogenes Laërtius' *Lives and Opinions of Eminent Philosophers*, written in the third century and containing information known in antiquity about countless philosophers.)

As far as the Cynic philosophers are concerned, their principles were not much different to the principles of simplicity and poverty that Jesus preached. Another striking parallel is that the Cynics did not respect or maintain family ties and held no form of fear, as can be found in the Gospels. Another similarity is that the Cynics often sought to disrupt public life. For example, one reads in Mark the story of the "cleansing of the temple" as Jesus forcibly chases the moneychangers out of the temple. It says, "And Jesus went into the temple, and began to cast out them that sold and bought in the temple, and overthrew the tables of the moneychangers, and the seats of them that sold doves; and would not suffer that an man should carry any vessel through the temple" (Mark 11:15-16). It is clear that the episode fits well with the way Cynic philosophers liked to disrupt public order.

The story requires a brief explanation. As mentioned earlier, Palestine was at the time a Roman province, where people paid with Roman coins. However, this caused a problem for the temple in Jerusalem. Anyone who wanted to bring a sacrifice, for example a dove (from someone who was poor) or a sheep (from someone who was rich), had to pay for it at the temple, where these sacrificial animals were sold. However, this Roman money was unclean according to Jewish religion, and therefore could not be used inside the temple. For that, there were moneychangers, who exchanged Roman coins for temple money. The practice was approved by the Roman authorities, and it was entirely according to Jewish law. So why did Jesus throw such a tantrum? Of course, there are many theological explanations for this. But historically it is a remarkable event, and some of the story may not be true either. For instance, it seems that the temple was more or less like a village church.

However, the temple had 13 entrances and the temple precinct was several soccer fields in size. That a single person could have made such a mess of things is rather unlikely. It would certainly be agreeable to some today to paint Jesus as an anticapitalist, but the storytellers undoubtedly exaggerated a bit.

In the New Testament, this incident is portrayed as the reason for his arrest: "And the scribes and chief priests heard it, and sought how they might destroy him: for they feared him, because all the people was astonished at his doctrine" (Mark 11:18). But why did they not have him arrested for disturbing public order? All they had to do was call some Roman soldiers, and they would have captured him right away. What were they waiting for? As a story, of course, it is well thought out; the arrest is subtly announced, but postponed, so that the tension rises. But this episode is not at all historically plausible.

Interestingly, John mentions the incident with a time difference of several years. In John 2:13-22 the same episode is narrated, but there the event takes place at the very beginning of the time when Jesus was preaching (so with no connection to his arrest). In Mark it takes place on the eve of his arrest, which is at least three years later. However, the episode clearly fits the way the Cynic philosophers liked to disrupt public order. Several specialists (including F. Gerald Downing, Burton Mack, John Crossan and R.B. Branham, and M.-O. Goulet-Cazé) see a great deal of correspondence between the ideals and rhetoric of Jesus and those of the Cynic philosophers.

Yet another interesting argument is that the city of Gadara, in what was then Palestine, was a center of Cynicism—and a mere day's walk from Nazareth. In any case, the influence of the Cynic philosophy was very much felt in Palestine 2,000 years ago. Was Jesus a Cynic philosopher? We do not know. Be that as it may, he fits almost seamlessly into this tradition, even though he was not a Greek, but a Jew.

Conclusion

In this chapter I have described the complex linguistic situation in which the New Testament was written. The fact that Palestine was a province of the Roman Empire did not mean that Latin, the language spoken by the Romans, played an important role in cultural life. It was the language of administration, justice and practical life. Therefore, the texts of the New Testament were not written in Latin. Through the empire founded by Alexander the Great, Greek became the most important cultural language, also in Palestine, where various cities were purely Greek in nature. However, Jesus' immediate environment consisted of low-skilled workers (peasants, fishermen, artisans, carpenters) who were certainly not able to speak Greek let alone read or write, even in their own language, Aramaic—a Semitic language related to Hebrew and Arabic, and spoken at that time by the majority of the Palestinian population (albeit in different dialects). This means that the Gospels were written by people who were not part of Jesus' immediate environment. Therefore, they are by no means direct testimonies. No known text comes from someone who knew Jesus himself. However, many anecdotes about Jesus fit a worldview that originated in Greece, namely the Cynical philosophy. So far, however, this view is only a working hypothesis.

A closer look at the Greek text of the New Testament, in which numerous miracles are recounted, revealed another remarkable result. In one possible interpretation, Jesus did not walk on water, but along water (the lake). This exercise showed the importance of carefully studying the original text. On the other hand, the analysis turned out to be contradictory to what is given in another Gospel, that of Matthew. During a brief excursion, I demonstrated how such "miracles" lead to a better, more exciting, more beautiful, and yes, a more "literary" story. That is why Matthew's version of Jesus' walk on the water is better known and more often referred to than Mark's and John's.

Another example, that of the virgin birth of Jesus, showed once again the importance of linguistic analysis in clearing up millennia-old mystifications.

Chapter 4

The Texts of the New Testament

This chapter will look at the texts of the New Testament on a deeper level. Where are these texts to be found? A simple (and correct) answer is: in the bookstore. And this bookstore gets the text from the publisher. But where does the publisher get the text? Well ... from earlier editions. And what about the even earlier editions?

We are delving into the history of the texts here. And the discipline that deals with this, philology, has developed appropriate ways to do so. When one reads the New Testament today, it is in translation. This is already evident in the word "Gospel" itself, from Old English god-spel, literally "good message" or "good story." The Gospels were written by the "evangelists" deriving from the Greek εὐ-αγγέλιον (eu-angellion). Eu means "good" in words such as "euphemism," "euthanasia," and "euphoria." Angellion means "message" or "messenger" from which the English word "angel" is derived. So an angel is a messenger, and the evangelists bring the "good news," the good message. I now look at the beginning of such a Gospel, in this case, Mark's (1:1):

Ἀρχὴ τοῦ εὐαγγελίου Ἰησοῦ Χριστοῦ [υἱοῦ θεοῦ]
(The beginning of the Gospel of Jesus Christ [the Son of God].)

This comes from the critical edition of Nestle-Aland (2012, p. 102). The last two words are between square brackets. Why? Because scholars strongly suspect that this part is a later addition, so that the original text did not say "the Son of God." The next sentence reads:

Καθὼς γέγραπται ἐν τοῖς προφήταις, Ἰδοὺ ποστέλλω
τὸν ἄγγελόν μου πρὸ κατασκευάσει προσώπου σου, ὃς
κατασκευάσει τὴν σου-
(As it is written in the Prophets, Behold, I send my messenger
before thy face, which shall prepare thy way before thee)

Here already is an example of a deliberate intervention in the
text. The translation according to Bible Gateway (https://www.
biblegateway.com/passage/?search=Mark%201:1-Mark%20
1:13&version=NABRE) is: "As it is written in the prophet
Isaiah." So, is it "prophets" or "prophet Isaiah"? To find out,
it is necessary to reconstruct what happened to the text here.
The author of the Gospel of Mark refers to a prophecy in the
Old Testament, namely to that of the prophet Isaiah: "Behold,
I send my angel." But there is no such quotation in Isaiah! A
clever monk, well versed in Biblical matters, must have noticed
this when copying. He probably wondered what to do now
since this quotation obviously did not exist, and came up with
a simple solution: leave out the name "Isaiah." Even in some
of the oldest manuscripts of this Gospel, the omission had
already happened. One would normally assume that the older
a manuscript, the more reliable it is, because it is closer to the
original. But that is not necessarily the case. So the age of a
manuscript does not guarantee its reliability.

Prophecies

The texts in the New Testament regularly refer to "prophecies"
from the Old Testament. There, the course of events surrounding
Jesus would have been predicted. But these predictions are
invariably denied by Jewish scholars. I examine the case more
closely. In the text Isaiah (Isa. 53:3) we read, "He was despised
and rejected of men; a man of sorrows, and acquainted with
grief: and we hid as it were our faces from him; he was despised,
and we esteemed him not." Christians saw this as a prediction

of Jesus' suffering and the redemption it brought to humanity. But the text of Isaiah is in the past tense, "was," and refers not to the future but to the past. This passage is about someone who has suffered. Furthermore, the prophet also makes it clear (in Isa. 49:3) who it is about. It is not a Messiah, but the people of Israel who suffered for the sins they committed against God: "He Yahweh said to me, 'Thou art my servant, O Israel; in whom I will be glorified.'"

In fact, none of the so-called prophecies listed in the New Testament are credible. These prophecies were all cases of what the Germans so aptly call *hineininterpretieren*, literally "to interpret into."

The type of intentional alteration of texts illustrated above is not limited to the ancient world. It still occurs today. To give a simple example, I recently reread the poem *"De herfst blaast op den horen"* (Autumn blows on the horn) by the Flemish writer, Felix Timmermans. One of the lines speaks of "a triangle of geese in the sky." But at school we had to learn the poem by heart, and I don't remember that phrase. I remember it was "a triangle of ducks in the sky." But because ducks don't fly in triangular formations, and geese do, someone—a reader with some ornithological knowledge—must have "adapted" the text, and accordingly protected the author from his ignorance. The copyist who changed "the prophet Isaiah" into "the prophets" was likewise trying to protect the text of the Gospel from itself.

Scholars are constantly on the lookout for such later adaptations. In any case, it must not be forgotten that the texts of the Gospels that we read now are at least three steps removed from what Jesus preached. Everything that Jesus would have said according to the New Testament is already a translation from the original that had been orally transmitted from Aramaic into Greek. So it is not known exactly what Jesus said in his native language. Also, we are reading a translation of the Greek into English, yet another step away from the original. Such a linguistically complex situation almost inevitably leads to misunderstandings.

Four gospels

Church authorities correctly assert that the New Testament was not written by one person. It is not clear what language the evangelists themselves spoke, although they knew Greek well, otherwise they could not have written these texts. Small variations in their Greek may say something about where they lived. It is unlikely that they themselves understood Aramaic well. In other words, they got their stories from what others said Jesus would have said.

In fact, we do not know who the real authors were. They wrote their texts decades after the events, in countries other than Palestine, most likely in urban settings, in a different language to that of Jesus. What they wrote was based on stories they had heard, stories that differed from each other and which they then adapted to their own vision of who Jesus was and what his message meant. Did they know the texts of the other authors? In some cases they did, as already seen for both Matthew and Luke who used Mark's text and the *Book of Q*.

Perhaps it is not entirely clear how scholars go about identifying authors. As already noted, small variations in Greek can give clues about where the evangelists lived or where they came from. For instance, here are some examples from the English language. The first thing that is immediately obvious is whether the spelling is British or American. Another is the choice of words. So, if a text contains words like *lass* (for "girl"), *bonnie* (for "nice"), *wee* (for "small"), *noo* (for "now"), or *bairn* (for "child"), we may be sure that the text originates in a Scottish environment, and that the author must at least be familiar with this language variety. Based on such word usage—and other aspects of language—scholars are able to determine that the text must in all probability have been written by a Scottish author. The same is true for the Greek language of two thousand years ago. But then, of course, one must master ancient languages at a very deep level.

The texts themselves

The first question to ask is how many of these New Testament texts exist. As mentioned earlier, there are over 27,000, and counting. But how did this vast number of texts eventually lead to the New Testament? A crucial figure in the process was Bishop Athanasius of Alexandria (295-373). His 39th letter, written in 367, is considered the basis for the current version of the New Testament; he listed the same 27 "books" that are still known today in our editions of the New Testament. Prior to this, there were many "lists" of texts that circulated among the various Christian communities, although they were quite different from the one by Athanasius, and from each other. Athanasius wanted to create unity in this multiplicity of lists, but also to clarify which texts were to be considered "recognized." His "list" was not his own unilateral decision, but the end result of a long process of investigation and consultation. At the council of Carthage, in 397, Athanasius' list would eventually be approved. In ecclesiastical jargon, this list is called the "canon," from the Greek κανών, which in Hellenism meant rule, regulation, guideline, standard.

Ultimately, then, the canon was written more than three hundred years after the death of Jesus, and the differences between the manuscripts are downright extreme: There are between 200,000 and 300,000 variations among all the manuscripts, more than there are words in the entire New Testament! Most of these variations are minor errors in copying or translation. Some, however, are clearly intentional. Moreover, the understanding of the New Testament was hampered for a very long period, in fact throughout the Middle Ages, for about a thousand years by the fact that few people in the West were skilled in the Greek language. For example, Dante, in his *Divina Commedia* (in Canto 26 of the *Inferno*), has Odysseus sail past the Pillars of Hercules (Strait of Gibraltar) into the Atlantic; the true outcome of the Greek epic was apparently unknown to him. And Dante certainly not the least in erudition! I'm not suggesting that no one in the Middle Ages knew Greek. But knowledge about Greek at that time was very limited. Therefore, Jerome of Stridon wrote a Latin translation of the Bible in the fourth or fifth century, the *Vulgate*, as mentioned in the previous chapter.

The knowledge of Greek increased considerably after 1453 following the fall of Constantinople (also known as Byzantium or Istanbul, which by the way is a derivation of the original Greek name: εἰς τὴν Πόλιν, *eis tein polin*, "in the city"). This was the capital of the so-called Eastern Roman Empire which had survived for a thousand years after the fall of the Western Roman Empire in the fifth century. In this Eastern Roman Empire, Greek was the language of administration and religion, of science and of the imperial court. During the siege of the city by the Muslim armies, many intellectuals fled to the West and passed on their Greek knowledge to Western scholars. Italy in particular was where many of these refugees ended up, directly contributing to the rise of the Renaissance.

The first editions

Here is an important and surprising fact: During the Middle Ages, ordinary people were forbidden to own a Bible. In 1199, Pope Innocentius III prohibited the private reading of the Bible. At the Council of Toulouse in 1229, possession of the Bible (especially translations in the vernacular) were strictly forbidden. In the words of the Council:

> We prohibit also that the laity should be permitted to have the books of the Old and the New Testament; unless anyone

from the motives of devotion should wish to have the Psalter or the Breviary for divine offices or the hours of the blessed Virgin; but we most strictly forbid their having any translation of these books.

(Peters 1980, p. 195)

It was punishable by death! Of course, high members of the church hierarchy had copies in their possession, mostly of the *Vulgate*, but not the priests and certainly not the faithful. Here, in brief, is the story of William Tyndale (c. 1494-1536) which shows how hard the church authorities tried to control the faith.

Tyndale left England in 1524 and stayed for a while in Germany, where he learned Hebrew. This was not possible in England after King Edward I expelled all Jews from the country in 1290. (They could not return until the seventeenth century, at the time of Oliver Cromwell.)

Meanwhile the first printed Greek version of the New Testament appeared in 1516, under the Latin title *Novum Instrumentum omne*, by Erasmus of Rotterdam. Tyndale used this edition as well as the German translation of the Bible by Martin Luther. He produced an English translation based on these texts in 1525. His translation of the Old Testament is the first direct translation from Hebrew into English. This translation made him unpopular because the possession of a Bible was punishable by death. Cardinal Wolsey therefore declared Tyndale a heretic. Tyndale fled to the Continent, to Antwerp. There he hid for a while, but the story ends badly. Spies of Henry VIII found him, captured him, and for a year he was imprisoned in Vilvoorde near Brussels. There he was accused of heresy, sentenced to death, and publicly strangled and then burned on October 6, 1536. A monument to him was erected in Vilvoorde and can still be seen there today.

Now I return to Erasmus of Rotterdam. Thanks to the spread of Greek knowledge, in 1516 Erasmus published the first Greek printed edition of the New Testament. He relied on six manuscripts, most of them from the twelfth century. Where these manuscripts were incomplete, he translated the text of the *Vulgate* from Latin back into Greek. This was necessary, of course, because Erasmus was trying to reconstruct the original text as best he could. So the situation was as follows:

1. Jesus' statements in Aramaic were translated into Greek.
2. Then they were translated from Greek into Latin (the *Vulgate*).
3. Then (through Erasmus) they were translated back into Greek.
4. Then (through Tyndale) they were translated into English.

How fate (or the cynicism of power) plays with people's lives: the official version of the New Testament in English today is the King James Version of 1611, prepared by order of King James I of England. This King James Version consists of ninety percent of Tyndale's text! ...

So much for the history of the translations. I turn now to look at the separate parts of the New Testament in more detail, to see where they overlap, but also to get a feeling of their individual character. As noted earlier, the New Testament contains 27 "books." Of these, the three synoptic Gospels form the core of the "good news." These stories — and the differences between them — are so important that I give them further attention in the coming chapter. For now, I discuss the Gospel of John, and then the other parts of the New Testament.

The Gospel according to John

A first thing to notice is that, with the exception of the Passion, none of the stories in John's Gospel occur in the synoptic Gospels. And the style of the synoptic Gospels is quite different from that of John. In John, Jesus speaks almost exclusively of himself as God (John 3:36, 95; 10:30; 14:6). He proclaims who he is, where he comes from, where he will go, how he has always existed (John 8:58), and that he is the way to eternal life. In this sense, the Jesus in Mark and the Jesus in John appear to be two completely different people. He does not preach in John what he preaches in Mark. Therefore, with John, Christianity fundamentally changes its character. In the synoptic Gospels, Jesus is an apocalyptic preacher who sees the world he lives in as unjust, and proclaims that its end is near. Then God will judge and reward the righteous and punish the unrighteous. The most important criterion is: "Inasmuch as ye have done it unto one of the least of these my brethren, ye have done it unto me" (Matt. 25:40). This end is to be expected very soon. So what Jesus preaches is a horizontal chronology:

NOW (BAD) → SOON (GOOD) → THE KINGDOM (ON EARTH)

But this anticipated upheaval does not happen, not even after his death. And the first contemporaries die without Jesus' prophecy being fulfilled. This poses a serious problem for the first Christians. John solves this by tilting the horizontal time axis by 90 degrees. The new order now applies vertically: above (heaven) and below (earth).

HEAVEN / HELL

↑

HEREAFTER

↑

LIFE ON EARTH

Justice now takes place after death, in the hereafter. However, this is not what Jesus himself preached in the synoptic Gospels. There Jesus proclaims a new kingdom *here* on earth, not in the hereafter. Access to this kingdom is for those who have followed the maxims of the Sermon on the Mount. Accordingly, John creates (alongside Paul's revolution) a completely new religion, Christianity, in which there is hardly a trace left of what was presumably Jesus' original teaching.

Acts of the apostles

The book of *Acts* (Πράξεις τῶν Ἀποστόλων) deals with the development of Jesus' followers in the years after his death, with special reference to the apostles Peter (Chapters 1-12) and Paul (Chapters 13-28). It was written around eighty or ninety years after Jesus died. But by whom? Among experts there is no doubt: It was the same author who wrote the Gospel according to Luke, and who was clearly a follower—or better still, an admirer—of Paul.

The story of Acts begins in Jerusalem (with the Pentecost) and gradually develops in opposition to Jewish religion. Judaism was at first open to Christianity, but increasingly opposed it, which led to an opposition between the two religions. Acts is about Paul's conversion and his travels, and ends with Paul's release from prison in Rome. The central theme is that the message of Jesus was given to the Gentiles because the Jews rejected it.

Luke clearly writes Acts as a tribute to his master. But there are also textual problems. For instance, in Paul's account we read of Paul's conversion: "And the men which journeyed with him stood speechless, hearing a voice, but seeing no man" (Acts 9:7). But a little further on, the text says, "And they that were with me saw indeed the light, and were afraid; but they heard not the voice of him that spake to me" (Acts 22:9). There is no sufficient explanation for this contradiction.

The letters of Paul

There are a total of 14 letters of Paul in the New Testament. But only seven of them are authentic. For example, the letter to the Hebrews is unanimously rejected by specialists; it is certainly not by Paul. Its style is more eloquent and sophisticated than any other New Testament text. Several scholars call it a forgery. The remaining six letters were written by authors who used (and indeed abused) the name of Paul to gain more persuasion for their views.

Paul's authentic letters are the oldest sources of Christianity, written in 48-56. The oldest Gospel, the Gospel of Mark, was written about twenty years later, around the year 70. These are the letters to the Christians of Rome, the first and second letters to the Christians of Corinth, the letter to the Galatians, to the Christians of Philippi, the first letter to the Christians of Thessalonians, and the letter to Philemon. Paul sees in the resurrection the sign that Jesus' prophecy about the coming new age will be fulfilled. Soon, all will be resurrected. But then this does not happen either. So, also in Paul's case, a solution must be found to the fact that in Christian groups people are constantly dying and not being resurrected. In Chapter 10, I will elaborate on the crucial role that Paul played in the formation of Christianity.

Other letters in the New Testament

There is first a letter of James, the brother of Jesus and his "successor." After the death of Jesus, James becomes the leader of the Christian group in Jerusalem. However, the oldest manuscript of his letter dates from the third century. According to several scholars, this letter is also a case of *pseudo-epigraphy*, which means that someone calls himself James to give more authority to his writing. Moreover, this brother of Jesus certainly could not write and probably did not speak Greek. The same is true of Peter's two letters.

In the year 62, at a time when for a while there was no Roman prefect, the high priest Ananus caused James to be stoned for blasphemy. The reason was probably James' relentless criticism of wealth and his spirited defense of the weak. His letter says, "Go to now, ye rich men, weep and howl for your miseries that shall com upon you. Your riches are corrupted, your garments are moth-eaten. Your gold and silver is cankered" (James 5:1-3). He is referring to the fact that Ananus abuses his office as high priest to enrich himself by keeping the taxes for the living expenses of the lower priests to himself. The facts are reported in Flavius Josephus' *Antiquitates Judaicae*. As previously described, there are problems with the authenticity of the letter, but not with the account of the stoning of James.

There are also three letters of John (written ca. 98-99), probably by the author of the Gospel of John. But a minority of specialists doubt this; the authorship is still a subject of debate. The authorship of the letter of Judas (not the betrayer, but another brother of Jesus) is also critically doubted. In summary: of the 21 letters in the New Testament, only one-third, the seven letters of Paul, are definitely authentic!

The revelation of John

The book of the Revelation of John is a form of apocalyptic literature. The author describes what was revealed to him in a vision of the future. It is also a form of eschatological literature, in that it concerns the imminent end of the world. Contemporary interpreters see this writing as an expression of conflict within early Christian groups. The Revelation of John rejects the viewpoint of Christians who seek a kingdom on earth according to the ideals of the synoptic Gospels.

Later additions to the texts

It is now clear that the stories of the Gospels changed over time, particularly when they were copied. Very often these changes consisted of additions by later copyists ("later" here meaning "much later," sometimes hundreds of years later). Let us consider a typical but very important example of this.

Mark, the oldest Gospel, says nothing at all about the virgin birth. Even Joseph, Mary's husband, is not mentioned in this Gospel. Jesus is described there simply as "the son of Mary."

The ending of this Gospel is also quite different from the other Gospels. The women go to the tomb and see that the stone has been rolled away. A young man (not an angel) tells them to go to Galilee; there they will see the risen Jesus. And then comes, "And they (the women) went out quickly, and fled from the sepulcher; for they trembled and were amazed: neither said they any thing to any man; for they were afraid" (Mark 16:8). There does follow another bit of text (Mark 16:9-20), but the Nestle-Aland critical scholarly edition (2012) puts it inside double square brackets: [[...]]. On page 10 of this edition, the meaning of these brackets is explained as follows:

> that the enclosed, usually longer piece of text certainly does not belong to the original textual inventory. Texts of this type, however, originated at a very early stage of transmission and often played a significant role in the history of the Church from an early date. Therefore, the texts have not been included in the scholarly compilation without being marked (cf. John 7:53 to 8:11).

Here it can be seen how the Gospels have grown over time. In this case (Mark 16) none of the manuscripts dating from before the fifth century contain verses 9 to 20. So these verses, which deal mainly with the apparition of the risen Jesus, were added hundreds of years later. For this reason, this part of Mark's Gospel is inauthentic. At the same time, the originally final verse 8 displays another, much deeper problem that should jump out at everyone. If the women, out of fear, did not tell anyone about what they saw, how can *we* know? Because there was no one there but the women, Mark presents himself as an omniscient narrator who sees and knows everything (see further details on this aspect of narration in Chapter 7). But clearly he was not in the tomb with these women. Since Mark wrote that the women did not communicate anything to anyone, it is questionable how he learned about it.

In the original Gospel of Mark, then, there are no apparitions, as in the other Gospels. In fact, the young man tells the women that Jesus will be seen in Galilee, not in Jerusalem, where the other Gospels have most of the appearances taking place. Why then are these later verses added? Probably because the abrupt ending of Mark's Gospel was experienced as unsatisfactory. But the history of the text shows that it was quite some time before verses 9-20 were added. Bruce Metzger, professor of Biblical Studies at Princeton University, writes in his book *A Textual Commentary* (2005) that neither Clement of Alexandria (150-215) nor Origen (185-253) in the third century knew of verses 9 to 20 in Mark. And the writings of Eusebius (260-340) and Jerome (347-420) attest that there are no verses 9 to 20 in the older Greek manuscripts known to them. This means that the corresponding section about the resurrection and appearances of Jesus was missing in Mark until about the third century! So, although it is a later addition, nevertheless many Bible translations, including the King James Version, print the passage as if nothing is wrong.

Chapter 5

The Four Evangelists

The previous chapter highlighted some general issues to keep in mind regarding the texts of the New Testament. The present chapter will now treat in more depth the four central texts, namely the four Gospels. They differ from each other, not just in trivial details, but fundamentally.

By now, it is clear that Matthew had taken large portions from Mark. Luke also did so, but he put completely different words into the mouth of Jesus. So why didn't Luke adopt the words of Mark in his text? Because Luke's Jesus is quite different from Mark's (and to a lesser extent from Matthew's). For example, Luke's account of the Passion is interwoven with dialogues with the women, and with the murderers who were crucified with him. This is in stark contrast to the Gospels of Matthew and Mark, in which Jesus says nothing to the others at the crucifixion. The talkativeness in Luke is all the more astonishing when one considers the agony Jesus must have already suffered at that moment. In the next chapter I will show that such dialogues would indeed have been medically impossible. So there must be another intention behind Luke's story.

John's Gospel is again quite differently ordered. It is about the plan established from the beginning of this Gospel, the Word who is God and who is at the origin of everything. And with Jesus, this eternal Word became flesh, or man, fulfilling the mission of liberating humanity. Jesus, in this Gospel, was a redeemer from birth, a task that was established with original sin and must now be fulfilled by him. After his preaching, after performing miracles and dying the horrible sacrificial death, he could cry out, "It is finished!" (John 19:30). If it were not disrespectful to believers, one could almost say, "Mission accomplished." For this is indeed how John sees Jesus: as one who comes to fulfill a promise, a mission, a divine task.

These differences between the Gospels are of a very different order to the inaccuracies and contradictions I spoke of earlier. Here one is dealing with existential differences. These are not simply different stories. Here, Jesus is a different Jesus each time. These four portrayals of Jesus are similar at first sight, but they differ dramatically in their nature. Therefore, it is useful to examine more closely the core of each of the four Gospels. How does Jesus appear in each one?

The Gospel of Mark

For the first time in history, the word "Gospel" appears in the text of Mark. In doing so, the author created an entirely new literary genre. When José Saramago published his novel *The Gospel According to Jesus Christ* in 1991, he spanned an arc of some two thousand years with a man named Mark, who had created this genre. Consequently, few things are as deeply rooted in our culture as the Gospel, created by a genius—an unknown Mark. And his creation has an immediate influence: about ninety percent of Mark's text is found in the Gospel according to Matthew, and about sixty percent of it in Luke's Gospel. Those who look for the historical roots of Jesus' life in the New Testament will find the most reliable source in Mark's Gospel (after the *Book of Q*).

There is the greatest possible consensus among experts that Mark's is the oldest Gospel. The text was written around the years 60 to 75. Mark 13:2 refers to the destruction of Jerusalem. From this, some conclude that this Gospel was written between 66 and 70. However, it is not known who this Mark was. "Mark" is a Roman name, the most popular male name in the Roman Empire at the time. There must have been thousands of them. So he was probably a Roman, or perhaps found himself in Rome, writing not for Jews but for a Roman audience. This Gospel says nothing about the birth of Jesus, his childhood, his parents, his ancestors, or Bethlehem. The story begins *in medias res*, when Jesus begins to preach. But it does mention his mother and brothers and sisters.

The reason the author Mark is considered Roman is because of his language. There are quite a few Latinisms (loan words from Latin) in his Greek. This could indicate that the author felt more at home in Latin than in Greek, or that he was considering a readership that was more familiar with Latin. For example, in Mark 15:39 and 44-45, the word κεντυρίων (*kenturion*) is mentioned three times, which is not a Greek word at all. It is Latin: *centurio*, derived from *centum*, hundred. (The English translation has it translated as "centurion," referring to the commander of a hundred soldiers.) Both Matthew and Luke use the Greek equivalent ἑκατόνταρχος (*ekatontarchos*). In Matthew and Luke there are no Latinisms. So it appears that Mark made concessions for his audience—probably a Latin-speaking audience—who were not so comfortable in Greek. Presumably Mark was writing for an audience that consisted mainly of non-Jews or Gentiles. This would explain why there are many explanations of Jewish practices (see, for example, Mark 7:3-4). Jews living in Palestine at the time certainly did not need such an explanation, so we can assume that Mark was at least addressing a substantially non-Jewish readership as well.

It is written for a Christian community, an εκκλησία (*ekklesia*), which means a gathering, a meeting, a community. These communities were largely independent of each other. There was not yet a central authority such as a "church." One may therefore assume that these communities differed from one another, in terms of what exactly they believed and professed, and how they put those beliefs into practice. The first Gospel is clearly written for such communities. Perhaps they were experiencing serious difficulties, so the author, Mark, focuses on suffering and the need to endure it, and to find comfort in the story. This is evident in the fact that about a quarter of the Gospel is taken up by the Passion story.

Anyone who begins to read the Gospel according to Mark is immediately swept up in a whirlwind of events. The first chapter begins with the baptism of John the Baptist, the temptation of Jesus by the devil, the calling of the disciples, a healing in a synagogue and the healing of Peter's mother-in-law, a summary of the healings and the proclamation of the message of salvation, a conversation with Peter and finally the healing of a leper. And all this in 45 verses! What is unmistakable is the urgency and passion with which the story is told. Mark has no time to lose!

Yet there is special attention to secondary characters and events, for example, the woman with blood loss (Mark 5:25 ff.), which is related to the fact that in this Gospel, Jesus is presented mainly as a human being. Repschinski (2016, p. 70) provides a nice list: Jesus is tired (Mark 6:31), hungry (Mark 11:12), has compassion (Mark 1:41, 6:34), is angry (Mark 3:5), surprised (Mark 6:6), beautiful (Mark 10:21), shaky (Mark 10:14), and does not always know everything (Mark 13:32). None of the other Gospels emphasize Jesus' humanity to the same degree. One gets to know Jesus here as a man of action, a healer, an exorcist who casts out devils almost like a magician—all bundled up in a wandering preacher, with no fixed abode, living in poverty and austerity, with no family but a multitude of followers.

There is another, somewhat surprising aspect of Jesus, that appears only in Mark. Jesus is first described as an outsider. In Mark, Jesus is an eccentric who is viewed with suspicion by his immediate family. "And when his friends heard of it, they went out to lay hold on him: for they said, He is beside himself." (Mark 3:21) The King James Version has a somewhat one-sided translation here. It is not "friends" that is meant, but "relatives." The Greek has οἱ παρ' αὐτοῦ (hoi par autou), literally, those who belong to him. A little further on in verses 3:31-35, reference is indeed to "his brethren and his mother." But think about it: Jesus as a madman! Such a characterization of their teacher must have been painful to the first Christians. That is why a generation later, in the texts of Matthew and Luke, such references to Jesus as an eccentric are absent. In this context, scholars use the *criterion of embarrassment* as an indication that these are authentic passages (I write more on this in the discussion of Matthew's Gospel).

The theme of Mark's Gospel is also very characteristic; Jesus' identity is shrouded in an atmosphere of mystery. He even forbids the disciples to make him known (Mark 3:12): "And he staitly (sic) charged them that they should not make him known." This creates a tension between Jesus' actions and his teachings on the one hand, and his constant insistence that his mission must be kept secret, on the other. This theme is accompanied by a similar aspect, that of the apostles' understanding. It is constantly evident that Jesus' followers do not understand him. At the end of the Gospel, they are also a little embarrassed. At the time of his arrest they flee, Peter denies his Lord three times, and at the end of the story there is no rehabilitation. The fear and misunderstanding of the followers contrasts sharply with the role of the women, who play a much larger role in Mark's work, for instance in the description of the women under the cross (Mark 15:40), and of the women discovering the empty tomb.

And then there is an abrupt ending; the women flee from the empty tomb and are filled with fear (Mark 16:8). Most experts (see Schröter 2010 for a recent overview) believe that this was indeed the end of the original Gospel. There is a sense that the story is not yet "finished." Therefore, there were some attempts in antiquity to "finish" it in most later manuscripts. But both the style and content of these additions differ significantly from the rest of the Gospel text. Abrupt this original ending undoubtedly is. On the other hand, it may be intended as a literary device. By suddenly breaking off the action, a surprise effect is achieved, similar to what was discussed earlier as "foregrounding" techniques in literature (see Chapter 3).

The Gospel of Mark was probably written around the years 66 to 70, coinciding with the Jewish revolt and the destruction of Jerusalem, and around the time of the persecution of Christians in Rome during the reign of the emperor, Nero. In this Gospel, Galilee is also strongly emphasized, perhaps an indication of some hostility between the north of the country and the Jewish Christian communities in the south, in Jerusalem. In this context, the end of the Gospel is also important. The resurrection and reunion with the risen Jesus will take place in Galilee, as it is announced to the women.

The writing style is not particularly elegant and is more attuned to spoken language. Typically, many sentences begin with "and" or "and immediately," as do the frequent changes between past and present.

The Gospel of Matthew

A striking difference between the Gospel of Matthew and the Gospel of Mark is that Matthew's name is Jewish, and the audience for whom Matthew writes is also markedly different. There are no Latinisms in his text, so his readers would have to have been Greek speakers. And the many references to Jewish customs and rituals are not explained here, from which one may conclude that he was writing for a Jewish-Christian community around the eighties and nineties of that era, most likely in Antioch, the capital of the Roman province of Syria, the second largest city in the Roman Empire, with more than half a million inhabitants around the time of Jesus.

A first impression after reading Matthew is that of delay. To express it musically, Mark's tempo is *presto*; Matthew's is *adagio*. This Gospel is twice as long as Mark's. The author takes his time and does not shy away from interruptions. And, as already mentioned, he takes over almost all of Mark's history, about ninety percent of Mark's text. Of the almost 1,100 verses, about 600 come directly from Mark's Gospel, about 220 are from the *Book of Q*, and the remaining 250 are typical of Matthew. In other words, Mark's message is substantially supplemented by Matthew, offering new content compared to his predecessors. What Matthew does not take from Mark is also noteworthy. In the first place, Matthew leaves out Mark 3:21, where Jesus' family say of him that he is mentally displaced. The second omission concerns the story of the blind man of Bethsaida. Mark narrates how Jesus wants to heal a blind man, but that this is only possible after a second "attempt" (Mark 8:22-26), which of course calls into question Jesus' perfection as a healer.

Both omissions can be explained. After all, both are episodes that must have caused embarrassment for early communities of Christians. These communities were still small and vulnerable; their doctrine was not yet stabilized, and there was competition between them. In such a situation, it is not pleasant to read that one's revered teacher is not perfect at all. These are understandable reasons for Matthew leaving out these episodes. But there is a catch here. When you compare these two Gospels and ask yourself which of the two is the most reliable, the criterion of *embarrassment* is generally used. One assumes that an author will not include something in his text if it causes embarrassment to himself and his readers. This leads one to the conclusion that such passages must have a high degree of authenticity and, therefore, reliability. In other words, the two passages in Mark are much more reliable than their omission from Matthew.

This also shows how the very human portrait of Jesus is considerably weakened in the Gospel of Matthew. The minor characters are also much less vivid than in Mark's Gospel. One conclusion is that Matthew paints a different Jesus, namely as founder of the church and as savior, but still bound to Jewish law and customs. The human Jesus undergoes a certain "flattening" here. He is presented as the Old Testament Messiah. Another relevant observation is that the Old Testament is quoted more frequently in Matthew than in the other Gospels, for instance in explanations of the Law of Moses and Pharisaic traditions and tracing Jesus' genealogy back to Abraham. This suggests that it is addressed primarily to Jewish Christians. In Mark, the emphasis is primarily on Jesus' actions; in Matthew, it is on Jesus' teachings. Therefore, one receives a very different theological message in Matthew.

According to tradition, Matthew was a tax assessor (not a fisherman; see Matt. 9.9), and tax assessors at that time were notoriously corrupt. This Gospel was probably written in Damascus, about twenty years after the Jewish revolt of 66-70. The author could have been a Hellenistic Jew, deeply rooted in Greek culture but still practicing Jewish rituals. Therefore, most of the references to the Jewish texts and traditions are found in him. However, all this is mere supposition; no one knows who this Matthew was. He was by no means one of the 12 apostles.

Matthew's Gospel tells the story of Jesus as it was previously written by Mark. But he adds a very different accent, which probably originated with a group of Jewish Christians who were confronted with a new, unexpected, and perhaps even threatening situation. Possibly the author's goal was to offer comfort and a way out of their difficulties. It is conceivable that this Jewish community was in crisis because of the influence of Christianity. Were they still to be considered Jews? In this sense, one can understand Matthew's criticism of the Pharisees. His criticism was not leveled at the Jewish people as a whole, but at political and religious leaders, especially the Pharisees, and against those who turned the temple into a trade fair. Matthew's strategy is very different from Mark's. In Matthew, Jesus' opponents tend to be the Pharisees. The disciples, on the other hand, are portrayed much more sympathetically. They stand in contrast to the Pharisees and form ideal figures for the readers to identify with—and implicitly to follow.

This is very well thought out from a story perspective. Matthew's goal is to draw the community he is writing for closer to the figure and message of Jesus. Mark writes much more from a neutral perspective, whereas Matthew creates the opportunity to identify with the teachings of Jesus. Were Jewish believers not in danger of losing their faith in God because of these new developments in Christianity? Or was it disappointment that Judaism did not accept this new religion? Matthew offers comfort to the community by telling them about God who gave Jesus and his mission to the people; he does so in and through the figure of Jesus. In addition to the Jewish people, he also focuses on the Gentiles. The "good news" is open and accessible to them as well. Matthew's criticism of Judaism does not yet have the virulent character it will later receive from John. In Matthew's case, the criticism is more about internal tensions within Judaism.

A striking passage in Matthew is the Sermon on the Mount (Matt. 5:3-10), which is much more elaborate than in Luke's Gospel (see Chapter 6). One may deduce from its occurrence in both Matthew and Luke that the authors must have taken the passage from the *Book of Q*, because the Sermon on the Mount does not occur in Mark. This passage is a core element of the Christian faith, namely the importance of love in a universal sense, in contrast to the view of the Jewish religion which understands only tribesmen as "neighbors." However, Matthew's view of love is not originally Christian. The emphasis on love's universality is also found elsewhere in the Mediterranean world and the Middle East, as will be seen in Chapter 7.

Quite notable in Matthew are the many cases of *parallelism*, not only in the Sermon on the Mount itself, but also in other passages, such as the statements about the salt of the earth and the light of the world (Matt. 5:13-16) and other parables (in

Matt. 13:24-33). Very often they are introduced with the same expression: "The kingdom of heaven is like ..." In Matthew one finds a masterly and complex artistic work.

The Gospel of Luke

In the famous German feature film *Das Boot* (literally "The Boat") about the vicissitudes of the crew in a submarine during World War II, the ship is damaged and they are given permission to return to their home port. The sailors are relieved, although they face a dangerous journey. But the captain hopes to be home by Christmas and gives vent to his longing for the coziness of his home with the words: "with the Gospel of Luke." For most readers, Luke is probably the most attractive of the three synoptic Gospels. The contrast with Matthew could hardly be greater. While Matthew focuses on Jesus and his teachings, Luke offers someone who stands out less for his teachings than for his actions and humanity. In Matthew, Jesus is worshipped by the apostles; in Luke, Jesus is the one who prays constantly himself (see Matt. 3.21, 5.16, 6.12), and he is the one who cares for the poor and oppressed. When asked who Jesus is, Luke answers right at the beginning, "Today the Savior has been born to you in the city of David, Christ the Lord" (Luke 2:11). The most important word here is "Savior," in Greek σωτήρ (sōtēr), a term that can also mean "redeemer" and was used in ancient Greek to describe several gods or rulers, for someone who comes to bring redemption and deliverance. This redemption can refer to earthly matters as well as to life after death. For Luke, Jesus is the figure who will bring salvation to humans.

Luke is a very different type of writer; in some ways he is much more important than the other authors. He was highly educated, well-to-do, and (unlike most contemporaries) did not look down on manual labor. Luke's language is characterized by its graceful style, similar to classical Greek and the Greek of the *Septuagint*. It also contains the features of Hellenistic historiography. His Greek name, Λουκας (*Loukás*), is a common one. Since his knowledge of the geography of Palestine was rather meager, it is assumed that he did not live there. Where he wrote his Gospel is not certain. There is a strong suspicion that it was in the Syrian city of Antioch about twenty years after the Jewish revolt. This city is mentioned several times in the Acts of the Apostles, of which Luke was also the author, at about the same time as Matthew. He was also a follower of Paul. Perhaps he was converted to Christianity by Paul; he is mentioned as such in an authentic letter of Paul (Col. 4:14). In Paul's letters Luke is mentioned by name three times (Phil. 1:23-24; Col. 4:14; and 2 Tim. 4:11). In total, Luke's writings provide almost 28% of the entire New Testament. He was also the only evangelist to give a detailed account of the birth and infancy of Jesus.

In fact, Luke saw himself primarily as a historian, not an evangelist. His models were those of Dionysius of Halicarnassus (c. 54-7 BC), an author of Roman history, and Flavius Josephus (already discussed in chapters 2 and 4), perhaps other Hellenistic authors as well. From this historical point of view, he indirectly criticizes the other evangelists, and announces that he will do better. See, for example, the opening of his Gospel:

> Forasmuch as many have taken in hand to set forth in order a declaration of those things which are most surely believed among us, even as they delivered them unto us, which from the beginning were eyewitnesses, and ministers of the word. It seemed good to me also, having had perfect understanding of all things from the very first to write unto thee in order, most excellent Theophilus, that thou mightest know the certainty of those things, wherein thou has been instructed. (Luke 1:1-4)

In other words, Luke writes that he never knew Jesus, and that his information comes second-hand—or even further back. This has led to a much more complex account of things than was formulated in your little assignment (see Chapter 1), in part because there are parables in Luke that are absent from Mark and Matthew, such as the parable of the Good Samaritan and that of the Prodigal Son. It is therefore assumed that there was an *L source*, a source that was only available to Luke and not to the other authors.

So now there are not only the *Book of Q* and Mark as sources for Matthew and Luke, but also the *sources M and L*, and a document about the childhood of Jesus which apparently only Luke had knowledge of, and also a possible *Antioch document*, which only Matthew knew. In addition, it is assumed that there existed a *proto-Luke* document as well as an earlier Gospel according to Luke that he reworked into this *proto Luke*. Likewise, there is a strong suspicion that there was an earlier version of Matthew. Scholarship does not rest, and there are still many unsolved problems, for instance, the inexplicable similarities between the Gospels of Luke and John. For example, only in these two texts do the figures of Martha and Lazarus and the cutting off of the servant's right ear by Peter during Jesus' arrest appear.

The other Gospels form a cohesive whole, but the Gospel of Luke is the first part of a two-part work; the second part is the *Acts of the Apostles*. The author of both works is the same, and together, the works form a unity. This is what the author of Acts himself says in the first lines: "The former treatise have I made, O Theophilus, of all that Jesus began both to do and teach" (Acts 1:1). The name Theophilus may refer to any believer, since the name literally means "beloved of God," but it could also have been a Roman official. In any case, the conclusion is clear: the Theophilus here is the same as at the beginning of Luke's Gospel.

The date of composition is fixed at around the year 80, roughly some time after the year 70 and probably before the year 90. This can be deduced from the fact that Luke assumed a peaceful coexistence of Christians in the Roman Empire (see Luke 7:1-10 and Acts 10:2-22). However, this situation ended with Emperor Trajan (who ruled from 98 to 117). One must therefore assume that Luke's Gospel was written before Trajan's reign. Another reason for this dating is that Luke warned against the expectation that Jesus' apocalyptic prophecy would soon be fulfilled (Luke 21:8 and 17:20 ff.). After all, two generations had passed by since Jesus' death and the new kingdom was not yet there. Luke's concern was not with the expectation that the kingdom would arrive in his lifetime, but rather with the essence of the kingdom (Luke 4:43, 8:1, 9:2, 16:16; Acts 1:3, 8:12, 20:25, 28:31).

Luke's Gospel is the strongest of the three synoptic Gospels because of its claim to universality, which I referred to earlier when discussing Matthew's Gospel. Matthew is still dealing with a Jewish community open to Gentiles in the Christian sense, but in Luke, this has become a matter of course. Any exclusion of a group is firmly rejected. This openness is most clearly expressed in the parables of the Good Samaritan and the Tax Collector. Injustice, oppression, poverty, exclusion: These are the things Jesus rejects. Luke was also less dependent on Mark; he adopted only around sixty percent of Mark's text. Of course, it is not known if this selection was deliberate, for it is also possible that the author had only an incomplete copy of Mark's Gospel. However, it is clear that many omissions relate to Jewish customs and traditions. It is also noticeable that the eight Aramaic expressions that appear in Mark are omitted by Luke. This probably has to do with his Greek background, but also with the fact that Luke was in an urban environment where Aramaic was less esteemed. He also takes less material from the *Book of Q*, only about twenty percent. Overall, only half of Luke's material comes from Mark and the *Book of Q*. In addition, Luke adds much new material. In fact, the stories of Jesus' birth and childhood come largely from Luke. This is especially noticeable in the first two chapters, where Mary's visit to Elizabeth, in particular, testifies to a great sensitivity to friendship between women. Luke also emphasizes the role of women (see Luke 8:2-3, 10:38-42, and 11:2).

Over the centuries, legends have grown up around the figure of Luke. One of them comes from Col. 4:14, where Luke is depicted as a physician. There are several descriptions of healings; in no other Gospel do the words "heal" and "recover" appear as often as in Luke's case. These passages can possibly be interpreted as referring to the art of healthy living, which, in medical terms, was considered important in antiquity. One is reminded of Juvenal's well-known *mens sana in corpore sano* (a sound mind in a sound body). From this perspective, the message in this Gospel is that faith in Jesus leads to a healthy life! This is evident in the stories about the healings of the watery woman (Luke 14:1-6) and the bent woman (Luke 13:10-17). Both healings take place on the Sabbath, the day God rested after creation. In this way, Luke creates an image of Jesus completing the creation through his miraculous healings.

In addition, Luke is portrayed as a painter. For this reason, many guilds of medieval and Renaissance painters, as well as present-day academies for the visual arts, are named after him. This reputation is probably based on his pictorial descriptions in this Gospel, such as when Elizabeth heard Mary's greeting, "the babe leaped in her womb" (Luke 1:41). He is also said to have painted the first Madonna, although this is probably a legend, based perhaps on the preference for the figure of Mary in his Gospel. For how could Luke have painted a portrait of Mary when he himself says he was not an eyewitness? This shows again how productive the descriptions were in the New Testament, and how they led to ever new stories.

Luke presents the message of his Gospel not in an abstract or theoretical way, but through his narrative art. His mastery is evident especially in the stories about the birth and childhood of Jesus and in the interweaving of the lives of John the Baptist and Jesus. John and his message precede Jesus, leading to the conclusion that Jesus as prophet and preacher surpasses John. The announcement of the births at Mary's visit to Elizabeth, the testimony of Simeon and Hannah, and the story of the 12-year-old Jesus in the temple all show the mystery of Jesus, which is then interpreted by Christians as a sign of his divinity.

The Gospel of John

With the Gospel according to John, the reader moves furthest from the historical facts. It was written almost a century after the events and there were no living contemporary witnesses left at that time. Meanwhile, many Christian communities in the Mediterranean region had already developed, most of them outside the Jewish cultural sphere. Matthew placed the events in a Jewish community, while Luke introduced the reader to the cultured world of Greek Hellenistic civilization. In John, the reader is in eternity! In John's Gospel, Jesus is the eternal Son of God who teaches people who God really is. In doing so, the world of the synoptic Gospels is left behind. John's Gospel is a completely different work, with a completely different content and message. So it must be considered as an independent—in a certain sense even idiosyncratic—work.

It begins with the profound prologue, which replaces the genealogy of Jesus or the stories about his birth and childhood. In John, Jesus is not born. There is no need for that, because he was always there. Now he has become "flesh." In Greek, this is Και ο λόγος σάρξ εγένετο, literally, "And the Word became flesh." Usually the Latin word *incarnatio* is used for this expression, which is the translation from the *Vulgate*. From this choice of words it is clear that a completely different spirituality is presented here, with a transcendental event that breaks through the boundaries of historical facts. In the three synoptic Gospels which preceded John, one has the impression that the

first oral traditions about Jesus were quite homogeneous. But
John's Gospel deviates strongly from this impression. Indeed,
it's so far removed from the other three Gospels that one must
assume that, even in the first century, different traditions were
circulating around the figure of Jesus. Here, it is necessary to be
aware of the complexity of historical reality. In the case of John,
one is no longer dealing with different emphases as provided
by the synoptic authors. Instead, a completely different picture
emerges. Those who believe that the four Gospels all deal
with or portray the same thing are seriously underestimating
this complexity. For example, two central and revolutionary
Christian messages "Thou shalt love thy neighbor as thyself"
(Mark 12:31) and "Love your enemies, do good to them which
hate you" (Luke 6:27) are completely absent from John! This
makes it sufficiently clear that the historical reliability of this
Gospel is extremely low.

Tradition has it that the author of this Gospel was the
disciple whom Jesus loved the most. This is how he is presented
in the text: ὁ μαθητὴς ὃν ἠγάπα ὁ Ἰησοῦς (the disciple loved
by Jesus, John 20:2) and ὃν ἐφίλει ὁ Ἰησοῦς (whom Jesus loved,
John 21:7). This description is repeated six times. Nevertheless,
the author could not have been a follower of Jesus. First of all,
the disciple John was like the other apostles, a poor, uneducated
fisherman. Second, he could not be because of the time. The text
of John's Gospel dates from around 100 to 120, in which case
he would have written the text when he was at least eighty,
perhaps even a hundred years old. This is wildly unlikely, if
not impossible, since those who survived infantile diseases
during the Roman Empire and reached the age of ten usually
lived up to the age of around 45. It is therefore hardly a point
of discussion among experts; this author John was by no means
the beloved disciple of Jesus. And again, John is a common
Jewish name. Who was he then? No one knows. However, it is
clear that he saw himself as a Jewish-Christian prophet. And it

is noteworthy that John the Apostle is not mentioned by name anywhere in this Gospel. This "favorite apostle" of Jesus is most likely a literary trick. Furthermore, unlike the synoptic Gospels, the influence of Gnostic teaching is evident here.

The author of this Gospel most likely lived in Ephesus, located in western Turkey, the ruins of which are visited every year by thousands of tourists. The Gospel is likely to have been written there, around 100 to 120, but this is not known for sure. Its social background at that time would have involved the contrast or conflict between Jewish and Christian communities that gradually grew further apart. John's Gospel adds a tooth in terms of anti-Jewish sentiments, and indeed it is a regular source of anti-Jewish sentiments.

But there is something else that characterizes this Gospel. John portrays Jesus as much more divine than the synoptic Gospels do. See, for example, the opening of his text: "In the beginning was the Word, and the Word was with God, and the Word was God" (John 1:1). This image of God as "Logos," the Word, is strongly spiritual. It is clear here that Jesus was already God before he came to earth, and has always been. This is a vision of Jesus not found in the synoptic Gospels. There, Jesus is man, preacher, seer, prophet, healer, exorcist. He is not presented as God—unless one includes later additions by copyists. In this sense, John (together with Paul) is the true shaper of the Christian faith.

John is also the author of the three letters of John. Their style is strikingly similar to that of the Gospel. It is also claimed, according to tradition, that he is the author of the final book of the New Testament: the Revelation. But there is serious doubt whether it is the same person, among other things because the Greek of John is correct, poetic and elegant, but that of Revelation is not. Specialists therefore refer to the author of Revelation as "John of Patmos," the person who speaks in Revelation.

If one compares John with the text that is the farthest away from him in chronological order—that of Mark—the conclusion is inescapable that the New Testament does not provide one unified picture of Jesus, There are at least four pictures that emerge. In a thunderous action story, Mark presents Jesus as a lonely and totally abandoned figure, who tried throughout his life and teachings to bring people to repentance until the extreme dark end. But John's Jesus is above all, a divine, uplifted creature, while dramatically embedded in sustained and solemnly poetic reflections on the form and meaning of everything, who ultimately knows how to stand above his own torment. His last words: "It is finished" sound almost like a triumph. This must have been someone other than the Jesus in Mark. The same applies to the figure of Jesus in Matthew and Luke.

The use of language is also different in John's Gospel. There is nothing in the synoptic Gospels that resembles the extremely lofty and poetic language of John's prologue which is strongly rhythmic. Each concept is further explored in the sentence that follows, and each stanza sketches a new, distinctly lyrical theme which imitates the beginning of the Old Testament, with clear hints of the creation story. The expression "And the Word became flesh and dwelt among us, and we beheld his glory" serves as the reading instruction for this Gospel.

This Gospel is characterized by long and meditative theological discourses and farewell speeches (John 14-17), the story of the raising of Lazarus, and abstract metaphors such as the "living water," the "light of the world," the "bread of life," and so on. The story is set mainly in Jerusalem, with only an occasional excursion into Galilee. Unlike the synoptic Gospels, the expulsion from the temple takes place very early in this Gospel (John 2:13-22).

A small fragment of the Gospel is the oldest extant piece of the New Testament that has been found. Papyrus 52 is only a few square inches in size and contains verses 31-33 from Chapter 8 on the front and 37-38 on the back. So far, specialists do not agree on the dating, which is supposed to be between the years 125 and 160; the Gospel itself was probably written around the year 100. Papyrus 52 is the oldest extant piece of manuscript (so far) containing something from the New Testament.

A whole series of explanations have arisen concerning the origin of John's Gospel. However, none of the theories is based on sources. In other words, no texts have been found to support the various hypotheses. The connection with the synoptic Gospels is also still unclear, and there is no consensus among researchers in this regard. It certainly is not an addition to nor a correction of the synoptic Gospels, but is a completely independent work. Most specialists in this field work with a hypothesis that several authors may have written the text together. Chapter 21 is clearly a later addition, because a conclusion is already formulated in John 20:30-31, while John 21:24 distances itself from the earlier concluding words. Later additions include the story of the adulteress and Chapters 15 to 17, but there are also coherence problems in Chapters 4 to 7: the Galilee-Jerusalem sequence is not always correct. It is possible that the pages of the manuscripts got mixed up over the centuries.

Conclusion

The New Testament brings not just one "good message" but four, each with its own focus and purpose, each with its own accents, and each with, yes, a different Jesus. This is not particularly surprising given that there are four different stories, each with its own background, purpose, and audience, written by different authors who probably didn't know each other. In this sense, the four stories in the New Testament, like all later imitations, are adaptations of stories. Each of these adaptations brings a different message and therefore needs a different Jesus. One could argue that these four Gospels simply contain different aspects of the same Jesus, which is a possible view of the matter. But the differences are very great, especially if one looks at the last words of each—from complete abandonment and despair in Mark, to dominant self-control in Luke, to complete and eternal authority in John.

Chapter 6

Passion Story and Resurrection

When I lecture on the topic of this chapter, I always play about 15 minutes of music from Johann Sebastian Bach's *St. Matthew Passion*, especially the chorus, *O Haupt voll Blut und Wunden* (O Head Full of Blood and Wounds). Here Bach aptly embodies the physical mutilation Jesus has undergone at the hands of his executioners. This profoundly moving music, in which the listener is immersed in the total abandonment of a tortured and mocked human being, stands in stark contrast to what can be found in Christian iconography. Nothing even remotely resembles the emotionality of Bach's music. In painting, Jesus is rarely depicted as having been so mistreated. His face in the paintings is always intact, yet the Gospels clearly describe him being beaten with fists and sticks. Except for a spatter of blood here and there, in most paintings one would not think that this man was severely beaten. And the total desolation and abandonment captured in the music is mostly absent from the paintings. It is obvious that painters were reluctant to depict the injuries Jesus had suffered in a vivid and realistic way— with one exception: the painter Matthias Grünewald (1470-1528), who tried, to some extent, to show the brutality to which Jesus had been exposed. Why was there so little realism in the depiction of the Passion, when painting generally aspired to far-reaching realism, such as that of the Flemish Primitives? An obvious explanation lies in the feelings of horror a realistic picture of a tortured human being might evoke. It is probably too painful for Christians to depict their bleeding and severely tortured God. And perhaps the visual medium is less suited to depicting the abandonment and shock of being tortured, at least compared to the possibilities that music seems to have. Be that as it may, the Passion story forms a theme that is ubiquitous in Western art.

There are two crucial reasons to pay special attention to the Passion. First and foremost, it forms the core of the Christian faith, namely that mankind was freed from original sin through the suffering of Jesus. Secondly, the Passion is the climax of each of the Gospels. After the resurrection, the stories stop (although *Acts*, of course, contains a continuation). But it is not only the end of the story; it is also the climax. The Gospels are constructed so that everything leads to this point. However, the major differences between the four Gospels are striking, as already discussed in the previous chapter. It is also noticeable that this final part of the Gospels contains more "quotations" from the Old Testament than the other parts, which must prove that everything recounted here had been predicted. However, this makes a historian suspicious, because so many correct predictions simply do not occur in history. And besides, many of these references are so vague that they cannot be located, for example, where they say, for instance in Luke 21:22, Matt. 26:54, Mark 15:28, and several others, that "the Scripture might be fulfilled." What "scripture"?

At the same time, a historical reconstruction of the facts in this case is facilitated. First of all, there is a wealth of historical material directly related to the Passion, concerning justice under Jewish and Roman law, about the person of Pilate, and on the forms of execution the Romans practiced. In this chapter, I will confront this information with the texts of the Gospels. It will then emerge that the Passion story is a litmus test for the historical authenticity of the New Testament. In terms of the origin of Christianity, the Passion story is also inescapable. Without crucifixion and resurrection, no Christianity.

However, for me as a writer, the Passion story presents an emotional dilemma. Should I detail the horror of a crucifixion in all its cruel detail, running the risk of succumbing to voyeurism? See Crossan (1995, p. 140) for a similar argument. On the other hand, I could hide or obscure the details — but that would violate the account of the events, and the true nature of the facts. I have chosen the first option, of not avoiding the accurate description of the horror for two reasons. The first of these is that only then can the real terror come to light. I know that such descriptions deeply hurt people's feelings. The great sociologist Norbert Elias has given fundamental and detailed evidence of the process of internalized self-compulsion to control our aggressive drives and affects. We are all children of these long-term social developments, whereby depictions of real violence deeply wound our feelings. We no longer go and watch bear-baiting or cat-burning as in the time of Shakespeare, and the idea of public executions is deeply disgusting. So to be confronted with the details of the crucifixion is inevitably shocking, for anyone and everyone.

The second reason is related to the first. Because one constantly refrains from such detailed descriptions of raw violence and relentless brutality in discourses about history, a completely distorted picture of the past emerges. Stories of history are now supposed to be entertaining, soft and pleasant — but please, no horror! The entertainment industry tends to play along with this approach. Historical feature films rarely manage to depict the real lives of people from past eras, the stench, the incurable diseases, the ragged brevity of life, the injustices crying out to heaven. Therefore, someone who wants to know "how it really was" (Ranke) should not avoid embarrassing realities. The icy brutality with which executions like crucifixions were carried out is frightening and hurtful. It should not be avoided, but confronted, in deep sympathy with the suffering of people in earlier times.

These then are the reasons why, in this chapter, the crucifixion is revealed in all its disgusting brutishness — not to shock, but to enlighten, even if this enlightenment exposes the current and largely flattering image of mankind.

The arrangement of the story of Jesus' arrest, condemnation, execution, and resurrection is chronological in the Gospels. It moves from the entry into Jerusalem to the Last Supper, the trial (the Garden of Gethsemane, the arrest, the interrogation, the condemnation), the scourging, the crucifixion, and the resurrection. Each of these six phases in the story will be analyzed in light of what is known historically.

The entry into Jerusalem

It is the year 30 (or perhaps 33). The Passover is approaching, the great Jewish festival. Jesus and his disciples go to Jerusalem to participate. Once there, Jesus sends two followers into the city to find a donkey. Here already is the first textual problem. Matthew 21:5 says, "Behold, thy king cometh unto thee, meek, and sitting on an ass, and on a colt the foal of an ass." (This echoes Zechariah 9:9.) Did Jesus ride two donkeys at once? Of course not. This is an example of Hebrew "parallelism," adopted here in Greek. The word "and" does not indicate a complement, but a reinforcement. This custom is typical of the style of the ancient Hebrew tradition: parallelism.

Jesus, sitting on this donkey, goes into the city. The disciples, as well as the people in the street, spread cloaks on the ground before him. Apparently they recognize him as a preacher and they lay palm branches on the road in front of him. The entry is triumphant (according to the Gospels). The people crowd around him and praise him. If this account is true, it shows that Jesus had only a small band of followers, but he was in a certain sense also popular. The first century is pregnant with expectation, with the desire for liberation, and that is precisely the message Jesus brings.

A good question is why people applaud Jesus so extravagantly at his entrance into Jerusalem but cry out for his blood a few days later (see Matt. 27:25: "His blood be on us and on our children"). From a mass psychological point of view, however, this is not really surprising. Hysteria in a large group of people is something volatile and changeable, and is therefore easily manipulated.

The Last Supper

After the entrance, Jesus and his disciples enter a room to have a meal together. This is not the Jewish Passover sacrificial lamb, but an ordinary supper. This "Last Supper" will later be the subject of numerous paintings and artistic projects (see also the discussion of Leonardo's painting in Chapter 1). It is the last time Jesus and his disciples eat together, and he gives instructions on how to proceed after his death. He predicts that Peter will deny that he is a follower of his, and that someone in the group will betray him. After that, Judas leaves the room.

This raises the question of the role of Judas, the "betrayer" as he is known in church tradition. It is striking to note that in the Gospels, Jesus never says publicly that he is the rightful king of the Jews. But privately, among his followers, he has tacitly agreed with Peter's statement: "You are the Christ" (Mark 8:29), although he strictly forbids them to speak to anyone about it (Mark 8:30). In this sense, there was no reason for the Romans to suspect him. This is exactly when Judas appears on the scene. Judas probably committed the betrayal, not only by kissing Jesus, but also by informing the Romans about what Jesus said privately about his kingship. Of course, this is only a hypothesis. However, in Chapter 9 I take a closer look at Judas' position while studying his Gospel. From that viewpoint, a completely different story arises, so that Judas can no longer be called "the betrayer."

During the meal, Jesus also establishes the rite of the Eucharist. But the Gospels describe the event in very different ways, so it is difficult to get an accurate picture of what exactly happened. The authors do not even agree on when the meal took place. According to Mark (14:12), Matthew (26:17), and Luke

(22:7), it took place on the first day of the Passover. But John (19:14) says it took place on the day before Passover, because on the day of Passover (according to John) Jesus is crucified. They also disagree about the supper itself. In Mark (14:22-25) and Matthew (26:26-29), the bread is eaten first, then the wine is drunk. But in Luke (22:17-20) the order is given in reverse: first wine, then bread. In John, there is no transformation of bread and wine into body and blood; this is also noteworthy. And only in John does the washing of the feet take place.

At the heart of the event is a text said to have been spoken by Jesus, and still repeated during Eucharistic celebrations in Christianity:

> For I have received of the Lord that which also I delivered unto you, That the Lord Jesus, the same night in which he was betrayed took bread: and when he had given thanks, he brake it, and said, Take, eat: This is my body, which is broken for you: this do in remembrance of me. After the same manner also he took the cup when he had supped, saying, This cup is the new testament in my blood: this do ye, as oft as ye drink it, in remembrance of me.
> (1 Cor. 11:23-25)

Believers immediately recognize this text, because it is one that has been engraved in their memory through frequent repetition of their central religious ritual. It is the earliest formulation of the Eucharistic rite. But where does the text come from? Believers may be a little shocked here, because the text comes from Paul, who was not present at the Last Supper. So how was Paul able to spread this text? Did one of the apostles tell him? Unlikely, since they were completely at odds with each other. Paul claims to have "received" (παρέλαβον) these words. How, where, and when (and from whom) he does not say. We must take him at his word. These and similar passages show that although Paul's self-chosen name means "the little one," he clearly has authoritarian characteristics, hence his open conflict with the apostles (see more on this in Chapter 10).

The text about the institution of the Eucharist is almost the same in each of the synoptic Gospels. But these Gospels were written much later (after the year 70) than Paul's letters (c. 55). So Paul could not have taken his wording from the Gospels, because they were not there yet. It is evident that it worked the other way round: the Gospels took Paul's wording. Do not forget that the authors of these Gospels were also not present at the Last Supper. So the text cannot be considered as authentic; it is improbable that it represents the words that Jesus himself had spoken. In fact, absolutely nothing is known of what he or the others said at the Last Supper.

At the core of the Christian rite is another serious problem: eating human flesh and drinking blood is expressly forbidden under Jewish law. See Lev. (17:10): "And whosoever of the house of Israel or of the strangers among you eats any blood, against him will I turn my face, and will cut him off from among his people." It is true that it is not expressly forbidden to eat human flesh; Leviticus does not mention it as a prohibition. But the reason is clear enough: it is simply inconceivable! It is therefore also inconceivable that this text would have been pronounced by Jesus. There is also no historical evidence at all that the direct followers of Jesus (under the leadership of his brother James) would have performed such a rite. On the contrary, such a thing was simply unthinkable for them. Fortunately, we have a text that confirms this, a text that was not influenced by Paul. This is the so-called *Didache* (Διδαχή), which dates most probably from the end of the first century, and is also called "The Lord's Teaching Through the Twelve Apostles to the Nations." This is the oldest church document still in existence, which contains a type of instruction for candidates for Christian baptism. Here is the instruction for the Eucharist:

Now, concerning the Eucharist, give thanks like this. First, over the cup: "We give thanks to you, our Father, over the holy vine of your servant David, which you made known to us through your servant Jesus. To you be the glory into the ages."
And over the broken bread: "We give thanks to you, Father, for the life and knowledge made known to us through your servant Jesus. To you be the glory into the ages."
(Tuson 2021, p. 15-16)

Clearly, there is no reference at all to the body and blood of Jesus in this Christian text. And it is the earliest source of the Christian Eucharist that exists. Apparently, the first Christians did not know this flesh and blood ritual at all. If Paul's description was actually based on what Jesus had said at the Last Supper, his words would probably have been included in this early text, the *Didache*. To sum up the situation (certainly troubling for devout Christians): the words of the Eucharist were never spoken by Jesus, nor could they have been, since Jewish law, which he rigorously adhered to, strictly forbade such practices. In fact, if he had been told that these words would ever be put into his mouth, he would have recoiled in horror! Conclusion: the words of the Eucharist do not belong to Jesus, but to the imagination of a man who had haughtily rejected the message of Jesus, for the benefit of his own imagination. The fact that this rejection of Jesus' message has become the ritual core of the Christian religion is amazing, to say the least.

The trial

After the meal, Jesus led his followers to the Garden of Olives (also called the Garden of Gethsemane). He urgently requested the apostles to pray, but they all fell asleep. Shortly afterwards, Judas arrived with a group of armed men to arrest Jesus — the four Gospels agree on this, but there are also some differences.

In the three synoptic Gospels Judas kisses Jesus, the so-called "Judas kiss," but this is missing in John. There is armed resistance from the disciples, but Jesus admonishes them to refrain from this (except in Mark). Then, in Matthew and Mark, Jesus accuses the armed men of treating him like a criminal, but says that the scriptures must be fulfilled, whereupon the disciples flee. However, these details are missing from Luke and John.

Interrogation by the High Priest

According to the Gospels, an interrogation and trial take place after Jesus' arrest. But there are a number of serious inconsistencies in the Gospels. Some of the minor inconsistencies are, for example, that Mark (14:53), Matthew (26:57), and Luke (22:54) have Jesus brought before Caiaphas, the high priest, while in John (18:13-24) he is brought first before Caiaphas' father-in-law, Annas, and only afterwards to Caiaphas. Several more such inconsistencies occur in the record of the trial, since none of the evangelists were actually present at this interrogation. For this reason, none of the accounts can be considered reliable. Two observations are important to make here: (1) no trial was necessary in order to convict someone, and (2) what the Gospels say about the trial conflicts with Jewish law.

First, no trial was necessary. Caiaphas, the high priest, had an excellent relationship with Pontius Pilate, the Roman governor. They had worked well together for a long time, and had certain mutual agreements, for example, that troublemakers should be put an end to right away. When it came to non-Roman citizens from the province who were troublesome, martial law was carried out, and crucifixion was the usual way to do this, as a deterrent. There was no reason to bring this case to court, much less to seek the opinion of a crowd. And look who was to be involved in this trial: the high priest, the Roman governor, King Herod himself. All for a vulgar insurgent? These high-ranking people had other things to do than subject an insignificant troublemaker to extensive questioning. In other words, it is extremely doubtful whether such a trial of Jesus ever took place. Why is the story nevertheless so extensively narrated? Perhaps for many reasons, one of which could be that the story absolves the Romans of guilt and places it entirely on the Jews (remember that Mark was writing for a Roman audience). But let's assume for the moment that such a trial did take place. In that case, almost all the rules of Jewish law were violated. Here are just a few of the violations.

According to Mark (14:53-65), the interrogation took place at night. This was expressly forbidden in Jewish law, for the reason that a possible death sentence required a great deal of concentration in weighing the question of guilt. Therefore, the Sanhedrin (high council) was not allowed to meet during the period between the evening and morning rituals. Moreover, such a trial had to take place in the courtroom (in Hebrew "*Lishkat ha-Gazit*"), especially if it was a serious matter, and definitely not at the home of the high priest, as claimed in the Gospels. But there is more. The Sanhedrin was not permitted to meet on the Sabbath or on the eve of the Sabbath, and certainly not on or just before a religious holiday (which was what happened because, according to Mark, everything took place on the eve of Passover). Imagine a criminal being interrogated by a judge at night, at home in his garden in London or Los Angeles! The idea of a night interrogation in the garden of a high priest in Jesus' time is equally far-fetched. However, in terms of narrating a good story, the use of foregrounding provides a strong drama which is enhanced by the deviant character of the events. But historically, it is false.

Of course, this is not entirely surprising, since Mark probably came from a Roman background and did not know the statutes of the Jewish Sanhedrin very well. In any case, he was not present, nor were any of Jesus' followers. Similar scenes occur in the other Gospels (Matt. 27:27 ff.; Luke 23:11 ff.; John

19:1 ff.). They have been largely copied from each other. This was also the easiest way. What do journalists do when they are not present at an event? They simply repeat what others have already written. Only, in this case, *no one* was present.

But if none of the disciples witnessed the questioning, where does this report come from? Not from Jesus himself, because at this stage he will no longer speak to his followers. Nor, of course, from the high priests, who will not chat with the followers of this agitator, whom they want to get rid of. In short, there is no source that the evangelists can rely on to support their story. It must therefore have been invented. And since Mark's is the oldest Gospel, he must have been its creator. One must admit that he makes quite a strong story, which is subsequently adopted by the other evangelists. John then adds some new elements, presenting little "scenes" of dialogues between Jesus and Pilate, as if he had witnessed them himself. But the conclusion is that the historical reliability of the interrogation scenes is almost zero.

In the Gospel of Luke, Herod Antipas suddenly appears on the stage, who, according to this story, was also staying in Jerusalem at that time. Coincidence? Herod also wants to have his fun with Jesus—as he did with his predecessor, John the Baptist—and with the firstborn sons of Bethlehem, whose deaths are commemorated on the Feast of the Holy Innocents. Herod and his soldiers mock Jesus; they put a cloak on him and send him back to Pilate. This episode serves to heighten the drama; the execution of the sentence is postponed, increasing suspense. Otherwise, it's not clear what the point of this interlude is.

But the most fictional element of the Passion story is the sentence that is then pronounced. According to the story, Jesus was condemned for blasphemy. But this is factually incorrect, because Jesus would then have had to slander God's name, which he did not do. Furthermore, the law stipulated that if he was condemned, a second session of the Sanhedrin should follow the next day, in which the sentence had to be confirmed. Finally, it was also expressly forbidden by law to mock an accused, let alone spit on him or strike him with his fist, as Mark 14:65 records. It is virtually impossible historically that the questioning took place in this way.

Then, if Jesus had indeed been found guilty of blasphemy, the Torah is clear: "anyone who blasphemes the name of the LORD is to be put to death. The entire assembly must stone them" (Lev. 24:16). This happened with Stephen, the first martyr: "They dragged him out of the city and began to stone him" (Acts 7:58). Not crucifixion, but stoning is the punishment for blasphemy according to Jewish law. Why stoning was not carried out remains obscure, as does the reason for the chief priests referring a blasphemy complaint to the Roman governor in the first place. Had this happened, the Roman governor would have simply said, "Solve it yourself; we Romans have nothing to do with it." Therefore, the complaint against Jesus could no longer be slander against God, but was changed to rebellion against the Roman emperor. That certainly was something the Romans were sensitive to.

The interrogation by Pilate

Pilate's interrogation is also a farce. Historical legal scholars have scratched their heads over Pilate's procedures, considering Roman law. Their conclusion is that Pilate was not acting in accordance with Roman law at all. Instead of condemning Jesus, he should have restrained the Jewish mob. Roman law at that time specifically stated that a judge may not be influenced by outsiders. Furthermore, it is this Jewish crowd that threatens Roman authority, not Jesus. It has all the air of a popular uprising that he should have put down. Later in his career, Pilate explicitly and cruelly did so with the Samaritan Revolt (in the year 37).

All of this is also somewhat ridiculous in the light of the

relationships of the time. Would a Roman governor listen to a shouting band of Jews? Roman rulers knew pretty well how to deal with such rabble. In any case, Pilate could have acquitted Jesus (in this regard, see John 19:12: "And from thenceforth Pilate sought to release him.").

There is also no specific charge under Roman law against Jesus. But in the Gospels, Pilate keeps shifting his responsibility. First he tries to have Jesus condemned by the Jews themselves. Then he interrogates Jesus, and finds him innocent. So he should have acquitted him. Instead, Pilate presents the crowd with a choice: whether to release Barabbas, a convicted murderer, or Jesus on the occasion of the Passover. This, again, is pure fiction! There is not a shred of evidence for such an action. According to the Gospels, it had been a custom of the Roman government to pardon a convict at the Passover feast. But there is not a single reference to such a custom in the entire Roman history of over 1,000 years. On the contrary, such a practice would have been diametrically opposed to the methods of rule used by the Romans, namely harsh and terrible oppression. Why would a Roman prefect release a notorious criminal and insurgent because of a strange (in his eyes) Jewish festival? Why would Pilate, who despised the Jews and had thousands of them crucified, allow himself to be associated with a rioter for a minute, let alone consult a roaring Jewish mob? And finally, he could have had Jesus executed as a rioter without any form of trial. He did not need the advice of a Jewish crowd to do so.

There is one small, significant detail in this account that should not be overlooked. According to Matthew (27:22): "Pilate saith unto them, what shall I do then with Jesus which is called Christ?" In this statement, the evangelists betray themselves and reveal the fictional nature of their accounts: Jesus was never called "Christ" during his life. The description of Jesus as Christ, the Anointed One, first appears in Paul's letters, some twenty years after Jesus' death, by someone who had nothing to do with the historical Jesus. The fact that the evangelist puts the word "Christ" in Pilate's mouth shows that the account cannot be contemporary, and is therefore not reliable. On the contrary, it is a later retelling in which elements have been included that had no factuality at the time of the events — a bit like the Hollywood movie about Jesus, in which a Roman soldier wears a wristwatch. But here we witness such an anachronism in the Gospel text itself.

According to the story, following Pilate's "offer" the people elect Barabbas. It is wildly improbable that anyone would give freedom back to a convicted murderer and bandit, rather than to someone who did little more than overturn a few tables of moneychangers in the temple. The whole story becomes clear, however, when it is put into the context of its time. Mark wrote his Gospel some time after Jerusalem was razed to the ground by the Roman armies. The Jewish branch of Christianity no longer existed in Jerusalem. Christians, including Jewish Christians who were now scattered throughout the Greco-Roman world, had to favor Rome in order to survive. One of the ways to do this with as little friction as possible was to entirely absolve the Romans of any blame for Jesus' death. Pilate washes his hands in front of the crowd (Matt. 27:24). It was the Jews who killed Jesus, not the Romans. After the interrogation, Pilate has Jesus flogged as punishment, hoping that this will put an end to the mob's insistence on execution.

So, really nothing of what the Gospels report about the interrogation and trial is historically plausible. Remember that it was a time when physical violence ruled the world. Torture, flogging, maiming, burning, crucifixion and all kinds of barbaric cruelty were the order of the day — on a colossal scale. It was a time when only military power prevailed. Genocides were carried out on a massive scale. Compassion for the suffering of others was almost entirely absent.

For people of today, it is difficult to imagine the matter-of-fact atrocities of the past. And here comes a crucial point. The picture painted of Pilate in the Gospels does not correspond at all with the historical Pilate, of whom we are well-informed through the work of Philo of Alexandria (c. 20 BC-c. AD 50), who was a contemporary of Jesus. He writes (in *Legatio ad Gaium*, On the Embassy of Gaius) that Pilate had a "vindictive and wild temperament" and was inflexible by nature, a mixture of "obstinacy and ruthlessness." Philo describes Pilate's rule as being characteristic of "his corruption and his brutality and his rapacity and his habit of hurting people, and his sodomy and his relentless killing of people without any form of trial, and his relentless and unnecessary and terrible inhumanity." This picture of Pilate is confirmed by another source. Flavius Josephus writes (in *Antiquitates Judaicae* 18.3.2) that Pilate used money from the temple to build an aqueduct. When a crowd gathered to protest this, Pilate had Roman soldiers mingle with the crowd, and on his orders, they began randomly killing and mutilating onlookers, to nip the protest in the bud.

Although not much about Pilate is known, these two independent sources seem sufficient to relegate the story of a mild-mannered judge to the realm of fables. Even at the time, when horrendous violence was commonplace, Pilate was considered particularly cruel. Roman rulers were generally not squeamish, but Pilate was recalled to Rome in the year 36 because of gross abuse of power and extreme cruelty. Is it conceivable, then, that someone like him would have taken the time to question Jesus? What interest could he have had in giving a complete nobody (from the Roman point of view) the chance to justify himself? The only plausible way to imagine the historical Pilate is that he would have had Jesus executed immediately. He didn't need a trial or excuses for that. And certainly he had neither time nor reason to deal with this kind of Jewish scum. Pilate as a doubting and compassionate Roman governor is a pure invention of the evangelists.

The scourging

Pilate hands Jesus over to the soldiers to have him flogged. This was customary before execution. Only one sentence is reported about it in the Gospels; more was not necessary, because contemporaries knew only too well how such a flogging proceeded. But since we are no longer familiar with this practice, it needs to be explained—though I caution the reader that it is not easy to read such a description, much less to imagine it.

The whips employed were nothing like those one can buy in an erotic store nowadays. Nor were they anything like the ones in Hollywood movies, which portray them in a way completely at odds with what is known about the Roman practice. Even a specialized historian such as Will Durant points out that "crucifixion was a Roman, not a Jewish, form of punishment. It was usually preceded by a flogging, which, when thoroughly administered, left the body like massive, swollen, bloody flesh" (Durant 1944, p. 572). This is expressed very euphemistically. In Europe, too, flogging was used as a punishment until the recent past, although it was quite different from the practice of the Romans. This fact must be considered for a moment, because it has implications for understanding the Gospels. As in painting, so in movies, the depiction of the actual violence in the Passion story is extremely limited. Its cinematic representation is understandably adapted to our contemporary sensibilities (see Elias' theory of civilization, which I referred to at the beginning of this chapter) and is therefore very misleading. I know of only one Hollywood production that comes somewhat closer to the reality of a Roman flogging, and that is Mel Gibson's *The Passion of the Christ*, although it too contains some inaccuracies about the crucifixion.

After the condemnation, the condemned person was doomed. But there were no precise rules about how this was to be carried out. It was left to the officer on duty and his assistants to "dispose" of the condemned person as they wished. And this is certainly what happened.

Before the flogging, the victim probably had to endure derision and beatings, possibly also gang rape. Among Roman soldiers, the game of *basileus* was well known and popular. The convict, bound and blindfolded, was pushed in a circle from one soldier to another, where a knee, foot, or fist was waiting for him. This corresponds with Mark (14:65): "And some began to spit on him, and to cover his face, and to buffet him, and to say unto him, Prophesy: and the servants did strike him with the palms of their hands." The story of the crown of thorns also fits this humiliation. A similar torment is certainly consistent with mockery and chastisement by the soldiers, so it could have happened. But ... where did they get those thorns in the middle of the city? And would Roman soldiers have had the patience to weave something like that, at the risk of hurting themselves? However, even if it happened as described in the Gospels, in the totality of the suffering imposed, the crown of thorns is more symbolic than real, as will be seen shortly.

To carry out the flogging, the convict was tied naked to a pole. On either side of him was a *lictor*, a Roman soldier, who had to carry out the punishment. The soldiers took turns, or else beat him at the same time. There were no rules. The beating was done with a *flagrum*, a whip made of leather straps (three, nine or twelve). These were fitted with pieces of glass, metal hooks, sharp bones and, most importantly, lead or bronze balls and rings, with sharp points. There was no limit to the number of blows or the duration of the flogging. But the *lictors* had to avoid flogging the condemned person to death, because then he could not be crucified. Cases have been cited in history where the convict died during or immediately after the flogging as a result of the type of instruments used. Unlike the later practice of flogging, it was not only the skin that was torn to pieces but the underlying tissue, blood vessels, nerves, and possibly even organs were affected. Fragments of flesh literally flew off the body during a Roman flogging.

While the convict's entire back was beaten to a bloody pulp, it also happened that the tissue was so badly damaged that the underlying ribs or vertebrae were exposed. Flavius Josephus mentions such a case: "There, though his flesh hung by threads" (*Antiquitates Judaicae* 6.302). The condemned man was horribly mutilated in this way. It also made the punishment a self-fulfilling prophecy: the man was so dehumanized by the beatings that he no longer looked like a human being. And so he must have been a criminal.

As a result of total physical and emotional shock, the victim, abandoned by all humanity, with horrifying pain deliberately inflicted on him, loses all orientation. The existential abandonment and the gruesome wounds leave him totally unhinged. But there are also serious medical consequences. In addition to possible organ damage, there is, above all, hypovolemic shock. This happens when the body loses more than one-fifth of its total blood and fluids, causing circulatory failure. After all, blood carries oxygen and other important substances necessary to maintain tissues and organ function. If the body loses these fluids faster than it can replace them, organs can fail, and the heart can no longer pump enough blood throughout the body to provide the necessary oxygen. Blood pressure drops sharply, as does body temperature. A crisis situation. In a way, therefore, excessive blood loss from flogging could be of "benefit" to the condemned, in bringing on death more quickly on the cross. Of course, this does not alleviate the hideous pain and suffering.

According to the Gospels, after the flogging, the uproar does not subside, and finally Pilate hands over (deliver: παρέδωκεν, *paredoken*; Vulgate: *tradidit*) Jesus for crucifixion and dictates the titulus, the inscription of the crime for which the crucified is punished: "Jesus of Nazareth, the King of the Jews" (John 19:19). When the Jewish priests protest against this wording,

Pilate suddenly seems to show backbone. "Then said the chief priests of the Jews to Pilate, Write not, The King of the Jews; but that he said, I am King of the Jews. Pilate answered, What I have written I have written" (John 19:21-22).

The conclusion is clear enough; the usual rules of Roman jurisprudence were violated by Pilate without any reason, and so the trial was actually null and void. (And here is another peculiarity: Pilate could very easily have postponed the trial.) In a purely technical sense, therefore, no judgment (*res iudicata*) was pronounced. The evangelists also agree on this. Matthew (27:26), Mark (15:15, 19:16), and John (19:16) all speak of an "extradition," not a judgment. But in Luke (23:24) the word *epikrino* is used, which can be roughly translated as "judged, sentenced, approved."

The crucifixion

The execution took place outside the city. In the Gospels, this place is called Golgotha. The meaning of the word is largely the same in the four Gospels: "skull place" (Κρανίου Τόπος). In Western iconography, one regularly sees images of Jesus carrying his cross on the way to Calvary (the Latin word for "skull place"). This representation is completely wrong, but understandably so, because from the fifth century onward, people did not know how a crucifixion was carried out. When Christianity was declared the state religion (in 380, by Emperor Theodosius I), crucifixion as a method of execution was abolished from the Roman Empire. Therefore, later painters did not know how it had been done. Here follows a description of the crucifixion based on factual historical and archaeological material.

On the Way to Golgotha

According to the three synoptic Gospels, Jesus was too weak to carry his cross: "And as they led him away, they laid hold upon one Simon, a Cyrenian, coming out of the country, and on him they laid the cross, that he might bear *it* after Jesus" (Luke 23:26). Almost literally, the same passage is found in Mark (15:21) and Matthew (27:32). "They," of course, are the executors of the sentence, the Roman soldiers. That Jesus was unable to carry the cross is easy to imagine, given the extreme shock (both physical and psychological) he had experienced during the flogging. On the other hand, Jesus was a vigorous young man who crossed the entire country on foot to preach, so he was most likely in good health. But to assume that Roman soldiers were so sensitive that they forced an observer to lend a hand is absurd. There were enough ways to make even an exhausted and tormented person continue.

But there was no cross. An entire cross weighed more than 260 pounds; it is impossible that a tormented man could have carried such a weight. Therefore, the common depiction in paintings of Jesus carrying this 260-pound cross is mere fantasy. The standard procedure for a crucifixion was that the convict had to carry a crossbar (*patibulum*) tied to his severely wounded shoulders and arms, to the execution site. The bar weighed between 60 and 100 pounds. So how would this Simon of Cyrene have helped to carry the crossbar if it was tied to the convict's shoulders? There is also no historical evidence of a bystander being forced to relieve a convict's suffering in the street, and it would have been completely against the Roman approach. On the contrary, further torment of the condemned on the way to the execution site was attractive in the eyes of the Roman soldiers. One should not forget that the soldiers took no pleasure in this task, and therefore took out their frustration on the condemned, whom they considered a criminal anyway and who by this time also looked completely dehumanized. So why should they feel sorry for such a person?

The way to the place of execution was hell for the convict. Crowds of people at the roadside would be mocking, cursing, and beating him. The heavy weight on his shoulders made it difficult for the victim to keep his balance. The stones were slippery and the convict was barefoot; stumbling and falling was therefore inevitable. These observations are not explicitly mentioned in the Gospels, but find expression in the Christian devotion to the Stations of the Cross (or Calvary). The Roman soldiers propelled the victim forward using their whips and weapons. The pressure behind him caused him to fall forward as he stumbled. He would try to break his fall by absorbing the shock with his knees, and after a few falls, his kneecaps would be completely destroyed. Apart from experiencing frightening pain caused by these fractures, he would be unable to straighten his legs because the quadriceps tendon (the thigh muscle) would no longer be connected to the lower leg. The convicted person would no longer walk upright and in some cases would only crawl forward.

Even worse is a fall that is not cushioned by the knees. Then the convict falls directly with his face onto the stones, with the heavy crossbar providing additional impact. Teeth, nose and chin would break, sometimes also the frontal bone. It does not take much imagination to see that these falls, in addition to the injuries from the blows, would completely mutilate the face of the condemned. His head is now just a bloody mass, adding to his hideous appearance. And all of this is only the prelude to the actual torture. The victim is already half-dead when he arrives at the crucifixion site, and from then on it is a matter of keeping him alive as long as possible.

Crucifixion Itself

Crucifixion as a death penalty was not invented by the Romans. The Persians, Punics and Macedonians also applied it. The Greeks knew of its use, but largely avoided its application. In the Roman Empire, this punishment was by no means exceptional. It is reported that Consul Publius Rupilius had 20,000 people nailed to the cross after the first slave rebellion of 135-131 BC. After the slave rebellion by Spartacus, Crassus had 6,000 prisoners crucified. And closer to the Gospels, when the Romans besieged Jerusalem in the year 70, Titus, the Roman leader, arranged for so many people to be crucified that there were not enough trees nearby to make crosses.

Sections of the Roman elite also found this punishment so abhorrent that some turned away from it. For example, the consul and orator Cicero (106-43 BC) calls crucifixion the most cruel and repulsive punishment: *"Nomen ipsum crucis absit non modo a corpore civium Romanorum, sed etiam a cogitatione, oculis, auribus"* (which means "The word 'cross' must stay away not only from the body of Roman citizens, but also from their thoughts, from your eyes and ears") (*Pro C. Rabirio perduellionis reo* 5,16, quoted in Moltmann 1972, p. 36).

As is the case with flogging, little is said about crucifixion in the Gospels, for everyone in Palestine at the time knew what it entailed. The term for the cross used in the Gospels is σταυρός (*stauros*, cross), but the actual practice varied greatly depending on the place and time. Sometimes it was a simple tree trunk (*crux simplex*) to which the condemned person was nailed with his hands above his head. Sometimes there was a pole on the tree trunk (*crux commissa*) in the shape of the letter T. And there was the shape as we know it from Christian iconography: an upright pole (*stipes*) with a crossbar just below the top (*crux immissa*). The shape of the cross on which Jesus died is not known.

What is certain, however, is that the condemned man was nailed to the cross naked. The religious scenes in paintings and statues where Jesus wears a loincloth are an invention from the prudish minds of later Christians. It's not difficult to imagine that the crucified man's complete nakedness was the object of ridicule and humiliation, and his intimate parts the target of torment. Any gang of boisterous young men would find it particularly entertaining to pelt the face and genitals of the crucified with stones, pebbles, and even small rocks. The crucified was at the mercy of the crowd's perverse entertainment and could not avoid them, nor could he fend off insects or carrion birds that would feed on his wounds.

The usual depiction of Jesus on the cross, with nails through his hands, is certainly wrong. The weight of the body would have ripped the palms of the hands. The nails (usually square, between five and seven inches long and less than half an inch thick) were each driven through the wrist. The joint there is capable of supporting the weight of a person. However, the extremely sensitive median nerve, which coordinates the muscles of the hand and gives the hand feeling, is also located there. This nerve was usually hit when the nail was driven through each wrist. As a result, control of the hand muscles was lost, and each hand cramped into a claw. Direct injury to a nerve is one of the worst pains in the human body.

Carrying out a crucifixion was not a pleasant task for the Roman soldiers. There was always the possibility that the mob would attack and overwhelm them. But even with Jesus, whose death was apparently (according to the Gospels) wanted by the Jewish cabal, it was a heinous affair. The crucified man must have roared in pain, horrendous to listen to. And the place of execution must have aroused disgust. There were still decomposing corpses hanging on crosses, and all kinds of scavenging animals (vultures, ravens, rats and the like) feasted on the corpses. And the stench was unbearable; natural bodily functions do not cease when someone is hanging on a cross, and a deceased person no longer has control over his sphincter muscles. Even a crucified person who is still alive has no choice but to let feces and urine run free. In short, standing guard over a crucified person was not a popular task for Roman soldiers. This must have led in turn to aggression against the condemned man. He was in any case a criminal and an enemy of the Roman Empire.

The traditional idea that the cross was high above the crowd, as one can see in many medieval paintings, is probably also wrong. That would have caused too many technical complications. Rather, one should imagine that the crucified person was hanging just above the ground, so that it was not very difficult to attach the *patibulum* to the *stipes*. First the victim was nailed to the *patibulum* through the wrists. When this was done, the feet were nailed onto the *stipes*, shattering the foot bones and causing terrible wounds. However, these wounds provoked little blood loss, which was precisely the intention, to prolong the torture as long as possible. Cases have been described of crucified people who remained alive for several days, enduring this chilling torture.

The Israel Museum in Jerusalem holds a pierced heel bone of a crucified man, named "Jehohanan son of Hagkol," executed in the first century.

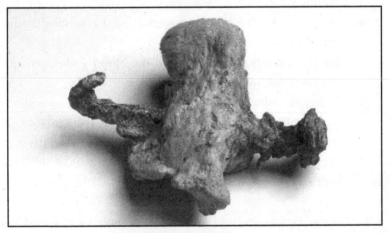

Jehohanan heelbone

A frequently asked question is what the crucified man finally died of. There is reasonably extensive medical literature on this question; see, for instance, Bankl 1989, Edwards et al. 1986, Maslen and Mitchell 2006, Samuelsson 2013, and Zugibe 1988, 2005. In the end, death came from exhaustion without food or drink in the hot Palestinian sun, after severe abuse. In the case of Jesus, all four Gospels report that Jesus died after only a few hours, and this was probably so. Although some documented cases exist of crucified persons living for a few days during crucifixion, they were more likely the exception than the rule.

I believe that the best explanation of the possible causes of death from crucifixion comes from Hans Bankl, an Austrian professor of pathological anatomy. They are:

1. Flogging having caused excessive blood loss.
2. Severe circulatory disturbances from the upright, standing posture, causing blood to sink into the lower limbs. This blood can no longer be circulated to supply organs in the higher regions of the body.
3. Neurogenic shock caused by the extreme pain and wounds.
4. Psychogenic shock from the emotional reactions to the torture.
5. Significant oxygen shortage in the blood and organs as the result of hanging by the arms.
6. Extreme dehydration from blood loss and excessive perspiration from shock. Consider the sponge soaked with vinegar that the soldiers offered Jesus; perhaps this involved the acetic acid drink *posca* that Roman soldiers carried.

All of these factors individually or in combination could be causes of death. But a central aspect is the respiratory problem. The full body weight of a crucified person hangs on the wrists, stretching the muscles of the chest, shoulders, and upper arms. The chest is therefore in the position for inhalation. Exhalation is impeded so that not enough carbon dioxide can be discharged from the lungs to the outside, which may become life-threatening in high concentrations. The only way to breathe is for the crucified man to pull himself up by his wounded wrists, creating immense pain. In addition, the fully broken back rubs against the rough wood of the *stipes*. One witness to a crucifixion used the expression *"equitabant in cruce,"* he "rode on the cross." The *suppedaneum* (a type of footrest) and the *sedile* (a type of seat board) could provide some temporary relief, but not much and not for long. The *sedile* was too short to rest on, and the Romans often applied the *suppedaneum* so that it was tilted forward, making it impossible to really lean on it. Without the support of the *suppedaneum*, the only way left to stand up was by leaning on the nails through the feet, which of course was accompanied by ghastly pain in the foot wounds. As a result, these supports brought relief only for a moment, but they prolonged the suffering. In the end, owing to exhaustion or coma, it was no longer possible for the crucified man to lift himself up in order to breathe. The lack of oxygen and the excess of carbon dioxide in the blood inevitably led to the loss of vital organs, and death from asphyxiation.

This was the reason why often the lower legs of the crucified were broken, the so-called *crurifragium*. Normally, Roman soldiers had to stand guard at a crucifixion until the prisoner was dead. In the absence of an explicit order to prolong the prisoner's life as long as possible, the soldiers preferred to go home. To hasten death, the lower legs were broken with a metal rod (or sword). As a result, the support in the legs fell away and the crucified man hung with his full weight on the nails. He could only breathe when he pulled himself up. But soon he succumbed to complete exhaustion, so that he suffocated. The Gospel according to John says that Jesus' bones were not broken: "But when they came to Jesus, and saw that he was dead already, they brake not his legs: But one of the soldiers with a spear pierced his side, and forthwith came there out blood and water" (John 19:33-34). But this is another medical error: no blood comes out of a body that has been dead for some time. The following verse is meant to excuse the error: "And he that saw *it* bare record, and his record is true: and he knoweth that he saith true, that ye might believe" (John 19:35). The fact that the author is so emphatic about the truth here must be understood as an attempt to convince his readers. With all the atrocities and public executions, contemporaries must have known that a corpse cannot bleed. After all, after death, the blood in the body begins to sink into the lower limbs and coagulate. And because the heart stops pumping, there is no longer pressure on the arteries, so the blood cannot flow. Bankl (1989) carried out an experiment with student volunteers to test whether asphyxiation was the cause of death during crucifixion. The result was that it was impossible for subjects to hang only by their arms for more than 12 minutes. Then blood pressure dropped to life-threatening levels and unconsciousness occurred.

According to the description of two evangelists, the death of Jesus led to a darkening throughout the land, although it was still noon (Mark 15:33 ff.; Matt. 27:45 ff.). What was the cause of the darkness descended in the middle of the day? It wasn't a solar eclipse. What then? In fact, this is a skillful insertion from a literary point of view, amplifying the impact of the event. If there really was such an inexplicable phenomenon, why was it not recorded in the writings of contemporaries? Historians like Tacitus and a naturalist like Pliny the Elder, who lived at that time, do not mention it. Pliny diligently wrote down all the natural phenomena from his time, from earthquakes to comets, but nothing about total darkness one afternoon in Palestine. Imagine a sudden total darkness in San Diego. Wouldn't that be in the newspapers? There were no newspapers at the time, of course, but in an oral culture the spread of news is pretty fast. Oral history research provides convincing evidence of this; see Chapter 8.

Moreover, the two evangelists mention that at the time of Jesus' death, the veil of the Jewish temple in Jerusalem was torn in half. But this, too, is implausible. The description of the crucifixion is based on a spatial view, namely the place of execution, Golgotha. But this place was about a good half mile or more from the temple. How could an eyewitness stand next to the cross and see what was happening in another place at the same time?

The Resurrection

For the early Christians, the resurrection was one of the cornerstones of their faith. The promise of the coming kingdom over which Jesus would rule was not fulfilled. Worse, their teacher had died a most shameful and cruel death. The psychological shock this must have caused to the disciples was so great that a solution had to be found. A simple solution would have been to admit that it was all a mistake. But such a thing would be difficult if one firmly believed in the promise of a new world. Compare this with what I have discussed regarding cognitive dissonance in Chapter 3. The solution developed by the early Christians was the resurrection: Jesus had died on the cross, but he rose from the dead.

Several passages in the New Testament contain testimonies of this resurrection. If one looks more closely at these stories, the first thing that stands out is that some attestations are mentioned in only one Gospel. For instance, Jesus' appearances to the people of Emmaus (Luke 24:13-32), to 500 people (1 Cor. 15:6), and to the followers at the Sea of Galilee (John 21:1-14) are each mentioned by only one author. The same applies to the appearance to Paul (around the year 36). He is the only one who reports that he saw the risen Christ—and even adds that his companions did not see anything! From a historical point of view, these testimonies are therefore suspicious. They are not necessarily wrong, but they cannot be verified historically, because there are no other records. Finding only one source makes the testimony suspicious.

However, this is not the case with the discovery of the empty tomb. For this, there are four different sources. According to tradition, Jesus' body was buried by Joseph of Arimathea in the tomb he had reserved for himself. The following Sunday, some women (Mary Magdalene, Mary the mother of James, and Salome) went up to the tomb with fragrant herbs to embalm the body. This is how Mark (16:1-8) describes it. But in Matthew (28:1-10), there is only Mary; in Luke (24:1-8) there is a Joanna instead of Salome, and in John (20:1-18) there is only Mary Magdalene. Although we have four testimonies, they are all different. But other details differ significantly as well. In Mark, the women find a young man in front of the tomb; in Matthew there is an angel. In Luke, there are two men, and in John, two angels. In the Gospels of Luke and John it is said that Peter also went to the tomb, but not so in Matthew and Mark. The "disciple who loved Jesus" also goes to the grave in Luke and John, but not so in the other Gospels. And in the texts of Matthew and John, Mary Magdalene sees Jesus herself at the tomb.

So there are enough differences to question the reliability of this visit to the tomb. When one considers these four sources together, with their contradictions, they do not provide a very strong testimony. What is perfectly clear from the four texts, however, is that the circle of Jesus' followers firmly believed that he had risen. Can current readers of the New Testament share in their belief? That depends. There is a much more convincing argument for doubting this resurrection. All the resurrection stories assume that Jesus was buried after his death on the cross. But this assumption is completely at odds with the Roman practice in this matter. The dead bodies of those crucified were usually left hanging for further deterrence. There is no reason to believe that this would have been any different in the case of Jesus, nor do the Gospels provide any reason. As mentioned earlier, it is known from all sources that Pilate, the governor who condemned Jesus, was extremely harsh, cruel and ruthless. Philo of Alexandria, a contemporary of Pilate, wrote of him that his style of government was characterized by "his corruption, his violence, his thefts, his attacks, his abuses, his frequent executions of unconvicted prisoners, and his relentless cruelties" (Smallwood 1961, p. 302). Why should anyone assume that the ruthless villain Pilate would allow a completely unknown insurgent from a remote area in the north the favor of a burial, directly contradicting the prevailing policy of oppression and deterrence in the Roman Empire? There is not a shred of evidence for this, and much to the contrary.

And Joseph of Arimathea? Suddenly he appears, at the very end of the story. Where does he come from? In none of the four Gospels is he mentioned as a follower of Jesus. It would therefore seem that he arrives here without any credible reference to the story as a whole, like a *deus ex machina*, a plot device that offers a necessary but unfounded solution. The most serious argument against this solution is that Jesus had no relations with rich and/or influential people in Jerusalem. None of the Gospels mention such a connection. As Crossan (1995, p. 175) succinctly puts it, "If they had power, they were not his friends; if they were his friends, they had no power." Why then does a wealthy, influential man like Joseph of Arimathea appear here, completely unexpectedly? Simply because a way had to be found to enable Jesus' buried body to arise from the dead.

But if after his death Jesus' body was left on the cross, just like those of other executed people, then he was not buried. So there was no tomb, and—this cannot be said more explicitly— then there was no empty tomb. And so the ground disappears underneath the belief in the resurrection of Jesus. One of the most important beliefs of Christianity is based on quicksand; there was no tomb at all! Every single element and detail of historical knowledge about the practices of the Romans in the provinces shows that Jesus was not buried. The stories about the empty tomb are historically untrue (which does not mean they are not foundational, beautiful, or touching).

For today's readers, there is not much more to be done than

to raise serious doubts about this belief. In our materialistic and scientific world, the only way to give credence to this resurrection is—yes, exactly, through faith. Those who do not subscribe to faith still have the possibility of auxiliary constructions: hallucinations, delusions, collective hysteria, and so on. Science, which sufficiently studies such constructions, demonstrates how easily people can become deluded, even collectively.

Conclusion

Analysis of the historical sources available inevitably leads to the conclusion that the Gospels are particularly unreliable with respect to the Passion of Jesus. In particular, the interrogations by the Jewish high priest and by Pilate are in no way consistent with the jurisprudence of the time. They are even less reliable regarding the brutal practice of violent oppression and sinister torture that was the order of the day at that time. However, this does not detract from the fact that each of the Gospels tells a poignant story, a story that truly cannot leave anyone unmoved.

Chapter 7

Tell A Story!

It is clear that the New Testament consists largely of stories. Some of these stories are strange, for example the book of Revelation which is a story about ... the future. Then there are the four Gospels themselves and the Book of Acts. The letters also contain many narrative elements. Where do these stories come from? Believers trace the Gospels directly to a divine authority. Whoever or whatever this may be, it is strange that this authority, an Almighty God, cannot communicate a clearer message. The ironic answer the great British philosopher Bertrand Russell once gave when asked what he would say to his Creator after he died and God demanded why he had not believed, was: "Not enough evidence, God! Not enough evidence" (Eakin 2002).

Since this view (that a God is the basis of the texts) involves a supernatural explanation, it has no place in science. Everyone is allowed to believe in such an explanation. Perhaps this also gives people something to cling to, or offers them comfort. But from a critical point of view, such a belief is unfounded.

Narrative perspective in the New Testament

The stories in the New Testament are the work of human beings, with all their imperfections. So who "tells" these stories? None of the authors were present at the events. But that doesn't mean that they can't tell an exciting story. This they do, from different points of view. In narrative theory, which studies the structure and effects of stories, a distinction is made between different types of storytellers. This is called a narrative perspective. Roughly speaking, there are about four ways to do this. To begin with, one can tell a story in the first person. This is clearly not the case in the

Gospels, since none of the evangelists speak in the first person. The beginning of Luke's Gospel (1:3-4; see the quote in Chapter 5) is the only place in the four Gospels and Acts where someone in the stories speaks in the first person. The first person perspective is often used in dialogues, of course, such as in Matthew (18:3) when Jesus answers the disciples' question about who is the greatest in the kingdom of heaven: "And he said: 'Truly I tell you, unless you change and become like little children, you will never enter the kingdom of heaven.'" Another example is when Pilate says, "I find no fault in this man" (Luke 23:4). But these are first-person accounts in a dialogue. The New Testament stories, by definition, are not told in first person, because the authors did not experience the events themselves. Where we regularly find the first-person narrator is in the letters of Paul, for example. The first person there is the one who speaks, as in the dialogues in the Gospels.

A story can also be told in the third person, in the "he" form. (I am using the male form here, but it will be obvious from the examples that the narrating instance can be female as well.) That is predominantly the case here. Generally, there are three variants of this mode of storytelling. One can tell the story from the point of view of one of the characters in the story. This form is called personal narrative (see especially Stanzel 2008). This could have been done by having the events narrated by Pilate, by Jesus, or by a bystander. But that's not the case here. The second of the "he" variants is when the story is told by a third person not known by the reader, but who seems to know everything about the events, and is therefore omniscient. This type of narrator is known in professional circles as an authorial narrator. There are again two variants of this. In the first case (so now the third possibility), the narrator is visible because he comments on the story he is telling. In Charlotte Brontë's *Jane Eyre*, for example, the narrator is constantly talking to the reader and also commenting on the story she herself is telling, for example, "Oh, romantic reader, forgive me for telling the plain truth!" (p. 95) It's obvious that we are not dealing with that kind of narrator in the Gospels either. Passages in which the reader is directly addressed in the text are fairly rare in the Gospels (although they do occur in the Letters, but from time to time there are comments on the Gospel story, to emphasize, for instance, that the events have been faithfully told). As just seen, the beginning of Luke's Gospel contains such a commentary, in which a particular reader, Theophilus, is addressed (Luke 1:3-4). Such comments appear here and there in the Gospels, always with the intention of convincing the reader of the truthfulness and importance of the message. Generally, however, the narrator remains invisible in the Gospels; one does not know who is speaking. This is the fourth possibility of narrative perspective, that the omniscient narrator remains hidden from the reader.

Here is a schematic summary of the different types of narrators:

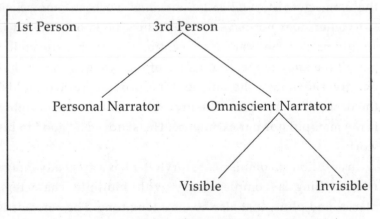

1st Person   3rd Person

Personal Narrator   Omniscient Narrator

Visible   Invisible

Types of Narrator

The omniscient invisible narrator of the New Testament

The fact that the Gospels are told by an invisible, omniscient narrator in the third person has a number of consequences.

The first is that there is something natural about this kind of narration. By far, most stories are traditionally told by such an omniscient but invisible narrator. Second, this narrator has unrestricted access to the inner world of all characters. In this context, it may be interesting to note that the position of the omniscient storyteller is often compared to the position of God: He knows everything, knows all the details, can explain everything. This becomes clear in many places in the Gospels. For example, when Jesus is 12 years old, the family travels to Jerusalem to celebrate the Jewish Passover. But suddenly his parents lose him. They find him in the synagogue only after three days of searching, where he is involved in conversations with scribes. Of course he is rebuked, but he replies that he had to be in the house of his "father," which the parents do not understand. The chapter ends, in the penultimate sentence, with the words, "but his mother kept all these sayings in her heart" (Luke 2:51). How do we know this? Because this is what the omniscient storyteller Luke claims. Such an omniscient storyteller does not have to justify how he knows this. It is simply part of the literary convention that such a storyteller has all the knowledge. In the case of the evangelists, this has one great advantage: he, and he alone, provides (or withholds) the desired information. The invisible, omniscient storyteller is the manipulator par excellence. He is indeed a "god" in his story.

In addition, an omniscient storyteller has a great advantage when telling a complex story with multiple characters, places, and plots, that also spans a long time. The narrator is not bound by time or place and can enter into the thoughts, attitudes, motivations and feelings of any character at any time. He himself is not part of the action, which allows him to maintain a certain distance from the events. The result leaves an impression of objectivity and authenticity. Moreover, the narrator always knows more than the individual characters.

Not only does he have access to their inner lives, but he also has an overview of *all* characters, something the individuals do not have. This makes his knowledge superior to that of the individual protagonists. And it gives him a special status because events can be portrayed much more credibly by the omniscient narrator than by the individual characters inside the story. Such a narrator can also divide his sympathy among the characters. He can portray some as suspicious or immoral, while with others he can emphasize their reliability or integrity. This allows him to control the distribution of sympathies. All in all, an omniscient narrator can develop a broad and wide panorama while at the same time probing deep into characters and events.

The Odyssey, *Pride and Prejudice*, *War and Peace*, *Oliver Twist*, *1984*, *The Brothers Karamazov*, *The Lord of the Rings*, and *The Trial* are just a few arbitrary examples of books with an omniscient storyteller, making it abundantly clear that this mode of storytelling is by far the standard. All these works paint a broad panorama in which the narrator forces us to perceive the characters and events through his eyes, with the value pattern he chooses. He decides; the reader has no choice. This inevitably leads to the conclusion that such an omniscient narrator clothes himself with authority. It is no coincidence that such a narrator is called "authorial." He is the only authority in the story.

But this omniscient storyteller also brings far-reaching problems. We have already seen one example. The last (original) sentence of Mark's Gospel states that the women fled when they saw the empty tomb and did not talk to anyone about it. But Mark can only know this because he acts as an omniscient narrator. He has direct access to the inside of all the characters, even those he was not together with or who said nothing. But an attentive reader will notice this.

Another example from Matthew's Gospel says that Jesus goes

with his disciples to the Garden of Olives (Matt. 26:36-45). He goes himself a little further to pray, but the disciples fall asleep. Three times he urges them to stay awake and pray. But we are told that "their eyes were heavy" (Matt. 26:43). Nevertheless, Matthew records the literal words of Jesus' prayer: "O my Father, if it be possible, let this cup pass from me: nevertheless not as I will, but as thou *wilt*" (Matt. 26:39). But wait ... all the disciples were asleep. And Jesus had gone a little further and was therefore alone. So how could Matthew know what Jesus' prayer involved? Not from the apostles, for they were asleep. Nor from Jesus himself, for he died shortly afterwards. So where did Matthew get this information?

We do not usually notice such problems as readers, because in most Western cultures, an omniscient narrator is the norm. He is the typical entity who tells myths and legends. And for the modern reader, "classic" stories like those of Dickens, Balzac, and Tolstoy are the kind of stories one immediately recognizes and feels at home with. This type of narrator is also the standard for most narratives in children's stories and young adult literature, so this is the model one actually grows up with (see Nikolajeva 2005 and Wall 1990). Psychologists call such a model a *script*. If you have grown up in a certain culture, you expect events to follow a more or less fixed script. For example, if you visit a hospital, you will expect to see people in white or green clothes that you would not see them wearing outside the hospital. But suppose you go to a restaurant and are served by a waiter or waitress in a white lab coat. Your hunger will be gone immediately, because the script for good food excludes doctors' white lab coats. One can think of an omniscient narrator as such a script in this context. We are so familiar with it that we experience the situation as "natural," and therefore do not question it.

Productive stories

Take a look at the next excerpt:

They want to make what happened to live forever, they told me. What is written down, they say, will change the world.

"The world?" I asked. "All of it?"

"Yes," the man who had been my guide said, "all of it."

I must have looked perplexed.

"She does not understand," he said to his companion, and it was true. I did not understand.

"He was indeed the Son of God," he said.

And then, patiently, he began to explain to me what had happened to me at my son's conception as the other nodded and encouraged him. I barely listened. I had other things to do. I know what happened. (p. 99)

This is an excerpt from a 2012 novel by Irish writer Colm Tóibín, *The Testament of Mary*. The first-person narrator is Mary, the mother of Jesus. The two men are followers of Jesus after his death. The novel describes how Mary feels after witnessing her son's preaching, his imprisonment and crucifixion, and how she was able to escape to Ephesus and now faces death, but is constantly harassed by two of her son's followers, whom she doesn't really want to know about. The story is a fictional continuation of parts of the New Testament.

This is a contemporary novel based on the New Testament, in other words, a story that continues the narrative of the New Testament. And it is not the only one. With the New Testament, the flow of writings about Jesus did not end, but only just took off. In the twentieth and twenty-first centuries alone, there has been a relentless stream of stories about the figure of Jesus. Below is a small (certainly incomplete) list of some English-language titles:

Naomi Alderman, *The Liar's Gospel* (2013)

William Edmund Barrett, *The Shape of Illusion* (1972)

Richard Beard, *Lazarus is Dead* (2012)

James BeauSeigneur, *In His Image* (1997)

Dan Brown, *The Da Vinci Code* (2009)

Taylor Caldwell, *Dear and Glorious Physician* (1958)

Taylor Caldwell, *I, Judas* (1977)

Morley Callagan and Nino Ricci, *A Time for Judas* (2007)

Jim Crace, *Quarantine* (1997)

Elizabeth Cunningham, *Magdalen Rising: The Beginning* (2000)

Marianne Fredriksson, *According to Mary Magdalene* (1997)

Margaret George, *Mary, Called Magdalene* (2002)

James Goldberg, *The Five Books of Jesus* (2012)

Robert Graves, *King Jesus* (1946)

Louis N. Gruber, *Jay: A Spiritual Fantasy* (2001)

Frank Turner Hollon, *The Book of Neil* (2012)

Donovan Joyce, *The Jesus Scroll* (1972)

Nikos Kazantsakis, *Christ Recrucified* (1954)

Charles Davis Kleymeyer, *Yeshu: A Novel for the Open-Hearted* (2013)

John Kolchak, *Next Year in Jerusalem* (2015)

Pär Lagerkvist, *Barabbas* (1950)

S.B. L'Aloge, *The Gospel According to Satan* (2007)

Stephanie Landsem, *The Thief* (2014)

A.J. Langguth, *Jesus Christs* (1968)

D.H. Lawrence, *The Man Who Died* (1929)

Reynold J. Levocz, *The Spear of Longinus* (2013)

Ki Longfellow, *The Secret Magdalene* (2005)

Norman Mailer, *The Gospel According to the Son* (1997)

Kathleen McGowan, *The Expected One* (2006)

Michael Moorcock, *Behold the Man* (1969)

Christopher Moore, Lamb: *The Gospel According to Biff, Christ's Childhood Pal* (2002)

James K. Morrow, *Only Begotten Daughter* (1990)

Fulton Oursler, *The Greatest Story Ever Told* (1949)

Paul Park, *Gospel of Corax* (1996)

W. Maxwell Prince, *Judas: The Last Days* (2015)

Philip Pullman, *The Good Man Jesus and the Scoundrel Christ* (2010)

Nino Ricci, *Testament* (2002)

Anne Rice, *Christ The Lord: Out of Egypt* (2006)

Michele Roberts, *The Wild Girl* (1991)

José Saramago, *The Gospel According to Jesus Christ* (1999)

Susan Shwartz, *The Grail of Hearts* (1992)

Tobias Skinner, *The Gospel of Lazarus* (2014)

Kenneth Smith, *Judas: A Biographical Novel of the Life of Judas Iscariot* (2001)

C.K. Stead, *My Name Was Judas* (2006)

Colm Tóibín, *The Testament of Mary* (2013)

Nick Tosches, *Under Tiberius* (2015)

Jonathan Trigell, *The Tongues of Men or Angels* (2014)

Philipp Vandenberg, *The Fifth Gospel* (1993)

Frank Yerby, *Judas My Brother* (1978)

Anyone eager to read stories based on those in the New Testament will soon find something to their liking. And there is no reason to believe that this trend will decline over time. Of the 49 books listed here, 55% were published after the year 2000 and nearly 30% after the year 2010.

What this shows is that stories themselves can become productive. This is not so unusual in the history of literature. More than 700 alternative versions and translations appeared of the 1719 story *Robinson Crusoe* by the English author Daniel Defoe, in all sorts of languages. And Cervantes' *Don Quixote* has produced eight adaptations for the theater and 31 film adaptations, 24 literary imitations, 29 adaptations for opera, ballet and music, and numerous visualizations in art by Gustave Doré, Pablo Picasso and Salvador Dalí, among others. Mary

Shelley's *Frankenstein* has 60 million pages in Google. There are no less than 300 different editions, 650 comic books, 150 spin-offs and parodies, and more than 90 film adaptations of the original 1818 novel in circulation today! And what about the word "utopia," which everyone knows, but which actually goes back to Thomas More's *Utopia* of 1516, with countless imitations?

I speak here of productive texts; they generate imitations and adaptations, and therefore millions of readers, generation after generation. As for the Gospels, the text of Mark is indisputably the first Gospel of the New Testament. This leads to an interesting conclusion: Mark is the most prolific author in the world. His literary imitators number in the thousands. No other author has ever produced so many adaptations, apart from, of course, Matthew and Luke, and perhaps John as well to some extent. And they too, in turn, have produced imitators of their own.

The seemingly endless stream of storytelling, however, has its origins in the New Testament itself, namely in the profound differences between the authors' theological views and practical goals. Let's take a closer look.

Theological differences

The invisible, omniscient narrator in the Gospels makes us perceive persons and events in ways that we ourselves cannot control. He "approves" of possible errors that we do not notice. The narrative situation enhances the credibility and authenticity of the stories, and is therefore in some ways a remedy for the many gaps, anomalies, and contradictions in the texts. One allows for the general human limitations and the limited information available to the evangelists, the lack of communication and the primitive means of disseminating written texts at that time. But even so, it still leaves a big black hole—a residue of inexplicable emptiness, a gap that cannot be filled with excuses, an inconsistency that cannot be tolerated. There is no solution for this problem, because it concerns the theological and purposeful differences between the authors. I would like to illustrate this with the "seven words of the cross." These are the last words spoken by Jesus before his death on the cross. The designation is not quite correct, for they are seven sentences, not seven words. And they are not all the last sentences, for there can be only four: one in each Gospel. But these seven phrases are traditionally called the words of the cross.

These seven have become the occasion for great musical compositions by Heinrich Schütz, Pergolesi, César Franck and many others. These words of the cross were inimitably witnessed in Joseph Haydn's unusually great work of art, *The Seven Last Words of Our Savior on the Cross* (Hob. XX/1:A) from 1787, edited in various versions by the composer until it received its final version in his oratorio in 1796.

Here are the seven sentences under discussion:

1. "Father, forgive them, for they know not what they do" (Luke 23:34);
2. "Verily I say unto thee, To day shalt thou be with me in paradise" (Luke 23:43);
3. "Woman, behold thy son!", "Behold thy mother!" (John 19:26-27);
4. "Eli, Eli, lama sabachthani? that is to say, My God, my God, why hast thou forsaken me?" (Matt. 27:46) and virtually the same in Mark (15:34);
5. "I thirst" (John 19:28);
6. "It is finished!" (John 19:30);
7. "Father, into thy hands I commend my spirit" (Luke 23:46).

This is the traditional order in which the words of the cross are performed in music. We see here an attempt to blend elements from the various Gospels into a harmonious whole, a form of "vertical reading" (see Chapter 1). This is necessary because the four canonical Gospels each tell different stories about the death of Jesus. Without detracting from the tradition and beauty of this intimate and deeply felt music, it is necessary to look more closely at the textual tradition here.

A first and obvious remark is that these seven sentences cannot all be the last words, in a double sense. From the Gospel of Luke come the three sentences (1), (2) and (7). It will be clear that only (7) can be the last sentence spoken by Jesus in Luke's Gospel. John also contains three sentences: (3), (5) and (6), of which only (6) can have been the actual last sentence. This leaves four final sentences, one for each of the four Gospels:

1. "Eloi, Eloi, lama sabachthani?" (Mark 15:34);
2. "Eli, Eli, lama sabachthani?" (Matt. 27:46);
3. "Father, into thy hands I commend my spirit" (Luke 23:46);
4. "It is finished" (John 19:30).

And again, these cannot all be the last words. Which of these four were the truly last? It is striking that the same last words appear in two Gospels, Mark and Matthew. More importantly, they are in the language of Jesus, one of the few places in the Gospels where expressions appear in Aramaic, and at a crucial moment in the story, the moment when Jesus gives up his spirit. These two factors (the same phrase in two Gospels and then both in Jesus' native language) together lend greater credibility to Mark and Matthew. Important to my argument here is the meaning of the sentence. In the Gospel text, the Aramaic phrase is translated into Greek; in English it reads, "My God, my God, why have you forsaken me?" This is an expression of total loneliness, utter despair. From a man in a state of shock, abandoned by all, without a spark of compassion from his fellow man. So here Jesus appears with completely human feelings. He preached the coming of a new and heavenly kingdom, and is now abandoned by the whole world and by God in a completely miserable and desolate way. At the same time, however, he appears elsewhere in the Gospels as God himself, so that one must ask about his "divine" status.

Was Jesus God?

An important question, then, is to what extent Jesus' followers, and later generations, regarded him as God. For most Christians, Jesus was and is both human and God. In the New Testament, there are three expressions that are important in this regard: "Messiah," "Son of Man," and "Son of God." These expressions are almost ubiquitous and therefore deserve special attention.

I begin with "Son of Man." This expression occurs a total of 82 times, only in the Gospels, and importantly, always in direct speech, namely in the words of Jesus himself. Here is a comparison of some of these references:

"Whosoever therefore shall be ashamed of me and of my words in this adulterous and sinful generation; of him also shall the Son of man be ashamed, when he cometh in the glory of his Father with the holy angels" (Mark 8:38).

"The Son of man shall send forth his angels, and they shall gather out of his kingdom all things that offend, and them which do iniquity" (Matt. 13:41-42).

"Watch ye therefore, and pray always, that ye may be accounted worthy to escape all these things that shall come to pass, and to stand before the Son of man" (Luke 21:35-36).

Jesus is speaking in the first person here, having been granted the floor by the invisible omniscient narrator. Especially important is the fact that in none of these statements does Jesus refer to himself—which is a crucial observation, since the early Christians probably thought that Jesus was the Son of Man, that is, the one who would bring cosmic justice. Believers today also often believe that these words of Jesus refer to himself, but this is clearly an inaccurate interpretation of what he says. In all cases, Jesus is referring to someone other than himself when he speaks about the Son of Man.

The Greek expression used in the Gospels (and nowhere else) is ὁ υἱὸς τοῦ ἀνθρώπου, literally, "the Son of Man." Matthew in particular takes up this theme and, as a Jew, naturally knows where the origin of this term lies. Chapter 7 of the Book of Daniel in the Old Testament mentions a visionary presentation of the world, similar to the Revelation in the New Testament, from the sixth century BC (but the manuscript is from the second century BC), referring to a person who will bring salvation and who will take vengeance on the enemies of God:

> I saw in the night visions, and, behold, *one* like the Son of man came with the clouds of heaven, and came to the Ancient of days, and they brought him near before him.
> And there was given him dominion, and glory, and a kingdom, that all people, nations, and languages, should serve him: his dominion *is* an everlasting dominion, which shall not pass away, and his kingdom *that* which shall not be destroyed.
> (Dan. 7:13-14)

This text deals with a human being; the power granted to him is described as "kingly," that is, worldly, not divine. But what about the expression in the New Testament? For the moment, it is noticeable that the term is almost always used by Jesus himself (with one exception in Luke 24:7). Finally, and most importantly, Jesus always uses the expression in the third person. Indeed, Christian believers identify Jesus with this Son of Man, but this is not in the text, because he always talks about the Son of Man in the "he" form. If Jesus had wanted to identify himself as the Son of Man, he would of course have done so in the first person, that is, "I, the Son of Man." But just as with the prophet Daniel, the expression refers to someone who will come in the future and establish a new eternal order.

This is a secular projection intended to deliver humanity from the present miserable and sinful valley of tears. The expression does not refer to God, but to a secular power. Allusions to the divinity of the Son of Man, however, increase in the textual chronology. This means that at the beginning and certainly during Jesus' life there could be no question whether Jesus referred to himself as God. Changes in this regard come from later times. And, in fact, they become more frequent from the year 100 onward, with John's Gospel having paved the way for them. But the Christian texts also connect to a much older tradition.

Christianity and Egypt

Christian tradition combines the person of the Son of Man with the concept of the Son of God, and sees both in relation to Jesus. In doing so, Christians believe that the expression is typical of their own religion, but this is by no means the case. Already the Egyptian pharaohs called themselves "son of God." Here is the name of Thutmosis III in the temple of Hatshepsut I in Deir el-Bahri in the necropolis of Thebe:

Cartouche of Thutmosis III

To the left of the cartouche, containing the name of the pharaoh, one sees a goose and a circle. Together they stand for the expression *sa re*: son of the (sun) god. This sign is regularly found in Egyptian hieroglyphs and refers to a very special person: the Pharaoh, who was considered a direct descendant of the deity. So the expression "Son of God" is not of Christian origin, because Thutmosis III lived from 1479 to 1425 BC.

Incidentally, this is not the only similarity between the Egyptian religion and Christianity. One of the central gods in ancient Egypt was Osiris. But he was not just any god with animal characteristics, as were the gods Anubis (the jackal), Horus (the falcon), or Bastet (the cat). Osiris was a god in human form who came to earth to bring moral laws to mankind: how to live and how to worship the gods. However, he was killed by the forces of evil (his brother Seth), then rose from death and resumed his place in heaven, where he will act as the supreme judge of all souls at the Last Judgment. The similarities with Christianity are unmistakable. Did Christianity borrow some things from the ancient Egyptians? Undoubtedly. Even more explicit is the borrowing of one of the central texts in the New Testament: the Sermon on the Mount, which was written already in ancient Egypt more than a thousand years before the New Testament. In the *Egyptian Book of the Dead* (Chapter 125): comes this text:

> I have not harmed a poor man.
> I have not done what the gods abhor.
> I have not slandered a slave before his master; I have not made anyone sick.
> I have not made anyone weep.
> I have not killed anyone.
> I did not order a murderer, I did not make anyone suffer.
> I gave bread to those who were hungry, water to those who thirsted, clothing to those who were naked.
> I gave a ferry to the stranded.
> (Pritchard 1950, p. 34-35)

The similarities with the Sermon on the Mount are unmistakable. Or, in a similar vein: in Chapter 25 of the *Instruction of Amen-em-Opet* (seventh to sixth century BC):

Do not laugh at a blind man, nor mock a dwarf, nor hurt a
cripple.
Do not challenge a man who is in the hand of God, and do
not be malicious to him when he errs. For man is clay and
straw, and God is his Maker.
(Lange 1925, p. 121)

In other words, there is nothing original about the Sermon on
the Mount, even if believers think the text is typically Christian.
The same is true of Jesus' advice to love one's enemies:

But I say unto you which hear, Love your enemies, do good
to them which hate you,
Bless them that curse you, and pray for them which
despitefully use you.
And unto him that smiteth thee on the *one* cheek offer also
the other.
(Luke 6:27-29)

Believers also think of this text as representing the renewal that
Jesus brought. But similar texts in older Middle Eastern cultures
clearly show that the text has antecedents, as the following
excerpt clearly shows:

Do not injure your adversary;
reward your evildoer with good;
do justice to your enemy.
Your oppressor (...)
let him rejoice over you.
(Pritchard 1950, p. 426)

This is a text in Akkadian, written in cuneiform script, around
the year 700 BC, quoted in *Counsels of Wisdom* (Macmillan 1906).
The texts of Matthew and Luke (and partly also from *The Book*

of Q) are simply "recycled" from older models that circulated in the Near and Middle East, just like the stories about Osiris. So it is clear that stories are also productive far beyond their boundaries of language-specific cultures.

The cult of Mithras

Osiris was not the only deity to demonstrate striking resemblances to the core of the New Testament Gospels. Mithras, originally a Persian deity, was also a "son of God." His cult consisted mainly of meals, which hardly differed from the Christian Eucharist/Lord's Supper. During these meals, Mithras was honored as well as the god Sol Invictus (the invincible sun). The day on which this honor took place was December 25, explaining where our Christmas date comes from. It may seem to you that similarities between Christian and non-Christian rituals are sought here to make them look alike. But that is not at all the case. Around the Mediterranean and in the Middle East, antiquity is full of similar myths and rituals. Christianity absorbed and somewhat transformed them and later denied and partially destroyed them. In other words, the message of the Gospels is not unique at all.

Jesus in the Jewish Tradition

But is or was Jesus God? The very idea was incredible in his own time. It is worth noting that in the ancient world it was mainly secular rulers who were elevated to divinity, for example Alexander the Great, often referred to as the "son of Zeus," the supreme Greek god. After his death, Julius Caesar was elevated to *Divus Julius*, the supreme deity of the Romans, alongside *Jupiter Optimus Maximus*. This tradition was taken over by his heir Augustus (63 BC to AD 14, i.e., a contemporary of Jesus) and was continued throughout the Roman Empire. Roman emperors were all called *Dei filius*, "Son of God." In other words, "Son of God" is a reference to a very special person, based on a long and venerable tradition in the Mediterranean and Middle East, and is by no means an invention of Christianity.

In Jewish tradition, the term "Son of God" is used to refer to charismatic leaders, sometimes kings, of the people of Israel, so not as the deity, and without ascribing divine attributes to the person. Therefore, the Jewish "Son of God" is actually much weaker than in the case of the Roman emperors. Crucial here is the word "Christ," a Greek translation of the Jewish "Messiah." In the Jewish tradition, the Messiah is a secular figure who will liberate the people of Israel, just like the "Son of Man" previously mentioned in the Book of Daniel. "Christ" did not have the connotation of God associated with it. However differently the various currents of the Jewish faith portrayed this Messiah, they at least agreed that this Messiah had to be a figure of impressive greatness and power. But Jesus did not fit that expectation at all. On the contrary, he was executed like a criminal. How could such a man be the Messiah? So there is an important reason why Jesus could hardly be seen as the Messiah in the eyes of his first followers during his lifetime and a little later, namely because of his degrading death on the cross. Such a dishonoring demise was the absolute opposite of how Jewish traditions envisioned the Messiah.

Nevertheless, there is evidence in the New Testament that Jesus saw himself as the Messiah. This is most clearly expressed in the answer Jesus gave to Pilate when asked if he was the King of the Jews: "Thou sayest it" (Mark 15:2; Matt. 27:11; Luke 23:3). One could argue that this is an evasive answer. But it is even clearer in John, where Jesus says of himself, "Thou sayest that I am a king. To this end was I born, and for this cause came I into the world, that I should bear witness unto the truth" (John 18:37). But also in a limited circle, Jesus says of himself that he is the Messiah. Jesus asks his followers who they think he is. "And Simon Peter answered and said, Thou art the Christ, the Son of the living God. And Jesus answered and said unto him, Blessed art thou, Simon Barjona: for flesh and blood hath not revealed *It* unto thee, but my Father which is in heaven" (Matt. 16:16-17).

That much is clear. But what does the word "Messiah" mean in these and similar passages? In Mark, it is not entirely clear in what sense he uses the term. What one can see in the later Gospels, however, is that the term is elevated above the human and into a divine person. Where initially it was about a gifted but human leader, in the later Gospels the Messiah is increasingly clothed with more divine attributes, in keeping with what happened to Roman emperors from Julius Caesar onward. In Mark, the references to the Son of God are still limited (and often questionable because probably added by later copyists). But even here Jesus is accused of blasphemy at the end, which means that there must have been a reason, such as Jesus having pronounced himself equal to God.

So Christianity has also heavily borrowed from Judaism. However, it is an incredible advance that Christianity brought about. From the Jewish tradition of "an eye for an eye, a tooth for a tooth" to the Christian "love your enemies" it is a quantum leap, culturally and socially. This has nothing to do with the divinity of Jesus; instead, it concerns the renewal that Christianity brings to the Jewish religion. If we were to confront the historical Jesus with the Christian view that he was the Son of God, he would probably be profoundly shaken. The Jewish religion to which he belonged did not even allow such a thought. The renewal that Jesus instituted might have stayed with him, within a small Jewish sect, had it not been for two other events: the destruction of Jerusalem by the Roman army in the year 70, and the conversion of Paul. But more on that in Chapter 10.

What one can conclude from this is that Jesus becomes more and more divine over time; least in the oldest Gospel, to most in the youngest. In other words, Jesus is gradually elevated from original prophet (certainly gifted, but still thoroughly human) to divine status, a process that takes place over a period of about a hundred years after his death. We see this in the additions to Mark up until the Gospel of John, where Jesus is and always was God, from the very first sentence. Even after John, this development is not yet complete. But history shows that this vision of Jesus, which attributes more humanity to him, could triumph over the other competing visions.

Chapter 8

Oral Traditions

Here's a personal example of how oral traditions work. When I worked as a young man in Algeria in the 1970s, in a small provincial town at the foot of the Atlas Mountains, my wife and I constantly had guests at home, neighbors or ordinary people from town (rarely women; they had to remain invisible). We spent time together, eating and talking. Conversations consisted of many questions back and forth, and answers that provoked wonder and new questions. We were all by ourselves, two young, naive people in a faraway land we knew nothing about, whose language we barely spoke and where everything was different. (There was no Internet, phone, e-mail or Facebook— nothing, just letters that took three weeks to arrive.) Across religious lines, we tried to understand each other, by eating and talking. And between questions, tea, curiosity, and attempts to build bridges between our very different cultures, stories kept emerging. One such story, told by a young neighbor six weeks after our arrival, during an evening visit (we barely knew each other), I wrote down in my journal that evening:

> The lion, strong as he is, has heard of the power of man and sets out to fight him. He goes from animal to animal and asks each of them, "Are you a man?" So he asks the goat, the horse, the chicken, the dog. But he always gets the answer, "No, but man makes me work very hard." He finally gets to know man. He asks him if he is strong. "Yes," says the man, "but I left my strength at home. Wait for me here, but be careful not to run away!" As the man was chopping wood, he says, "Put your paw here in this gap, so you won't run away!" The lion does so, the man pulls the axe out of the stump, and the lion

is trapped. The man kills him with his axe.

This story is somehow recognizable to Westerners. It contains elements of the Greek fables and their imitations. The point here is not how these similarities came about, but that the story united us with our Algerian neighbor. In terms of background, upbringing, religion, social norms and values, we were light years apart—yet the story established a connection. Why did our young neighbor tell us this story? He could only speak French, read and write a little and had no prerogative, except that he was our neighbor and we were his. And it was not a written story. Only now, several decades later, it ends up in the book you are reading. But the original story took place orally, in conversation.

None of the people involved took the story literally. Of course, the lion in the story is not a lion, but someone who overestimates himself, or someone who relies solely on his physical strength, or something like that. The intention of the story was to make our conversation entertaining, but at the same time to provide a moral lesson. We find it funny that the lion acts so foolishly, underestimating the value of modesty and rationality. Entertaining and instructive; that's how we might understand the function of stories like these. Our neighbor could have simply commented that it's better to rely on one's wits than on one's physical strength. The message would have been the same, but without the entertainment.

The combination of instruction with entertainment is old. It goes back at least to the dictum of the Roman poet Horace (who died a few years before Jesus was born), who wrote, "*Omne tulit punctum qui miscuit utile dulci*" (*Ad Pisones* 343), which means: he who knows how to combine the useful (*utile*) with the pleasant (*dulci*) will get the highest marks. Horace, like Jesus, lived in this Mediterranean culture. One important difference between them is that Horace could read and write. In fact, he was already a celebrated poet in the Roman Empire at the time. Jesus, on the other hand, was a poor, illiterate Jewish preacher in a remote corner of the same empire. Both built on existing traditions of their culture. My Algerian neighbor was barely literate, but he was living 2,000 years later in the same tradition. When one reads the Gospels, it helps to understand them in this context of storytelling.

Some of these traditions found expression in written lore. The fact that animal stories are widespread is primarily the result of oral tradition. Fortunately, people started to record parts of these oral traditions in writing; otherwise, they might have been lost forever. This happened for the animal stories already in the fables of Aesop, in the sixth century BC. In the time of Jesus, it also happened in the *Pañcatantra* in Sanskrit (the ancient Indian language from 1500 BC), which led to numerous adaptations in more than fifty languages, among them the wondrous Arabic collection *Kalilah and Dimnah* by Ibn-al-Muqaffa'.

Why did my neighbor tell this particular story? He had countless stories to choose from. We were foreigners; welcome, but distrusted as Westerners, because of colonialism. A story can be a bridge, but it can also be a test. And in any case, it was just an innocent conversation that did not lead to any action. But history (and culture) stood between us.

This is what this chapter is about, because such stories appear again and again in the Gospels, and they are usually put into a context. For example: the people are hungry, and evening approaches. A large crowd has gathered around Jesus, and the disciples suggest sending the people away. But Jesus says they must eat. However, there seem to be only five loaves and two fishes. Jesus blesses them, and suddenly there is enough food for everyone. "And they did all eat, and were filled: and they took up of the fragments that remained twelve baskets full" (Matt. 14:20). This "catering" story according to Matthew was probably based on a somewhat exaggerated estimate: "And they that had eaten were about five thousand men, beside women and children" (Matt. 14:21). One might be inclined to think that because there were no newspapers, television or telephones at that time, such stories may have been slow in spreading. But on the contrary, oral stories can spread incredibly fast. Opie and Opie (1959) cite several instances in the 1950s in which a new nursery rhyme or song in exclusively oral form spread throughout all of the British Isles in less than a month.

There is also experimental evidence for this. Two psychologists, Kent Harber and Dov Cohen (2005), studied how quickly stories about an emotionally charged event could spread. They took 33 of their psychology students to a morgue, where several bodies were laid out for medical study. A few days later, the students were asked who they had told about their experience. The results were astonishing: 97% of the participants had told one or more others. These persons were then tracked down and asked the same question: How many other people had they told this story to? Eighty-two percent of them had, and 48% of those people had told the story again to others. Net result of the experiment? Within three days, 881 people had heard a story from these 33 students.

Oral versus written

So what is the relationship between the oral tradition and the written Gospels? In the previous chapters, I have focused on the historical person, Jesus, as far as written sources allow. From this emerged the image of an enthusiastic preacher traveling through Palestine proclaiming the imminent coming of a new world order. The vision he spread was rooted in Jewish worship and traditions, but added new (and sometimes divergent) elements, such as the importance of spiritual renunciation. A group of followers joined him and shared his commitment. None of this was exceptional, and Jesus was probably not the only itinerant preacher with an apocalyptic message. Although there is still much which is not known, one can reconstruct this part of Jesus' life with a high degree of reliability. (Important publications directly related to the oral antecedents of the New Testament include Rodriguez (2013) and Ehrman (2016).)

But then came an unexpected turn of events, described in detail in the previous chapter. Jesus' message cast a political shadow on the Roman occupation, and perhaps on the sterile experience of Jewish religion. The reaction was not long in coming. As we have seen, death on the cross was the most horrible and also the most degrading form of public execution. For Jesus' followers, it must have been a shattering experience.

At that time, the followers did not yet see God in Jesus. As explained in the previous chapter, the Gospels show that the references to Jesus as God in the written texts increase with time. This gradual multiplication of Jesus' divine attributes now allows one a hypothetical look back in time. For there is no reason to assume that this shift in the perception of Jesus is found only in the written texts. Rather, it is plausible that such a development occurred even before that, during the phase of the oral histories. But if this assumption is justified (and it already seems very plausible), then a reliable reconstruction of the past leads to a point where Jesus was not yet God in the oral tradition.

Here an analogy is appropriate. Astronomers agree that the universe continues expanding, after it had started doing so in a remote astronomical past. Reasoning backward, therefore, the universe must have been infinitely small in the beginning. Similarly, one could also imagine a starting point in the evolution of Jesus' divinity, and should conclude that this inevitably leads to a starting point where that divinity was zero. There must have been a point in the oral tradition where there was no mention of a divine Jesus at all. So the very earliest oral stories about Jesus will not have considered him a god. The image of the divine Jesus, as it prevails in today's Christian faith, is the result of a longer development. And at the beginning of this development is the historical figure of Jesus of Nazareth, as a man, not as God.

Oral texts

One may now assume that oral stories were in circulation during the period of forty years between Jesus' death and the first Gospel. It would be strange indeed if this had not been the case. So the beginning point must be in the time before there were written texts; that is, at the time of oral texts.

Oral texts? Is there any such thing? Certainly. It's just that they are unfamiliar, because we write everything down nowadays. But there are rudiments of oral culture in our society, although they are usually quite short. Some texts (types) are very short. For instance, when people get married, both parties have to pronounce a very small text: "I do." Without this tiny little text (not hard to remember) there is no marriage. Our use of language also shows how important the oral form of communication is, in expressions like "giving one's word," "keeping one's word," and "breaking one's word." And then there are fragments of text that people drop into conversations, for example from poems, such as "to be or not to be" or "no man is an island," "what doesn't kill us makes us strong." There is also the reciting of poems, but this is coming under increasing pressure today. Professionals such as actors, however, still have to memorize large amounts of text in order to be able to recite it, which also applies to singers. That's not so bad for pop songs, but if you want to sing Schubert's *Winterreise* (Winter Journey) by heart, it's a major task.

There is one typical form of oral text that has survived in all Western cultures, and that is the joke. Although there are collections of jokes in book form, a joke only comes into its own when it is told, preferably in a group. The joke is a thoroughly oral text which is tied to the spoken word. As we all know from experience, there are good joke-tellers, but there are also those who just can't manage to tell a joke. In oral cultures like those of 2,000 years ago, it must have been the same, in that there were good and pathetic storytellers. In the transition to written texts, the versions of the really good storytellers remained, while those of the less good storytellers were forgotten, or polished up by others until they became equally good.

Oral texts also play a significant role if one belongs to a religious faith. Then one has prayers to recite from memory, often together, in group. In this way, believers in Christianity know the Lord's Prayer by heart. It is still written down, but never really "read." Instead, it is prayed, silently, or recited aloud. In a religious context, such oral texts are still common. For example, the Qur'an exists in written form, but is recited mainly—if not exclusively—by devout Muslims. As a point of interest, the Arabic word "Qur'an" simply means "recite," or "to recite."

At the time of Jesus there were few people who could read and write, at most about three percent. So texts necessarily had to circulate orally. Therefore, after his death, there were oral stories about his life and teachings. These stories gradually gave rise to the written Gospels.

From oral to written

Such a transition from oral to written tradition is well documented for several literatures. In the West, this was most profoundly the case with respect to Homer's epic stories about the Trojan War and its aftermath. They were written down in the eighth century BC, having most likely been based on oral versions from the twelfth century BC. They were then performed in front of an audience, a bit like an open-air pop concert, with a professional singer called a *rhapsode*, who recited the whole poem (of more than 15,000 verse lines) by heart, accompanied by a type of harp, either played by the singer or by another musician. In this way, the Greek epics were performed in front of an audience by professional singers who lived off the income from their performances. This was not the case with the Gospels. The authors were skilled and educated writers, but they did not earn their living by writing down oral stories they had heard.

The Greek singers needed years of training to memorize the long texts, at which they were extremely adept. This does not mean, however, that people in oral cultures are fundamentally better at remembering things or have more reliable memories. Because people in oral cultures rely more on their memory, they train it more, but certainly not to the extent that what they recite in a performance is error-free or completely reliable.

At a certain point in classical antiquity, the oral traditions were written down. The form in which they have come down to us is in a fixed meter. "Meter" is the regular alternation of syllables of a certain structure. In Germanic languages such as English, this structure is a sequence of stressed versus unstressed syllables, as in *iambs*, which may be familiar from Shakespeare and many other English poets. Listen, for instance, to a famous example:

To **be** or **not** to **be**

The syllables in bold are stressed; the others are unstressed.

In languages like Latin or Greek, this structure is a sequence of long versus short syllables. Now one would think that sustaining this metrical structure for 15,000 verses would cause additional difficulty in remembering. But in fact the opposite is the case. In a study, I was able to prove that exactly this metrical pattern is a great help for memory (see Van Peer 1990). Furthermore, using fixed expressions, so-called *epithets*, also aids memorization. For example, in the heroic poems attributed to Homer, morning is usually referred to as "rose-fingered dawn," and the main heroes are always given an epithet; for example, the hero Achilles is "the swift-footed" or "the radiant," and Odysseus is "many-sensed." Such references are also found in the Gospels when Jesus is called "Son of Man" or "Son of God."

The man who profoundly changed the way oral culture is understood was Milman Parry, a young American researcher who defended his dissertation at the Sorbonne in 1928. In it, he showed how the Homeric heroic poems in their original oral form were based on formulas, fixed phrases such as the epithets just discussed, and metrical structure. As a young professor at Harvard University, he made audio recordings (then a revolutionary technology) of Serbo-Croatian singers of traditional poetry in the Balkans between 1933 and 1935. The study also showed how singers memorized their performance while adapting it to local conditions. This made Parry the founder of research in oral literature, a flourishing discipline, as publications by Finnegan (1992), Havelock (1988), Ong (1982), Rubin (1998), and others convincingly demonstrate. Parry died young; he was only 33 when he was killed in an accident. His assistant, Albert Lord (1912-1991), continued his work in *The Singer of Tales* (1960).

Poetic texts

However, the New Testament cannot really be called an epic in this respect. Nor can it be called poetic. If there are verses in it, they are almost always quotations from the Old Testament, which is in fact characterized by several books cast in poetic form, such as the Book of Job, the Psalms, Proverbs, and the Song of Songs. Compared to the Old Testament, the New Testament is factual, prosaic, and dry, without many poetic phrases. And there lies the power of the book, in that it clearly conveys a message (in Greek, an *eu-angellion*), a good message. There are some texts in Paul's letters that can be called poetic, for example:

> If I spoke with tongues of men and with tongues of angels,
> and had not love, I should be a sounding brass or a tinkling
> bell. ...
> Though I speak with the tongues of men and of angels,
> and have not charity, I am become as sounding brass, or a
> tinkling cymbal. And though I have the gift of prophecy and
> understand all mysteries, and all knowledge; and though I
> have all faith, so that I could remove mountains, and have
> not charity, I am nothing.
> (1 Cor. 13:1-2)

Such partial repetition is called *parallelism* in literary studies. Usually it has a distinctly lyrical character and is also meant in this quote from Paul as a hymn of praise. Also in Luke (1:46 ff.), one finds such poetic structures in the so-called *Magnificat*: "My soul doth magnify the Lord, and my spirit hath rejoiced in God my Savior, for he hath regarded the low estate of his handmaiden" (Luke 1:46-48). The beginning of John's Gospel is read and experienced by many as a sublime form of poetry: "In the beginning was the Word, and the Word was with God, and God was the Word" (John 1:1). And, of course, the Sermon on the Mount can also be described as poetic because of its parallelisms. In all these cases, one may assume that this structure was also an aid to memorizing, in the time when stories about Jesus were passed down orally. One would expect such poetic structures to appear in the (reconstructed) *Book of Q*, which was recited and passed down orally, but this is not the case; the poetic content is quite low there as well. And the same is true of the apocryphal Gospel of Thomas, which is probably very close to the *Book of Q*. It is clear that the authors of the Gospels were not interested in creating a poetic message.

Images

If we want to speak of poetic elements in the New Testament, they are certainly not in the form. But poetry is characterized not only by its form, but also by its images. For example, what are we to make of the next passage:

> And I turned to see after the voice that spake with me. And being turned, I saw seven golden candlesticks, and in the midst of the seven candlesticks one like unto the son of man, clothed with a garment down to the foot, and girt about the breast with a golden girdle. His head and his hair were white as snow, and his eyes were as a flame of fire, and his feet like unto fine brass, as if they burned in a furnace, and his voice as the sound of many waters; and he in his right hand seven stars, and out of his mouth went a sharp two-edged sword; and his countenance was as the sun shineth in his strength. And when I saw him, I fell at his feet like dead. And he laid his right hand upon me saying unto me, "Fear not. I am the first and the last."
> (Rev. 1:12-17)

Is this poetic? It certainly is! Do you understand it? Probably not. But that is precisely a sign of poetry, that it is not in everyday, matter-of-fact language. This passage is a clear example of dark and visionary poetry. It is the beginning of the Revelation of John. This whole book in the New Testament is a vision: it describes what will happen when the prediction of the apocalypse, of the new kingdom, comes true—at the end of time. It projects an image of the end of time before our eyes, through the mind of a clairvoyant who knows what will happen. Such visionary moments also occur in the individual Gospels, but there they are very moderate and often isolated. Think of images like that of the leaven (Matt. 13:33) or the comparisons of the kingdom of God to a hidden treasure (Matt. 13:44) or a dragnet (Matt. 13:47).

The literary figures of speech that appear most frequently, mainly in the Gospels themselves, are those of comparison, metaphor, and allegory. All three are rooted in oral traditions. In everyday life, when we say that a politician is a "fox," we don't mean that he has red fur, a tail, and a pointed snout, or that he steals chickens at night. The image is familiar to everyone and needs no explanation. Such ways of speaking and writing are called *metaphor* in literary studies. A metaphor is basically a word or expression referring to one thing (a fox) but meaning another (slyness). In all these cases, everyone knows that the words are not meant literally, but must be understood figuratively. This is also the case in the Gospels. When Jesus says of himself several times, "I am the light of the world," of course he does not mean that he is literally the sun. Such images are so deeply embedded in our everyday oral culture that they need no explanation.

It gets a little more difficult when using images that are no longer part of everyday life. The "good shepherd" image is already somewhat removed from normal life, although it's not hard to imagine a shepherd caring for his animals. But things can get tricky, as in:

> It the kingdom of God is like a grain of mustard seed; when it is sown in the earth, is less than all the seeds that be in the earth; but when it is sown, it growth, and becometh greater than all herbs, and shooteth out great branches; so that the fowls of the air may lodge under the shadow of it.
> (Mark 4:31-32)

Admittedly, I have never seen a tree grow from a mustard seed in my life. But even without that experience, I understand what it's all about: I can picture it. And I understand the underlying message, which is that many great and important things in life start from small and humble beginnings, but later grow into something great. When the comparison becomes elaborate, as is the case here, we no longer call it a metaphor, but an *allegory*. For instance, medieval plays and stories about Everyman were meant to morally elevate the audience. It uses characters like Good Deeds or Death in an elaborate construction of virtues and vices. To give a modern example, George Orwell's *Animal Farm* can be interpreted as a twentieth century allegory of communism, with the various animals standing for particular figures in Russian Bolshevism. In the Gospels one encounters such extended metaphors, and they are called *parables*. Famous examples are the parable of the Prodigal Son or that of the Good Shepherd.

Sometimes, however, we cannot understand these images at all because they come from a culture to which we have no connection. When reading in Matthew (19:24): "And again I say unto you. It is easier for a camel to go through the eye of a needle than for a rich man to enter into the kingdom of God," one doesn't realize that the "eye of a needle" referred to a narrow gate in the city wall. The New Testament bristles with such similarities, which have their origin and use in everyday life and oral culture in the Palestine of 2,000 years ago. The deeper meaning has nothing to do with a mustard seed, but with the growth of the Christian faith. To understand how such forms of figurative language work in oral culture, it is necessary to look at human memory.

Remember

In any discussion about memory, it is vital to refer to Frederic Bartlett's seminal 1932 study. He had his students at Cambridge University read a story, "The War of the Ghosts," borrowed from the Kwakiutl (now called the Kwakwaka'wakw), a Native North American tribe of British Columbia, in the northwestern United States and Canada. After reading, students were asked to retell the story as accurately as possible, and then do so again at several intervals after that. The results showed how elements that did not fit well with the readers' world were omitted or replaced with elements with which the subjects were more familiar. Here is the story (left) with a retelling (right) in the original version:

So the canoes went back to Egulac. And the young man went ashore to his house, and made a fire. And he told everybody and said: "Behold I accompanied the ghosts, and we went to fight. Many of our fellows were killed, and many of those who attacked us were killed. They said I was hit, and I did not feel sick." He told it all, and then he became quiet. When the sun rose he fell down. Something black came out of his mouth. His face became contorted. The people jumped up and cried.
He was dead.

In the evening he returned to his hut, and told his friends that he had been in a battle. A great many had been slain, and he had been wounded by an arrow; he had not felt any pain, he said. They told him that he must have been fighting in a battle of ghosts. Then he remembered that it had been Queer and he became very excited. In the morning, however, he became ill, and his friends gathered round; he fell down and his face became very pale. Then he writhed and shrieked And his friends were filled with terror. At last he became calm. Something Hard and black came out of his mouth, and he lay contorted and dead.

Of course, the retelling does not seamlessly follow the original text. Human memory is not perfect, not even the memories of outstanding Cambridge students. What is important here are the distortions. For example, in the original version the man becomes "quiet" the next morning, but in the retelling he becomes "ill" and "very pale," neither of which occur in the original. And about the fight it is said that it was "queer," which was not mentioned in the original. No cause of death is mentioned in the original story, which may have been considered strange in a Western context, so terms like "sick" and "pale" were added as possible explanations. The original story said, "I accompanied the ghosts," which was remembered as "fighting in a battle of ghosts."

What Bartlett noted in this study, then, was not just the limits of remembering, but the constructive aspect of memory: we do not simply remember the facts; we create "facts" to fit our worldview and expectations. Is it conceivable that such distortions occurred in the original and later stories about Jesus? Why wouldn't they? Why should it have been any different? Our brains have not suddenly changed in the last 2,000 years. If one accepts this insight, it becomes clear that very little is known about the true nature of the events in the New Testament.

Which text is true? Did Jesus drink from the vinegar that the Roman soldier handed him at the cross, as John writes (John 19:29-30), or did he not drink from it, as Luke claims (27:48)? Or was it not vinegar at all, but wine mixed with myrrh, as one can read in Mark (15:23)? One could argue, of course, that all these are mere trifles, and in a sense they are, because they scarcely alter the core of the story. Whether Jesus was crucified at the ninth hour (Mark 15:25) or after the sixth hour (John 19:14) is hardly relevant to the "good news" of the New Testament. But in other aspects, the differences between the Gospels play a considerably greater role. Take, for example, the fact that the virgin birth is mentioned only by Matthew and Luke. This is strange, to say the least. Suppose a virgin actually becomes pregnant and gives birth, surely everyone in a wide circle would talk about it, and certainly in the case of someone who was considered so important. But there is not a word about it in Mark and John. And it's noteworthy that even in the very earliest texts, those of Paul, we find nothing about it. In fact, Paul writes that Jesus was born "of a woman" (Gal. 4:4), not a virgin. Another piquant detail: the English translation is "of the seed of David" (Rom. 1:3). But what does the original say? Σπέρματος (*spermatos*)! The Greek word is clear, literally, "the seed" of David. So no divine intervention. A natural fertilization. On top of it, Paul adds κατά σάρκα (*kata sarka*), literally, "according to the flesh."

Church authorities have maintained for two millennia that Jesus was not conceived "in the flesh" but by the divine spirit, while the oldest New Testament source, Paul, clearly says the opposite.

Unbelievable

So what is undeniable is that these details point to the unreliability of the texts. Why should one of them be believed and not the other? Why, in other words, believe Matthew and Luke, but not Paul? The texts themselves offer no clear motivation to do either. But here the study of oral traditions helps us: probably differences in the oral narratives were reflected in the written version. The oral stories that were told about Jesus at the time most likely corresponded to the compositional techniques that Parry (1988) and Lord (1960) have uncovered. They show that in oral cultures the events of a story are not literally repeated. Parry found that Avdo, a singer he knew, recited a story for him in which Parry took closely worded notes. The story was 12,323 verses long. A few years later, when Parry asked Avdo to recite the story again, it was only 8,488 verses long. Another time, he asked Avdo to recite a song by another singer. Avdo stated that he had sung the same song as his colleague. But Avdo's version was three times as long. Parry's findings were later expanded upon by Jack Goody (1977) in his book *The Domestication of the Savage Mind*, making similar observations among the Bagre, a tribe from Ghana in West Africa. Although the singers themselves as well as local listeners insisted that there was only one correct version of the myth, Goody also found significant differences in the length of their performances, which were sometimes up to five times as long. Also, some elements of the myth considered essential in a 1951 performance were omitted from a 1970 recitation. The Belgian historian and anthropologist Jan Vansina (1985) came to exactly the same conclusion in his research in Rwanda and Burundi.

In short, the transmission of stories in oral cultures is not stable, but subject to all sorts of influences. There is no reason to assume that this would have been different in the stories about Jesus. There must have been such constant changes, because oral culture is subject to the nature of human memory. It begins with eyewitnesses who speak about what they saw and experienced. Such witnesses are, of course, the surest source of information about who Jesus was and what he did. At least that's what common sense tells us. Unfortunately, common sense is often wrong.

The fallibility of eyewitness accounts

A very convincing proof of this was provided in 1993 by the Dutch psychologist Hans Crombag (1996). It concerned the crash of a Boeing in the Bijlmermeer near Amsterdam on October 4, 1992, in which the occupants and many apartment dwellers perished. Understandably, this accident dominated all conversations in the days that followed. Ten months later, Crombag asked if people had seen the film of the plane crash. In a first round, the question was asked of 193 people who worked at universities (professors, staff, students). Of these, 55% said they had seen the film. In a second round, the same question was asked of 93 law students. Of these, 66% said they had seen the film at that time. These responses appear to bear testimony to what respondents had seen. Except that there was no film at all; not a single shot! About 60% of the respondents, all intelligent people at universities, were firmly convinced that they had seen a film that did not exist. Things got even stranger when they were asked how the plane crashed. All respondents gave descriptions of the accident: some said the plane had crashed horizontally, others that it crashed vertically, some that it was on fire, others that the fire started after the crash.

History and reality

Do you see the connection to the stories in the Gospels? And how easy it is for people to make up stories that have little or no basis in the real world? The examples given above allow a realistic explanation of the differences (and also contradictions) between the various Gospels. Indeed, human memory was also very creative in the recording of the Gospels. This does not mean that memories are completely separate from what happened. But a memory is not a photographic representation of what we perceive.

Thorough research shows that witnesses are often not very reliable. Please check this out for yourself in the following Internet video: www.youtube.com/watch?v=vJG698U2Mvo

The researchers, Christopher Chabris and Daniel Simons (2010), the creators of this experiment, convincingly show how people often fail to notice things, even though they are particularly noticeable. (You can read more about their research on their website, www.viscog.com.) If this is true for very noticeable incidents where people have been forewarned to pay attention and watch carefully and intently, it is even more true for small details in situations where people were not forewarned and where the observation situation is less than ideal. Jesus spoke in the open, without a microphone.

In addition to the constructive, creative nature of memory, *selective perception* also plays a crucial role. We simply do not register everything that takes place in our surroundings, because our perceptual and cognitive abilities are limited. There is no doubt about this among professional psychologists. Even if eyewitness accounts permeated the New Testament texts, these testimonies were not necessarily accurate. But there is more.

In an oral culture, obviously stories must be passed on orally. Now, in this process of retelling, significant biases arise, as can be seen from Bartlett's research. Today, no one doubts the vulnerability of orally transmitted messages. The distortion that occurs is caused by limitations of the human brain, of memory, but also by specific interests and purposes of the teller and listener, as the next section will show.

Collective memories

Bartlett's study (and the research beyond his work) is concerned with the distorted memory of individuals. But oral stories about Jesus soon became collective. This insight is just as fundamental to the impact of memory. In *La mémoire collective* (1950) by French sociologist Maurice Halbwachs, for the first time attention was drawn to the fact that there is not only individual memory, but also group memory. This memory is formed by the specific group to which one belongs. Halbwachs uses the French term *cadre* for this, which can be translated as "framework." This framework forms and nourishes the collective memory. The group of Christians to which one belonged determined the memory of Jesus' life, and these memories took on a life of their own, perhaps even contradicting the details of the historical life of Jesus.

A striking example of collective memory is provided by the experience of tourists visiting Masada in Israel, the fortified castle on a difficult-to-access mountain where, according to legend, the last Zealots took their lives when it became clear that their defenses against the Roman army could no longer hold out. Masada plays an important role in the Jewish identity (their *cadre*) as a symbol of their unity and steadfastness. The explosive aspect of this story, however, is that Masada is not mentioned anywhere in the Bible, not in the Old Testament and not in the New Testament, nor in any of the sacred texts (Ehrman 2016, p. 236). It is, in Halbwachs' sense, a collectively construed "memory." This is not to say that it is not important. On the contrary, it is precisely around this type of shared "memory" that a group, a party, a people or a nation, crystallizes. Such collections of memories usually contain a historical core, but other elements, often ideological, develop around it. And with Masada, historical material exists, namely the writings of Flavius Josephus, by now a familiar name. He tells how Eleazar, the leader of the insurgents, tried to persuade the occupants of the mountain to commit collective suicide to escape humiliation and slavery at the hands of the Romans. But many lost heart, so Eleazar made a second attempt to persuade his followers using all the rhetorical means possible. According to Cohen (2014, p. 36):

> After this second speech, wrote Flavius Josephus, all enthusiastically agreed to Eleazar's plan: In the end, not a man failed to carry out his terrible resolve, but one and all disposed of their entire families, victims of cruel necessity, who with their own hands murdered their wives and children and felt it to be the lightest of evils.

The memory of Masada had almost disappeared from Jewish memory until it was updated with the birth of Zionism. Masada now became a symbol of the determination to defend together against the threat of external forces. The rise of this collective memory has been extensively and thoroughly researched by Yael Zerubavel (1995, but see also Cohen 2014, pp. 33-36). This research demonstrates how this kind of collective memory becomes especially important in times of uncertainty or crisis.

Jesus' death fits seamlessly into this scenario. The stories about his life and deeds were certainly determined by a situation of great uncertainty. They emerged from disillusionment and grief over the death of the beloved teacher, but at the same time the stories provided explanations and, above all, a way out of the fear and uncertainty.

One would expect that participants would correct each other in collective memory. Suppose we were at a party last weekend and it so happened that one of the couples had an argument with each other in public. How is this event processed in the group afterwards? Do all who were present tell the same story? They all witnessed the same event. The party guests will tell different, very different, even contradictory stories, fed by their identification with one of the arguing parties. Some found the woman reasonable, others the man. Does one correct the others' differences? Not really. Mostly, they remain side by side, a testimony to the various interpretations by the witnesses. Our emotional and social involvement with people and actions deeply colors how we perceive and remember things. This is how one must imagine the creation of stories about Jesus: several versions exist side by side. And such oral stories, which are strongly emotionally charged, spread quickly. How the various versions of the story evolve depends on what listeners think and feel is important—and these differences can be profound.

Literary success

In addition, the literary quality also plays a significant role in the story's survival. A good storyteller will be more successful than someone less skilled. This is most evident when one compares the versions of a story that appears in both Mark and Matthew. Look first at this passage in Mark 5:21-32:

And when Jesus was passed over again by ship unto the other side, much people gathered unto him: and he was nigh unto the sea. And, behold, there cometh one of the rulers of the synagogue, Jairus by name; and when he saw him, he fell at his feet, And besought him greatly, saying, My little daughter lieth at the point of death: *I pray thee*, come and lay thy hands on her, that she may be healed; and she shall live. And *Jesus* went with him; and much people followed him, and thronged him.

And a certain woman, which had an issue of blood twelve years, And had suffered many things of many physicians, and had spent all that she had, and was nothing bettered, but rather grew worse, When she had heard of Jesus, came in the press behind, and touched his garment. For she said, If I may touch but his clothes, I shall be whole. And straightway the fountain of her blood was dried up; and she felt in *her* body that she was healed of that plague. And Jesus, immediately knowing in himself that virtue had gone out of him, turned him about in the press, and said, Who touched my clothes? And his disciples said unto him, Thou seest the multitude thronging thee, and sayest thou, Who touched me? And he looked round about to see her that had done this thing. But the woman fearing and trembling, knowing what was done in her, came and fell down before him, and told him all the truth. And he said unto her, Daughter, thy faith hath made thee whole; go in peace, and be whole of thy plague.

While he yet spake, there came from the ruler of the synagogue's *house certain* which said, Thy daughter is dead: why troublest thou the Master any further? As soon as Jesus heard the word that was spoken, he saith unto the ruler of the synagogue, Be not afraid, only believe. And he suffered no man to follow him, save Peter, and James, and John the brother of James. And he cometh to the house of the ruler of the synagogue, and seeth the tumult, and them that wept and wailed greatly. And when he was come in, he saith unto them, Why make ye this ado, and weep? the damsel is not dead, but sleepeth. And they laughed him to scorn. But when he had put them all out, he taketh the father and the mother of the damsel, and them that were with him, and entereth in where the damsel was lying. And he took the damsel by the hand, and said unto her, Talitha cumi; which is, being interpreted, Damsel, I say unto thee, arise. And straightway the damsel arose, and walked; for she was *of the age* of twelve years. And they were astonished with a great astonishment. And he charged them straitly that no man should know it; and commanded that something should be given her to eat.

Now compare this excerpt with the same content in Matthew 9:1-26:

And he entered into a ship, and passed over, and came into his own city.

And, behold, they brought to him a man sick of the palsy, lying on a bed: and Jesus seeing their faith said unto the sick of the palsy; Son, be of good cheer; thy sins be forgiven thee. And, behold, certain of the scribes said within themselves, This *man* blasphemeth. And Jesus knowing their thoughts said, Wherefore think ye evil in your hearts? For whether is easier, to say, *Thy* sins be forgiven thee; or to say, Arise, and walk? But that ye may know that the Son of man hath power on earth to forgive sins, (then saith he to the sick of the palsy,) Arise, take up thy bed, and go unto thine house. And he arose, and departed to his house. But when the multitudes saw *it*, they marveled, and glorified God, which had given such power unto men.

And as Jesus passed forth from thence, he saw a man, named Matthew, sitting at the receipt of custom: and he saith unto him, Follow me. And he arose, and followed him.

And it came to pass, as Jesus sat at meat in the house, behold, many publicans and sinners came and sat down with him and his disciples. And when the Pharisees saw *it*, they said unto his disciples, Why eateth your Master with publicans and sinners? But when Jesus heard *that*, he said unto them, They that be whole need not a physician, but they that are sick. But go ye and learn what *that* meaneth, I will have mercy, and not sacrifice: for I am not come to call the righteous, but sinners to repentance.

Then came to him the disciples of John, saying, Why do we and the Pharisees fast oft, but thy disciples fast not? And Jesus said unto them, Can the children of the bridechamber mourn, as long as the bridegroom is with them? but the days will come, when the bridegroom shall be taken from them, and then shall they fast.

No man putteth a piece of new cloth unto an old garment, for that which is put in to fill it up taketh from the garment, and the rent is made worse. Neither do men put new wine into old bottles: else the bottles break, and the wine runneth out, and the bottles.

While he spake these things unto them, behold, there came a certain ruler, and worshipped him, saying, My daughter is even now dead: but come and lay thy hand upon her, and she shall live. And Jesus arose, and followed him, and *so did* his disciples.

And, behold, a woman, which was diseased with an issue of blood twelve years, came behind *him*, and touched the hem of his garment: For she said within herself, If I may but touch his garment, I shall be whole. But Jesus turned him about, and when he saw her, he said, Daughter, be of good comfort; thy faith hath made thee whole. And the woman was made whole from that hour.

And when Jesus came into the ruler's house, and saw the minstrels and the people making a noise, He said unto them, Give place: for the maid is not dead, but sleepeth. And they laughed him to scorn. But when the people were put forth, he went in, and took her by the hand, and the maid arose. And the fame hereof went abroad into all that land.

I am not sure which version you as a reader would prefer. But the chances are pretty high that you will go for Mark's version: it's much more dramatic and penetrating, both from a theological and a psychological perspective. Not only is it almost three times as long (although Matthew's entire Gospel is about twice as long as Mark's), but it is also much more penetrating. The core of the story is the same in both Gospels, which may indicate that both authors follow the same tradition (oral or written). But the suffering of the characters in Mark is rendered in a much more "biting" way. First of all, the event is spatially located in Mark, while it hangs in the air in Matthew. Mark also opens a much more dramatic event, by allowing the young daughter to live, while the message that later comes from the house tells us that she has since died. Moreover, the woman's discomfort and misery with the doctors is described in a much more human way, and her physical sensation of healing, as well as her fear of confessing that she had touched Jesus' clothes, involves the reader in her illness and healing. At the same time, the psychology of Jesus himself is also highlighted: his sensitivity contrasts sharply with the somewhat blunt and insensitive reaction of his disciples, though he does involve the circle of three intimates. The appeal of the girl who gets up and starts walking around, and Jesus' advice to feed her, underline his humanity. Moreover, the fact that Jesus says this in his native language is an indication of the authenticity of the story. Finally, there is the typical theme of secrecy in Mark.

A basic question arises: why did Jesus not write his story down himself? He could have done so before the Passion. It would have been much more convincing for future generations if he had written down his own view of the facts himself. Then there would be no disagreements and no ambiguities. Why didn't he do that? The answer is as simple as it is important: Jesus could not write, just like 97% (or more) of his countrymen. So, to put it accurately, Jesus was illiterate. But how can that be, the believing Bible reader will wonder. Jesus did write, didn't he? John's Gospel relates it clearly:

And the scribes and Pharisees brought unto him a woman taken in adultery; and when they had set her in the midst, They say unto him, Master, this woman was taken in adultery, in the very act. Now Moses in the law commanded us, that such should be stoned: but what sayest thou? This they said, tempting him, that they might have to accuse him. But Jesus stooped down, and with *his* finger wrote on the ground, *as though he heard them not*.
(John 8:3-6)

First, note that this statement appears in only one Gospel, that of John, the least historically reliable Gospel. And there is a devastating argument against the authenticity of the story: it does not appear in the most reliable manuscripts of John's Gospel. Whoever inserted it in later copies must have been a brilliant writer. But historically, the story is not about the historical Jesus.

Unfortunately, John does not tell the reader what Jesus wrote in the sand. Maybe he did not consider this important. Indeed, if it had been important, according to our copyist, then of course he would have told it. Ultimately, the whole scene exudes an air of indifference of Jesus to the trick question he has been asked. So maybe he just drew some figures in the sand. What can one deduce from this? Nothing really, apart from the general observation that it is extremely unlikely that the son of a poor laborer in a remote province in the north of the country could read and write. He certainly could not have written his autobiography either. So readers must content themselves with the ironic *Gospel According to Jesus Christ* by José Saramago (1999).

Traces in the works of the Church Fathers

There is a suspicion that traces from oral sources, before the actual Gospels were written, may be found in the works of the early Church Fathers. The term "Church Fathers" (also "apostolic fathers") refers to a group of early Christian authors who left behind texts in which they wrote about the Gospels, among other things. The oldest of these date from the end of the first century and the course of the second century. Because Christianity was still very young at that time, their writings may contain traces of earlier versions of these texts, and perhaps these lead to sources before the Gospels. Here I discuss three of the oldest texts of Church Fathers in existence: Clement of Rome, Ignatius of Antioch, and Papias.

The oldest source is Clement of Rome (also called Clement I, because he was the fourth Pope, according to tradition, after Peter, Linus, and Anacletus). He died toward the end of the first century, in other words relatively soon after the writing of the Gospels. A letter he wrote dates from around the year 95, from the time shortly after the creation of the Gospels of Luke and Matthew. The letter is addressed to the Christians in Corinth and illustrates the struggle between competing groups of believers, already at the very beginning of the new religion. The letter was triggered by the revolt of a group of young Christians in Corinth, who had deposed the elders of the church. Clement argues that the elders cannot be deposed and therefore must be restored in their function. Here is a clear illustration of what was explained earlier, that from the earliest beginnings of Christianity there has been disunity among Christians. And, perhaps more importantly, the discussions involve power — on the one hand, the power of the young to push aside the older generation, and on the other hand, the power of the older generation (represented in the person of the Pope) to force them to obey.

What is important here is that Clement uses texts from the Gospels in his discourse. Here is an example from his letter:

> Be merciful, that you may obtain mercy; forgive, that you may be forgiven; as you do, so shall it be done to you; as you judge, so shall you be judged; as you are kind, so shall kindness be done to you; with what measure you measure, with the same shall it be measured to you.
> (1 Clem. 13:2; see http://www.newadvent.org/fathers/1010. htm)

In this fragment there are references to several passages in the Gospels. Those who search will find them in the following places: Matthew 5:7, 6:14-15, 7:1-2; and Luke 6:31 and 6:36-38, but without Clement mentioning the names of the two evangelists. This is somewhat disconcerting. The church was still very young, and it is by no means certain that Clement could assume that his readers were familiar with the texts of the Gospels. So he should have mentioned these authors, especially since they refer to two different evangelists. There is, however, a reasonable explanation for this omission, namely that at the time of Clement the four Gospels were in fact not yet truly differentiated. In other words, there was no New Testament at that time. It was still "in the making," "in preparation," "in press."

These undifferentiated references are also found in the other early Church Fathers, for instance in the letters of Ignatius of Antioch (who died around the year 110) or in the letter of Barnabas, written between 70 and 132. The following text comes from the third paragraph of the letter of Barnabas:

> He should loose every band of iniquity, untie the fastenings of harsh agreements, restore the liberty them that are bruised, tear in pieces every unjust engagement, feed the hungry with thy bread, clothe the naked when thou seest him; bring the homeless into thy house, not despise the humble if thou behold him, and not (turn away) from the members of thine own family.
> (Schaff 2020, p. 59)

Here again are clear references to the Sermon on the Mount as it is known from the Gospels according to Matthew and Luke, but the authors are not mentioned by name. Such undifferentiated references to Gospel texts are also found in the *Didache*, once again without mentioning the names of the evangelists who wrote the Sermon on the Mount in their respective Gospels.

And then there is a name that keeps coming up in this kind of discussion: Papias. The case of Papias is of utmost importance, because it involves a distinction between oral witnesses and written Gospels. Papias (c. 65-130) was a bishop in Hierapolis, near present-day Pamukkale in Turkey, and is considered one of the earliest Church Fathers. Around the year 100, he wrote a five-volume work, the *Exposition of the Sayings of the Lord* (Λογίων Κυριακῶν Ἐξήγησις). It would have been the very first source on the authors and history of the Gospels—but unfortunately it no longer exists. We know of it only from references and quotations from later authors, especially Irenaeus of Lyons (c. 180) and Eusebius of Caesarea (c. 320). From the puzzle of all these pieces, the following emerges.

Papias was familiar with the written stories about Jesus because he rejected them, saying that he preferred "living" testimonies, referring to interviews he had conducted with people who knew others who had followed Jesus. Although he did not mention the evangelists Mark and Matthew by name, the references to them are clear. So, Papias was three steps removed from Jesus. At the first step were the disciples after Jesus' death in the year 30, who were probably also between 20 and 40 years old at the time, and who later told their experiences to others, who constituted the second step at say around the year 50. And one assumes again a little later, say around the year 70, that those others were interviewed by Papias (now three steps removed), around the year 90. Papias himself was then about 25 years old. His books came from about the year 100 when he was 35; such a scenario could apply. It certainly is quite savory what Papias had to say about his "living" sources. And this is all possible. Papias himself must certainly have been influential in early Christianity, or others after him would not have quoted him at length. So, although it is a great pity that these five books of Papias have been lost, it is fortunate that some passages from them were adopted by later Church Fathers. By comparing the oral evidence Papias reports with the written Gospels we have, we get a clearer picture of the situation at that time. Only in this case, the matter is not very revealing. Let's take a closer look.

One such interview of Papias (quoted by Irenaeus at the end of the second century) deals with the death of Judas. I take the quote in its entirety because it so colorfully describes what the interviewee says happened:

> But Judas went about in this world as a great model of impiety. He became so bloated in the flesh that he could not pass through a place that was easily wide enough for a wagon—not even his swollen head could fit.
> They say that his eyelids swelled to such an extent that he could not see the light at all; and a doctor could not see his eyes even with an optical device, so deeply sunken they were in the surrounding flesh. And his genitals became more disgusting and larger than anyone's; simply by relieving himself, to his wanton shame, he emitted pus and worms that flowed through his entire body.
> And they say that after he suffered numerous torments and punishments, he died on his own land, and that land had been, until now, desolate and uninhabited because of the stench. Indeed, even to this day no one can pass by the place without holding their nose. This was how great an outpouring he made from his flesh on the ground.
> (Ehrman 2006, p. 45)

The intent of the interview is clear. Because Judas committed such a terrible betrayal of Jesus, his punishment and downfall must be portrayed as being repugnant. For the Biblical scholar it is fortunate that this interview still exists, because it can be compared with what Matthew's Gospel says about Judas' death: "And he cast down the pieces of silver in the temple, and departed, and went and hanged himself" (Matt. 27:5). At least that's a bit more straightforward. But it raises a huge problem. Papias refers to the Gospel of Matthew in other places. So then surely he must have known the account of Judas' death in that

Gospel? Was he talking about the same text of Matthew as that which exists now? Sure, because he speaks elsewhere about this Gospel. He knows the text, he says. It is written in Hebrew and consists exclusively of statements by Jesus ... By now I imagine that you, the reader of this book, will be convinced that none of these statements are correct. The Gospel of Matthew contains mainly the life story of Jesus and to a much lesser extent his words. Against this background, it becomes clear that the story of Judas' death told by the "living witness" is also unreliable, not to mention that the description is hard to imagine, his head as big as a house, worms crawling out of his penis, a stench that is still unbearable a century later. Did the witness really see this?

What was before the Gospels?

From this consideration some conclusions can be drawn. First, in the works of the earliest Church Father, no solid sources from the time before the Gospels can be found. Second, all references to the Gospels lack any reference to their authors. This means that during the early stage of Christianity, the stories about Jesus were not yet linked to the names of any of the evangelists. The references then were still a thick soup from which the four Gospels would emerge over the next centuries. Finally, nowhere do the texts refer to eyewitnesses. They simply tell the reader that Jesus said this. The first manuscripts of the Gospels in existence date from about the year 200; before that time, the manuscripts never mention the name of an evangelist as the author.

In the first centuries of Christianity, small local groups came together. These groups were probably fewer than fifty people, and the meetings were not held in special buildings or churches, but in the homes of the members. It is likely that the Gospels arose from these communities in providing for local needs, and that is why they are so different from each other. When one group eventually received such a Gospel from another group, there were three possibilities: it did not correspond to the picture they had themselves made of Jesus, so they did not accept it; or, they fully recognized and adopted it; or (and this was perhaps the most common response), some elements of it corresponded to their own picture of Jesus, others did not, and so the text was adapted and "corrected," in other words, changed. And then competition arose between the different versions. It is conceivable that two (or more) versions coexisted for a while after that. But in the end, a "winner" emerged, probably being the numerically strongest group. And what happened to the versions that didn't make it? Probably they disappeared from the scene. It is not known how many of these texts were in circulation, but there could well have been hundreds. The Gospels we have now are the result of a long filtering (and consequent destruction) of texts. By the end of the second century, the vision had emerged that there were four Gospels and that these were the only reliable ones. The others were probably carefully destroyed.

Conclusion

This chapter dealt with the oral traditions that emerged after the death of Jesus, which eventually led to the written texts of the various Gospels (including apocryphal ones). Because no documents from such an oral tradition exist, one needs to reconstruct the process according to the most reliable methods available. This chapter has brought to light a number of factors that played a role in this oral tradition. Chronologically, the process proceeded in different phases.

First, the witnesses to the events in Jesus' life must have perceived things happening. There is good evidence that witnesses' observations do not always reflect the reality of things for various reasons (the action was too fast; they were distracted; someone was in their field of vision, and so on). Or there are things that they interpret and therefore distort (for instance, not comprehending that something happens because they do not want to "see" it). Second, there are external constraints. For example, the Gospels often say that Jesus was speaking for a large group. The famous Sermon on the Mount is a striking example of this. Matthew writes that a crowd had gathered and that Jesus went up a mountain and preached from it (Matt. 5:1-2). The author does not say how large the crowd is. But after Jesus speaks, the episode ends (in Matt. 8:1) with the addition: "When he was come down from the mountain, great multitudes followed him." How large? Fifty, a hundred, five hundred? We don't know. But I imagine there must be at least fifty to be called a "multitude." Suppose I am standing at the back of the group listening. Can I hear everything? Probably barely. The multitude is outside, with no sound amplification. I ask a neighbor what Jesus just said. As a result, I miss what Jesus is saying right now. In short, even when I see things in front of me, many details, even important ones, escape my perception.

The next phase involves such witnesses telling others what they have observed, and this process is also subject to limitations. What language does the witness speak? Aramaic? As a listener, is my Aramaic perfect or just flawed because my native language is Persian? Is the witness a woman? Then you are already on guard as a man. If this narrator is a Jew and I am not, then other problems of credibility arise. Did the witnesses describe in detail what they saw, or was it just a brief summary? Was the way the story was told convincing, compelling, amusing? Was the witness curious, or skeptical? Did the narrator say what I've heard someone else say—or is their story divergent? Does this witness clearly belong to a different group of Christians than I do? Is the narrator an old and thoughtful man, or a passionate young woman? All of these factors play a role in listening to the witnesses.

And then the report has to be passed on to others again and again, and distortion occurs each time. In addition, listeners need to remember what they heard from the witness (or witnesses).

Sometimes they have to remember the story over a long period, for example, when they tell it after a sea voyage—which was very slow in those days. Sometimes they have to remember stories from multiple witnesses who may have reported different things or put different emphases in their stories. Psychological research on remembering has now come to the clear conclusion that human memory is not only fallible, but that it is also "built" to construct things itself. Consequently, what listeners have heard from witnesses is not literally preserved in their memory. There are omissions, distortions, and additions. Remembering is not repeating, but repairing and reconstructing.

In a final phase, memory is cast in a particular form. Probably some forms of a story survive better than others. Memorable imagery and repetition are important aspects of this process. The Gospels we have were probably better told than those that have disappeared into the mists of history. In each of the four stages of the oral tradition (seeing, hearing, remembering, telling) adjustments take place. Generally, there are three possible processes involved in remembering: things are left out, others are added, and others are replaced. Does all this mean that one cannot believe anything that is written in the Gospels? Not at all. What it does mean is that one cannot simply believe what is written in the texts at face value. It is necessary to proceed carefully and methodically when finding out what happened historically.

Chapter 9

Christian and Yet Forbidden

This chapter deals with one of the most complex aspects of the New Testament, namely, how it emerged out of a stream of texts in the early days of Christianity. At first glance, this may seem strange. After all, for us right now, there's no problem, is there? There is only one New Testament. One can buy it or order it from a bookstore. And as different as the various forms of Christianity may be (Catholicism, Orthodoxy, Protestantism), when it comes to the text of the New Testament, there is actually little disagreement. So what's the problem?

History, that's the problem. We forget our history. We forget that we came from somewhere, and that the situation was not always as we know it now. For example, the text that we now buy in the bookstore is from the year 367. That is more than three centuries after the death of Jesus. Imagine that 300 years from now a text will appear with the orally transmitted insights of a preacher from India or Africa. It would surprise no one that numerous changes in content had taken place over such a long period. This is also the case with the New Testament. Didn't the New Testament exist from the beginning? No, in fact, it did not exist. Or to put it differently, before the year 367 there were many "New Testaments," all different from each other—and no unity in sight.

Although nowadays there seems to be agreement, a relic of the former disunity still exists. These texts are called the *Apocrypha*, from the Greek ἀπόκρυφος (*apókruphos*), meaning hidden, concealed. They are early texts around the figure of Jesus, including Gospels, that are not accepted by the Christian faith, although they are thoroughly Christian. The New Testament contains four Gospels. These are called "the canon" after the

211

Greek κανών, meaning "rule" or "measure." The canonical Gospels are those that have been accepted by church authorities over time as the only ones that are considered "trustworthy." In addition, there are more than 30 other Gospels that have not achieved this ecclesiastical status. These are the so-called apocryphal Gospels. This fact recognizes that there were other texts besides the canon, texts that were not approved. From this lack of agreement, lists of texts considered canonical emerged early in Christianity. Some of these lists still exist today:

- the canon of Muratori (from about 150-200, in ungrammatical Latin),
- the canon of Origen (born 185),
- the canon of Eusebius, the "father of church history" (10 volumes, published in 311),
- the canon of Athanasius from 367 (for the first time containing the 27 books known today in the New Testament).

Furthermore, it is known that discussions took place at the Council of Hippo in 393. Hippo (in present-day Tunisia) was the city where Augustine lived. With all his theological authority, he stood behind the canon of Athanasius. The minutes of this meeting are lost, but the minutes of the Council of Carthage (in 418) contain a summary of what was said and decided in Hippo. Even then, it was recorded that this canon was not binding. To this day, there are groups that do not accept the canon, but the vast majority of Christians do. But that was far from the end of the disagreement. Ultimately the current New Testament dates back to the Council of Trent, which took place from 1545 to 1563. This means that the New Testament as it is now known was only agreed on 1,500 years after the facts! Until then, there was much disagreement. And even after this council, there are still differences between Catholic, Protestant and Orthodox churches.

It is not possible to give an adequate account of this complex history within the scope of this chapter. For that reason, the chapter focuses on three fundamental issues. After an introductory explanation of some concepts, a good example of such an apocryphal text is discussed, namely the Gospel of Thomas. Then I examine what is meant by Gnostic texts, texts that come from an influential but vanished movement in early Christianity. Finally, attention is turned to the Gospel of Judas, recently revealed as a spectacular discovery that sheds an entirely new light on the origins of the New Testament. But first I look at a less well-known aspect of Christianity: the origins of its own intolerance.

Persecution?

Church authorities and devout believers often insist that Christians were persecuted in the past (and sometimes still are). Stories of these persecutions in ancient times are often greatly exaggerated by Christians themselves. Persecutions took place only in the first half of the third century (under Emperor Decius) and between 303 and 313 (under Emperor Diocletian). The Roman government did not ban Christianity outside of these periods. Why would they? All other religions were also tolerated. This does not mean that there were never any forms of local harassment or discrimination. But with the Edict of Milan in 313, under Emperor Constantine, these forms of intimidation ended.

Completely ignored, however, is the fact that a few centuries later, Christians themselves became the persecutors. Thanks to the scholarly work of Catherine Nixey (2017), among others, we are informed of how the advent of Christianity ushered in these persecutions, when Christians deliberately sought to destroy classical culture, especially the Greek and Roman mythologies and religions. Nixey's book begins with a description of an attack on the Temple of Athens in Palmyra (in what is now Syria):

When the men entered the temple, they took a weapon and smashed the back of Athena's head with a single blow so hard that it decapitated the goddess. The head fell to the floor, slicing off that nose, crushing the once smooth cheeks. Athena's eyes, untouched, looked out over a now-disfigured face.

Mere decapitation wasn't enough. More blows fell, scalping Athena, striking the helmet from the goddess's head, smashing it to pieces. Further blows followed. The statue fell from its pedestal, then the arms and shoulders were chopped off. The body was left on its front in the dirt; the nearby altar was sliced off just above its base. (...) On the floor, the head of Athena slowly started to be covered by the sands of the Syrian desert.

The "triumph" of Christianity had begun.

(Nixey 2017, p. xx)

Her book ends, after a detailed account of the fate of the philosopher Damascius in Athens in 529, with the conclusion, "The triumph of Christianity was complete" (Nixey 2017, p. 247). Fortunately, the attempt at destruction was not entirely successful, since we still have a broad and deep knowledge of classical ancient culture. Nevertheless, this episode casts a deep shadow over Christianity. The God who preached charity did not love the cultures of those who thought differently.

One may wonder, by the way, if it is a pattern of history that people who were persecuted at one point in time later become persecutors themselves ...

The Apocrypha

The Greek ἀπόκρυφος (apokryphos) is a word composed of "apo," meaning "away," and the verb "kryptein," "to conceal." Apocryphal texts are therefore literally "hidden" texts. For practical purposes, "apocryphal" is used in this chapter for all texts not considered canonical by the ecclesiastical authorities in Christianity.

In addition to the four canonical Gospels, several other Gospels, histories, apocalypses, epistles, and so forth circulated at that time. It is not known exactly how many there were. These non-canonical texts are all dated later than the four Gospels in the New Testament. None of them are older than the Gospels of Mark, Matthew, Luke and John. But this alone does not mean that there is no interesting information to be found in them. Dating is only one of many criteria for assessing the reliability of the information or its significance. The apocryphal texts contain a surplus of mythical, sometimes fantastic, funny or even grotesque stories. But several of these stories have had a great influence on popular pious traditions. The story of the ox and the donkey, for example, which still plays a role in popular accounts of the birth of Jesus, comes from the seventh century pseudo-Gospel of Matthew.

The process of selecting and narrowing down to the four Gospels took more than three centuries. In the meantime, there were passionate discussions between groups of believers who all called themselves Christians—and who all claimed to represent true Christianity. The present Gospels are the result of this struggle, in which the victorious party systematically condemned and also destroyed the texts of other Christians. Those that were not destroyed and still exist today are called the Apocrypha. To give an example of how far the views diverged between these groups, Ehrman (2006) explains:

In the early centuries, of course, there were Christians who believed in only one God. But others claimed there were two gods (the Markionites); yet others said there were 30 gods, or 365 gods (various groups of Gnostics) (...). There were Christians who maintained that this world was the creation of the one true God; others said it was the creation of the just but wrathful God of the Jews, who was not the true God; others said it was the creation of much inferior ignorant deities who were malicious and evil. There were Christians who believed that Jesus was both human and divine; others said he was human but not divine; others that he was divine but not human; others that he was two beings, one divine and one human. (p. 174)

Scholars have published numerous apocryphal texts, for example *Lost Scriptures* (Ehrman 2003), including books that did not make it into the New Testament: 47 apocryphal texts, some very short, others quite long. (This is not a complete collection, which can be found, however, in Elliott (1993).)

The Gospel of Thomas

So there are not only four, but at least 45 Gospels that have been preserved in whole or in part as manuscripts. A few examples of these are the Gospel of Peter, the Gospel of Ebion, the Gospel of Philip, the Proto-Gospel of James, and the Gospel of Mary. Unfortunately, it is not possible to discuss them all here. Therefore, I limit myself to one of them, namely the Gospel of Thomas, which experts believe could be one of the oldest sources. It was possibly written at the same time as the *Book of Q*, approximately between the years 40 and 70, so coming before the oldest Gospel, that of Mark. For this reason, the Gospel of Thomas has received by far the most attention from scholars. It should be noted, however, that there is no consensus on dating. Estimates range from the year 40 to the year 200! In any case, it was known in much of the ancient world from the year 230. Its status as an apocryphal text is remarkable in itself, as one of the oldest and most interesting texts to be excluded from the New Testament by church authorities.

The manuscript, as mentioned above, was found in 1945 in Nag Hammadi in the Egyptian desert. It is written in Coptic, but is almost certainly a translation of an original Greek text. This can be clearly deduced from the numerous Greek loan words in the Coptic text. Although the text is called a "Gospel," it is not a story about the life of Jesus as in the other Gospels. It is instead a collection of 114 statements of Jesus, very similar to the *Book of Q*, containing (some fifty percent) similar statements to those that can be read in Matthew and Luke. Other previously unknown statements are often difficult to understand because of their Gnostic origin (see later in this chapter). Some scholars believe that the Gospel of Thomas is closer to what Jesus himself said—but there is not yet a consensus among researchers on this. It is clear, however, that the picture of Jesus in this Gospel is quite different from that in the four Gospels of the New Testament. It is also much shorter, only fifteen percent of the length of Luke's Gospel. The author, Thomas, is unknown, but he probably wanted to give the impression that he was a follower (or brother) of Jesus.

Perhaps one of the most striking peculiarities of this text is that it does not mention the death and resurrection of Jesus. On the other hand, like the other Gospels, it contains an apocalyptic message. But the spirituality here is a bit different. This emerges directly from the second saying:

> Jesus said, "Let him who seeks continue seeking until he finds." When he finds, he will become troubled. When he becomes troubled, he will be astonished, and he will rule over the all.
> (translation Ehrman 2003, p. 20)

It seems that this kind of paradox leads back into the synoptic Gospels, where it says, for example, "but many that are first shall be last; and the last shall be first" (Matt. 19:29-30). But the idea that seeking and wondering lead to dominion is a very different perspective from that of the synoptic Gospels. The third saying expresses a similarly unfamiliar message:

> Jesus said, "If those who lead you say to you, 'See, the kingdom is in the sky,' then the birds of the sky will precede you. If they say to you, 'It is in the sea,' then the fish will precede you. Rather, the Kingdom is inside of you, and it is outside of you. When you come to know yourselves, then you will become known, and you will realize that it is you who are the sons of the living father. But if you will not know yourselves, you dwell in poverty, and it is you who are that poverty."
> (translation Ehrman 2003, p. 20)

So the spiritual, timeless kingdom exists by the grace of knowledge, and it is found in oneself and in the world.

In many of the sayings of the Gospel of Thomas, there are (oddly enough) some striking parallels to Zen Buddhist *koans* or to expressions from the art world, for instance saying 19, which is: "Blessed is he who came into being before he came into being." We are almost in the world of the avant-garde here: "Bevor Dada da war, was Dada da." In other sayings, echoes of the canonical Gospels may be seen, such as the emphasis on fasting, prayer, and almsgiving—generally expressing an abstinence from the world. "Become passers-by," reads saying 42. What is common, however, is that this Gospel has a stronger emphasis on philosophical contemplation, which suggests one reason why it may have been intended for philosophers in Alexandria. In any case, it is clear from the text that it was intended for a small elite group. This elitism is also reflected in the fact that some of these sayings of Jesus must at least be called enigmatic. For example, what are we to make of saying 37?

> His disciples said, "When will you become revealed to us and when shall we see you?"

Jesus said, "When you disrobe without being ashamed and take up your garments and place them under your feet like little children and tread on them, then (will you see) the son of the living one, and you will not be afraid."
(translation Ehrman 2003, p. 23)

It's not very likely that today's believers, on reading this, will start taking off their clothes. But why not? It's in a Gospel, after all! Granted, it's not one of the "approved" Gospels, but who decided that? Not the Holy Spirit, not God himself, but human authorities. And on what is this decision based? On opinions, the opinions of proponents, called "bishops." Actually, the etymology of the word "bishop" is interesting. It comes from the Greek ἐπίσκοπος, epi-skopos, literally "to look around," or "to see around." So the bishop is someone who looks around, someone who keeps an eye on everyone. A type of policeman, then. The religious police. (In Islam, such a police force still exists: in addition to the *sjorta*, the ordinary police, the *mutawwi* is responsible for controlling religious transgressions.) But who appointed these policemen? (And they are *always* men, of course.) Other bishops, for sure, and ultimately those in power who did not need to be held accountable.

The last saying of the Gospel of Thomas is perhaps the most shocking, at least for today's readers:

Simon Peter said to them, "Let Mary leave us, for women are not worthy of life."
Jesus said, "I myself shall lead her in order to make her male, so that she too may become a living spirit resembling you males." For every woman who will make herself male will enter the kingdom of heaven.
(translation Ehrman 2003, p. 28)

Is this an example of the misogyny of Christianity? Yet it is not

Jesus who says it, but Peter, while Jesus intercedes for Mary Magdalene. But how is the reader to understand that he makes her "male"? Does this mean that she has to put on men's clothing when she goes around with Jesus and his followers? Or that she must acquire a male "attitude"? It remains mysterious. This may be a piece of Gnostic tradition. What is that?

Gnostic texts

In the first centuries after Jesus' death, numerous movements arose, collectively known as "Gnosticism." These movements were concerned primarily with secret knowledge, accessible only to initiates. The Gospel of Thomas, for example, begins with the phrase: "These are the secret sayings which the living Jesus spoke." Gnostic groups were at odds with the official church groups and were therefore fiercely opposed by the Church Fathers, among others.

This should not be surprising when one considers the debates within Gnosticism. There were fierce debates about the question whether the death of Jesus had brought salvation to mankind or whether this death was unimportant for the salvation. Or, perhaps shocking to modern believers, even whether Jesus had really died. The fact that we can no longer imagine such debates and that we take the answers for granted is a consequence of the victory of a group that has rewritten history from its perspective and whose "children" we are.

Gnosticism is a very special world in which man is seen as a spirit who has fallen from the kingdom of God and is now trapped in matter. Salvation from this is possible only by gaining insight into secret knowledge. The worldview conceived in the Gnostic movements is of cosmic dimensions and is fundamentally foreign to contemporary ideas, especially if Gnostic movements are considered Christian. What they have in common with Christianity is that they seek salvation from present material or physical captivity, and strive for spiritual liberation and perfection. I consider some of these insights here, keeping in mind that they come from a multitude of groups that were also often in conflict with each other.

One idea that lives in many Gnostic groups is that before the universe existed, there was a divine order. This *pleroma* is the "fullness" of the divine realm; the word also means "fullness" and so refers to the place of perfect divine order. But during a catastrophe, one of the gods fell out of this order, resulting in a new kind of deity, not within but outside of the pleroma. This deformed and imperfect divine being, usually called Jaldabaoth, proclaimed himself as the only god of the Jews, unaware that there are gods far more powerful than he is. In turn, he created new gods to join him in creating the material world. Jaldabaoth and the new gods then created people with divine but flawed attributes to populate the world as it is now.

Why is this world a place of suffering, misery and pain? Because it was not created by the last true God. It is a flawed creation of a lower, inferior, ignorant and sometimes malicious deity. Therefore, it is not a matter of establishing a kingdom of paradise on earth (which is impossible), but of escaping the bonds of earthly matter through secret knowledge and returning to the ultimate divine order.

To illustrate this movement, I look at some texts. *Ptolemy's Letter to Flora* is a good example of Gnostic thought. Ptolemy was one of the most famous Christian Gnostics in Rome in the second century. His letter to Flora, a non-gnostic Christian, was intended to instruct her about gnosis. The argument is this: You Christians believe that the Bible is the product of the perfect God the Father. But how is this possible when the Bible contains laws that are not perfect? And this is clearly seen in what Jesus taught on the subject of divorce:

(4) When the Savior was talking with those who were arguing with him about divorce—and it has been ordained (in

the law) that divorce is permitted—he said to them, "For your (plural) hardness of heart Moses allowed divorce of one's wife." Now, from the beginning it was not so. For God, he says, "has joined together this union, and what the Lord has joined together, let no man put asunder."

(5) Here he shows that the law of God is one thing, forbidding a woman to be put asunder from her husband; while the law of Moses is another, permitting the couple to be put asunder because of hard-heartedness.

(6) And so, accordingly, Moses ordains contrary to what god ordains; for (separating) is contrary to not separating. (Ehrman 2003, p. 203)

On the other hand, the world cannot have been created by God's adversary, the devil. For there is also good in the law, for example, the possibility of separating according to the law of Moses and therefore not being destroyed by God. The devil could not have accomplished such a thing. So neither the devil nor God brought forth the world. Accordingly, there must have been another being who created everything. This must have been a "mediating" intermediate God, a God who stands between the perfect God and the devil and who created both good and evil. (Against the background of this reasoning, the question of how many gods there are becomes somewhat more understandable to the reader.)

In the Gnostic texts we also find a strong preoccupation with sexuality. This is true of Christianity in general, and of most other religions where the main concern is the control of women's sexuality. But in Gnostic texts, this preoccupation is even more pronounced. The *Pseudo-Titus*, for example, contains a virulent attack on sexuality in general. *Acts of John* (150-200) is a good example of the tortured attitude toward human sexuality. It is a poignant story of passion and asceticism. Drusiana, a deeply religious Christian, wants to renounce carnal pleasures in her

222

marriage to Andronicus. He insists, however, on locking her in a tomb and giving her the choice of physically surrendering to him or being buried. Drusiana prefers her piety to life — whereupon Andronicus converts to Christianity. But a pagan, Callimachus, lusts after Drusiana, who therefore dies of grief because she was the object of another man's desire. Callimachus then enters her tomb and wants to have sex (with the corpse), but is devoured by a giant snake that guards the tomb.

Another example of the Gnostic approach to sexuality is found in the *Acts of Thecla* (end of the second century). Thekla, Thamyris' fiancée in Iconium, hears Paul proclaim his life of chastity and decides to become a follower of Paul. Therefore, she is condemned to burn at the stake by order of Thamyris, but is saved by God. This is not the end of the story, however, because in Antioch she resists the advances of an important aristocrat. After that, all sorts of surprising adventures take place, including Thekla baptizing herself in a pool of dangerous seals, from which she is again rescued by God. Finally, she is spiritually reunited with her beloved apostle Paul, who allows her to preach the faith. The clear message is that a woman may spread the Christian faith only if she renounces her own sexuality. Thekla became an extremely important saint in the Middle Ages and was an object of veneration, especially for women who could not avoid abiding by the rules of patriarchy. The Gnostic traditions are full of such attacks on sexuality. The *Gospel of the Egyptians* (from 100-150), for instance, even condemns marriage and procreation. And the main message in *Acts of Thomas*, probably written in the third century in Eastern Syria, is to detach from physicality and value chastity above all!

Amazing stories

In addition, several Gnostic texts contain fantastic stories, although in the *Acts of Thomas*, these stories still remain somewhat within limits. This Gospel is said to have been written by the identical twin brother of Jesus. ("Thomas" means "twins" in Aramaic, but also "doubter" in Greek: *thaumazein* means "to wonder.") In this story, Jesus sells Thomas as a slave to the king of India, where he works as a carpenter for the king, but also performs numerous miracles and brings Christianity there. Things get even stranger in the *Acts of Paul* (from about 200), in which Paul converts and baptizes a talking lion, who later saves his life in the arena. The *Acts of Peter* (from about 180) is a kind of Kung-Fu story, a fight between Peter and a satanic sorcerer, Simon Magus. The climax of the story is when Simon flies like a bird over the temples and hills of Rome and Peter attacks him in full flight. Simon falls to the ground and is stoned by a crowd.

These tales are far from the "good news" that the Gospels would bring. Some texts are even further from the center of the canon, such as the *Second Treatise of the Great Seth* (from the third century). This text states that it was not Jesus who was crucified, but Simon of Cyrene, while Jesus looks on from a distance, laughing. In many of these Gnostic texts, the "ordinary" Christians are also mocked because they do not understand anything about the truth; the text says that they are ridiculous. Similarly, in the Coptic text *Apocalypse of Peter* (from the third century): the heretics here are the bishops of Orthodox Christianity, who tell their faithful that Jesus died on the cross.

There are also a number of texts about Jesus' childhood, such as the *Proto-Gospel of James* (from shortly after 150), which played an important role in the iconography of the Middle Ages, or the *Infancy Gospel of Thomas* (100-150). These stories are mainly about Jesus' pranks with his friends or episodes in which Jesus corrects his father's carpentry, or in which he denounces the ignorance of his teachers at school. Some of these texts come from the Nag Hammadi find and are among the oldest such legendary stories about Jesus as a child.

And then there is the strange letter of Barnabas. This is

found in the oldest manuscript of the New Testament available to us, the Codex Sinaiticus (from about 350). The letter is extremely anti-Jewish and even claims that the Old Testament is a Christian book which the Jews misunderstood. Jewish laws were to be understood and followed not literally, but spiritually. Circumcision, for example, should not be understood literally but only symbolically, namely as proof of one's faith in Jesus. How does Barnabas come into this? In Genesis 14:14, Abraham leads 318 of his men in battle against their enemies. According to Barnabas, 318 is a symbolic number. Here is his reasoning:

(For the Scripture) saith, "And Abraham circumcised ten, and eight, and three hundred men of his household." What, then, was the knowledge given to him in this? Learn the eighteen first, and then the three hundred. The ten and the eight are thus denoted – Ten by I, and Eight by E. You have the initials of (the name of) Jesus. And because the cross was to express the grace (of our redemption) by the letter T, he says also, "Three Hundred." He signifies, therefore, Jesus by two letters, and the cross by one. He knows this, who has put within us the engrafted gift of His doctrine. No one has been admitted by me to a more excellent piece of knowledge than this, but I know that ye are worthy.
(Schaff 2020, p. 77)

You will no doubt agree that we have landed very deeply in esotericism here. But the strange thing about the text is that the letter is in the oldest manuscript of the Bible in existence. Its ideology also fits well with later developments in Christianity such as hatred of the Jews, and the incorporation of the Old Testament into the new faith. So why was it nevertheless considered apocryphal? This question must remain unanswered for now, as research on the subject has not yet led to clear conclusions. For one who studies the New Testament from a historical-critical perspective, religion offers more questions than answers. And the question marks are constantly multiplying, also because new texts are regularly discovered. One such spectacular discovery concerns the *Gospel of Judas*.

The Gospel of Judas

The *Gospel of Judas* is one of the oldest apocryphal Gospels we have. The first thing to note is that Judas is portrayed completely differently in the synoptic Gospels. In Matthew, he throws the 30 pieces of silver into the temple and hangs himself. With the money, the chief priests buy a field, which they call "the field of blood" (because it was bought with blood money). In *Acts*, Judas himself buys a field on which he stumbles. His stomach rips open and his intestines come out. He dies in his "field of blood." In both texts, he betrays Jesus by kissing him. In John, Jesus knows in advance everything that will happen. In this Gospel, Judas is portrayed as the actual devil. A band of soldiers and assistants to the high priests comes to arrest Jesus. He asks who they are looking for. "Jesus the Nazorean" is the answer. Jesus himself answers (in Greek), *"Ego eimi"* ("I am he") (John 18:5), whereupon they all, including Judas, recoil and fall to the ground. So there is neither a kiss of Judas in John, nor a story about the death of Judas.

The figure of Judas, and his betrayal have always been somewhat mysterious. He led the authorities to Jesus, but that was not really necessary, because Jesus was a publicly known figure. And in some Gospels, Judas unleashed a riot in the temple a few days earlier. So it's hard to call Judas' actions "betrayal." Almost everyone knew who the itinerant preacher named Jesus was, so the authorities did not need Judas in order to find and arrest Jesus. Therefore, what was the role of Judas in the New Testament is an intriguing question. Jesus never says in public that he is "king," but only within the group of apostles. Could the betrayal of Judas be that he gives this inside information to the Roman authorities, who then have enough reason to see him as a rebel and condemn him?

All this may seem somewhat surprising, but it took a spectacular turn when a copy of the *Gospel of Judas* was discovered in 1978 in the province of Al Minya (in central Egypt), 180 kilometers south of Cairo, by two illiterate peasants whose names are no longer known. What happened to the manuscript after that is truly fascinating. The Gospel was ultimately published in 2006 by a team of specialists in *National Geographic* magazine. In the published edition, the literal similarities with the synoptic Gospels are marked in red, making it easier to compare with the traditional story of Judas (see Kassel et al. 2008). The text is now in the possession of the Maecenas Foundation in Geneva.

Such a *Gospel of Judas* must have been known long ago. The first mention of it is found in Irenaeus, in his work *Against Heresies* (from 180). He calls it one of the oldest Gospels outside of the New Testament and says about it:

> Judas also, the betrayer, it is said, had exact knowledge of these things, and since he alone knew the truth better than the other apostles, he completed the mystery of the betrayal. Through him all things in heaven and on earth were destroyed. This fiction they propose and call the Gospel of Judas. (1.31.1)

It is noteworthy that this passage in Irenaeus is remarkably similar to the recently discovered and published text.

The manuscript is a codex of 31 folios (leaves), or 62 pages, which was intensively studied for three years after its discovery. The manuscript is authentic, but after 1978 it was severely neglected owing to poor treatment by its various owners. Ten to fifteen percent of the pages are so damaged that they are illegible. It is written in Sahidic, a Coptic dialect, but the text is clearly a translation from Greek. The manuscript dates from around 400; the text itself is much older. It must have been composed between 120 and 150 by a Gnostic author under the name of the apostle who betrayed Jesus. So the author is definitely not the historical Judas, just as the other Gospels were not written by disciples of Jesus.

In terms of content, this Gospel is almost the opposite of what is said about Judas in the New Testament. He was the apostle closest to Jesus and to whom Jesus revealed the truth necessary for eternal life. According to this Gospel, Judas accepted the knowledge Jesus had given him and fulfilled Jesus' destiny by doing what Jesus had commanded him to do, allowing Jesus' soul to escape from its earthly "shell" and return to the divine order. According to this Gospel, Judas was not the enemy, but the closest friend of Jesus; for an edition of the Gospel, see Archer (2007).

The structure of this Gospel is completely different from the Gospels in the New Testament, which is why I discuss it here. It begins with an introduction, namely the secret account of the revelation Jesus gave to Judas. (Note how the tone immediately changes with the use of Gnostic terminology.) This is followed by four lines about Jesus' life and then a first encounter of Jesus with the apostles during a ritual meal, εὐχαριστέω (*eucharisteo*). Jesus laughs, the apostles are grumpy, and Jesus explains to them that his God is different from theirs. Judas stands up and explains the truth about Jesus: that he comes from the realm of Barbelo, a divine being who is the mother (i.e., female!) of all creation and dwells in the pleroma, above the realm of the God of creation. Jesus suddenly gets up and leaves. The next day he comes back, and the apostles want to know where he was the night before. Jesus answers that he was in another realm where mortals cannot enter. Then he disappears again. When he returns, the apostles ask him to explain a vision of theirs. Then Judas says that he too had a vision in which he was stoned by the other apostles. Jesus explains to him that the others will hate him. Then Jesus takes Judas aside to teach him the mysterious truths that no one has ever seen before. They contain the Gnostic explanation of the world. Judas wants to know if it is possible for people to exist in the afterlife. Jesus answers that some have only an earthly existence, but others have a divine spark in them and will survive forever, even beyond the end of time. Judas belongs to this group because he understands the mysteries and does what is required of him. Jesus says that he will surpass them all. For he is the one, Jesus says, "who will sacrifice the man that clothes me." (56:17-21) (Quoted in Ehrman 2006, p. 130). So Judas' "betrayal" is really his faithful obedience to Jesus, who must die so that he can escape his material existence and return to the *pleroma* where he came from. And Judas will make this possible. Judas then has a vision of his own exaltation and glory. Finally, Judas hands Jesus over to the Jewish authorities. This is the end of the Gospel: then the title is given. Unlike the other Gospels, which are all titled "The Gospel According to," here the title is "The Gospel of or 'by' or 'about' (the Coptic is ambiguous) Judas." In other words, the divine plan of salvation for mankind was made possible only through the obedience of Judas Iscariot.

It is striking that Jesus laughs in this Gospel. Four times, in fact. He does not do so in any other Gospel. He also runs away a few times for no reason. The apostles express their confidence that Jesus is the Son of their God. But Jesus denies that, because "their" God is an inferior God. He says: "this world was made by a wrathful, bloodthirsty rebel, and humans were created by a fool" (Ehrman 2006, p. 95). The apostles realize that Jesus does not have much sympathy for them, and become quite angry and indignant. They even blaspheme him! Jesus challenges them, asking who is strong enough to "bring forth the perfect human and stand before my face"? Only Judas succeeds, saying, "I know who you are and where you have come from. You are from the immortal realm of Barbelo. And I am not worthy to utter the name of the one who sent you" (Ehrman 2006, p. 90). Jesus takes him aside and tells him that with his help he will reach the kingdom of the mysteries, but that this will mean some pain for him, because his place will be taken by someone else when he has separated himself from them. When Jesus is arrested, all the other apostles flee; only Judas remains with his Master as a faithful disciple. He delivers Jesus, gets a sum of money and ... there, the Gospel stops. Nothing is said about the crucifixion and nothing about the resurrection.

Researchers had previously noted that Judas is gradually portrayed more and more negatively in the New Testament. Is it possible that in earlier versions (which we no longer have) Judas was seen as an apostle who was very close to Jesus, as in the *Gospel of Judas*, but that these texts were lost or destroyed?

No one knows what would have happened if these Gnostic traditions had "won" or if the different currents of Christianity had continued to coexist. Nor is it clear for what reasons one current won out over the others. But the fact that the figure of Judas is portrayed quite differently in church tradition than in some other groups of early Christianity arguably makes the *Gospel of Judas* explosive. The apocryphal texts generally cast a questionable light on the official version of Christianity as propagated by the dominant churches.

Chapter 10

A Christianity Without Jesus

The first Christians were faced with a major problem. They needed to convince people, who had worshipped pagan gods for thousands of years in the Roman Empire, of the new "order" offered by Christianity. One man knew how to do this: his name was Saul. Later he would change his name to Paul. (In this chapter, I use the two names interchangeably; they both refer to the same person.) His solution was to travel tirelessly to proclaim the new "good news" everywhere. He traveled alone, on foot, on horseback or by sailing ship, and he did this like no other, tirelessly wandering through the vast empire to spread his conviction.

What is known about Paul and his life is inversely related to the countless stories traditionally told about him. Apart from the Christian scriptures, there are no other sources about him. There are many legends, none of which can claim trustworthiness. His own letters, therefore, are the only source we can rely on, besides the description of his projects in the Acts of the Apostles, written some 20 to 30 years later, by Luke. But which letters? His so-called correspondence with Seneca was completely invented. And the third letter to the Corinthians is also a forgery. The authentic letters of this Saul are only half of the 14 letters that have survived. They are the letters to the Thessalonians, Corinthians (two letters), Galatians, to Philemon, to the Philippians and to the Christians in Rome.

The situation

After the death of Jesus, sometime around the year 30, small groups of his followers spread his teachings (or what they thought were his teachings) mainly in Jerusalem and the

231

surrounding area. One could think of them as small revolutionary cells proclaiming that their executed leader had risen from the dead, because he was God. However, this immediately caused controversy because, according to Paul, Jesus would be resurrected after his death and would be the "Messiah," which was something unheard of in traditional Judaism. In addition, however, there were groups in the city who were not Jewish but respected Jewish traditions and were sympathetic to this new movement. They did not follow Jewish law, but saw salvation in this new religion. But since they were not Jews themselves, this created tensions with traditional Jewish communities, and very soon this led to violent conflicts at times. According to tradition, Stephen, the first martyr of Christianity, was stoned to death in Jerusalem for his alleged blasphemous remarks (from a traditional Jewish perspective).

This was the situation when Saul appeared. As a Jew, he wanted to stop this new Christianity movement, and he did so violently by persecuting and exterminating the Christians. Maybe he was present at the stoning of Stephen and also saw groups of Christians fleeing the city. As far as we can tell from his attitude, he must have been in full agreement with this execution, and it wasn't too long before he was hunting down Christian fugitives.

Perhaps he was born in Tarsus, in southern Turkey, but even that is uncertain. However, Jerome, who lived in the fourth century, reports that another story was also circulating at the time, that Saul's parents were from Gischala in Galilee, a town about 25 miles north of Nazareth, and that Saul was born there. He and his parents were exiled by the Romans to Tarsus in Turkey in the midst of a mass deportation following an uprising after the death of Herod the Great in 4 BC. If this tradition is based on truth, it casts serious doubt on Saul's claim that he was a Roman citizen. Would Rome have granted citizenship to someone from a troubled province? Highly unlikely.

Possibly he was the son of a tentmaker. In his letter to the Christians of Philippi, he calls himself a Pharisee, a Jewish sect known for strict adherence to Jewish laws (Phil. 3:5). Perhaps for this purpose he went to Jerusalem, nearby, to study under Gamaliel, one of the famous rabbis of that time. But Luke may have intended to elevate the status of his teacher (for that is how he regarded Paul), since Gamaliel was known for his tolerance, also of non-Jews, and even of the Roman occupiers. His gifted teacher, however, would certainly not have agreed. Saul was an ardent advocate of strict adherence to Jewish observances. He was not a member of the political movement that sought to overthrow the Romans. He could well have been described as a fanatical zealot for the preservation of Judaism. All deviations from Jewish law and all compromises with the goyim (Gentiles) had to be forcibly eliminated. Christians behaved in a deviant manner, and therefore his persecution of them was based on indignation. In his view, these Christians posed a threat to Jewish identity, partly because of their extravagant claims about Jesus, and partly because they interfered with Gentiles. According to the Pharisee Saul, the view that this Jesus was the Messiah had to be relentlessly suppressed.

So, this was a persecution of Christians, not by the Romans, but by other Jews. It was a purely internal matter within the Jewish communities. It is not known exactly what this persecution meant, and Paul himself does not speak about it. Acts says, "As for Saul, he made havoc of the church, entering into every house, and haling men and women committed them to prison" (Acts 8:3). However, Ehrman (2018, pp. 49-50) points out that this is highly unlikely. By what authority could Saul enter homes? He had no official appointment, and was a foreigner in Palestine. And in what prison could he have locked up Christians? There were no Jewish prisons, only Roman ones, which were certainly not available to Saul. The Romans had their own political agenda, which did not include interfering in internal Jewish affairs. Perhaps he had his victims flogged. This was a Jewish punishment for blasphemy that he himself had suffered, since in Galatians (1:13) he confessed that he had acted "immoderately." He uses the Greek word ὑπερβολή (*hyperbolé*: "exaggeration"), which is still recognized in the word "hyperbole." In the English King James Version of the Bible, the word is translated as "violently." Perhaps, in retrospect, he only meant it as actually "hyperbolic," the way he initially persecuted Christians. But it will certainly not have been friendly; that much is clear from the story.

From that point on, the paths of Saul and the Jerusalem community diverged. For James, the brother of Jesus, the new faith was still completely anchored in the Jewish tradition. Paul radically broke with it to open the way to a universal Christianity in which everyone, regardless of birth or origin, could become a member of the new community without additional requirements. This had colossal consequences. Without Paul, Christianity would never have become a world religion, but would have remained a small and controversial sect within Judaism. Through Paul, Christianity became accessible to everyone. The only condition is the belief in the crucifixion and resurrection of Christ.

After his vision on the road to Damascus, Paul became the strongest defender of the Christian communities, several of which he founded, but with whom he also lived in constant tension. Especially with the Christian community in Jerusalem under the leadership of James, the brother of Jesus, the tensions were considerable, even leading to open conflict.

Paul's travels

The main sources for Paul's travels are the Acts of the Apostles and his own (authentic) letters. These two sources do not always agree completely, and dating the travels is sometimes problematic, but it is clear from these texts that he was almost constantly on the road, proclaiming the Christian message. Paul really is the engine of the earliest Christianity.

First, he travels south from Tarsus (where he probably lived) and arrives in Jerusalem via Antioch and Damascus. According to his own testimony (in the letter to the Galatians), he goes from Damascus to Arabia, more precisely to Mount Sinai, symbol of the Jewish Law, because on this mountain Yahweh gave the stone tablets with the Ten Commandments to Moses. Then he travels back to Damascus, to Antioch and Tarsus, then from Antioch to Cyprus, and from there to Galatia, in the interior of present-day Turkey, then back to Antioch and to Jerusalem, some time later to Thessalonica, then to Athens, to Corinth, then to Ephesus, to Colossae and back to Jerusalem, then to Troas and Philippi, and back to Corinth, and finally to Rome, where his journey and (according to tradition) his life ended. And I'm skipping over lots of other destinations in this summary. This was all done without motorized transportation, under often harsh conditions. Certainly some of the destinations are uncertain, and sometimes the authenticity of his reports is disputed. But what cannot be denied is Paul's totally restless character, always eager to proclaim the new order among ever newer groups. He was not only concerned with expressing a different inner attitude; at least as important was the creation of a new political order. It is no exaggeration to say that Paul was the most successful politician in the history of the West. His personal commitment to this cause was almost superhuman. He describes his own life in this way:

I am more; in labours more abundant, in stripes above measure, in prisons more frequent, in deaths oft. Of the Jews five times received I forty stripes save one meaning the 39 lashes as punishment for blasphemy (against the Jewish religion). Thrice was I beaten with rods, once was I stoned; thrice I suffered shipwreck, a night and a day I have been in the deep. In journeying often, in perils of waters, in perils of robbers, in perils by mine own countrymen, in perils by the heathen, in perils in the city, in perils in the wilderness, in perils in the sea, in perils among false brethren; in weariness and painfulness, in watchings often, in cold and nakedness. (2 Cor. 11:23-27)

Here speaks someone who has gone to extremes. You may wonder why the man was so passionate, so inexhaustible in his energy and so tenacious in his perseverance. The answer is not far away. Paul was obsessed with urgency. He literally expected Jesus to reappear and thought a new world was in the making. So there was no time to lose. Everyone had to cooperate, and he the most of all. Ultimately, he was the one called to share the great plan God had for the world. This made him not only restless, but also indefatigable, although not free of depression. In the second letter to the Corinthians, this is abundantly clear: "that we were pressed out of measure, above strength, insomuch that we despaired even of life" (2 Cor. 1:8).

Paul as a missionary

How did it go in practice, this missionary work? Well, let's imagine that Paul arrives in a new city. As a Jew, he could immediately contact the local synagogue, but that was risky. Many Jewish communities were downright hostile to the new movement, to Christianity, and this he experienced firsthand several times. Think of the corporal punishment of the "forty stripes save one" mentioned earlier. Probably the best hypothesis proposed in this regard, and the one that seems most historically plausible, is by Ronald Hock (1980); his explanation runs as follows. If it is true that Paul was a tentmaker, then he had a profession that he could practice anywhere. In ancient times tents were very often made of animal skins. Not much material was needed to do this: knives, awls, alders and some other tools. One could buy the leather on the spot; it didn't have to be carried around. Like the guilds in the Middle Ages, crafts in ancient times were concentrated in the center of the city—ideal for spreading his new message. Paul looked for a suitable place as a workshop, rented a room there and began to receive customers, from sunrise until after sunset. While working and talking to customers, he talked about the new good message. Of course, this didn't always work, and disillusionment must have been the order of the day. But there are two things to remember. One is the enormous population density of the cities at that time. And Paul preached exclusively in cities, unlike Jesus, who went from hamlet to hamlet in the countryside. Antioch, near today's Antakya in southeastern Turkey, had a population of about 200,000 at the time, and was crowded by our standards today, having twice as many inhabitants in Paul's time. "The average population density in Roman cities was about 200 persons per acre, matched today in only the densest inner cities. There was little space and even less privacy. One result was that news could spread very quickly indeed. And rumor. And gossip" (Ehrman 2018, p. 63).

At the same time, one must imagine the spread of new ideas and how they could arouse attention and interest. The vast majority of people in these cities were poor and engaged in a daily struggle for existence. Inequality and injustice existed on a scale that can hardly be imagined today. If a man arrived proclaiming a liberation from poverty, preaching that all people are equal and that a new order was coming, he would be assured of a lively interest. And if he could convince someone, then others would become curious; people would come by to watch, listen, comment, discuss. And this in turn would lead to even more interest in the neighborhood—and beyond. Moreover, Paul was a worker who earned his living like other people, someone who lived an ordinary life. (Don't forget that hardly anyone in early Christianity came from the upper classes.) This interest, together with the speed at which news spread in such densely populated cities, ensured Paul's success. This is also evident in the story of his life. He actually succeeded in planting new churches in many cities, and his letters to these churches testify to his partial success. The rapid spread of Christianity in the first century is certainly due in part to Paul's relentless efforts.

But it was not always easy. The vast majority of people were "pagans," in the sense that they were polytheistic. In every city there were several temples for dozens of gods to sacrifice to, and most people did so. The general religious view was that the world was ruled by all sorts of supernatural beings who had to be satisfied, but who could also grant favors. The emperor, Caesar, was also worshipped as a god. After all, he was responsible for the welfare of his subjects. And then there were the household and family gods who were worshipped in smaller circles. It must have been a very strange spectacle for the city's inhabitants to see someone proclaiming that there was only one god. Not only that, but a god who had been executed by the government in the most shameful way, and who had risen from the dead (even more insane), who could not be sacrificed to, and whose believers gathered for communal meals, a ritual in which his body was eaten and his blood drunk in remembrance. It was completely different from anything the people were used to. For Paul, it was just a matter of convincing the visitors to his tent workshop. But how did he do this?

Rhetoric

As a Greek speaker, Paul must have been familiar with rhetoric, the art of persuasion which had been practiced and taught as part of Greek philosophy for centuries. Moreover, as a Pharisee, he was well versed in Judaism with its long, venerable, and lively tradition of discussion, of the word.

For many, a transition from polytheism to a belief in a single God would have seemed improbable. It meant not only leaving behind the views of all relatives, neighbors, friends, and acquaintances—in fact, almost everyone in town—but also no longer being able to participate in local rituals, festivals, processions, and sacrifices.

In effect, this transition required a leap from the concrete to the abstract. Allow me to explain. The images of the gods were tangible; one could perceive them, they appeared physically in the material of bronze, marble, and wood. And they were artfully made by craftsmen who knew how to make a beautiful statue of a god or goddess. These statues exerted a powerful attraction. This is still true today in Eastern religions—think of the Ganesha statues that can be seen all over India and also in the West. In Christianity, one thinks of the famous Madonnas of Lourdes, Fatima, Czestochowa, Medjugorje, and Guadelupe. These statues are similar to the statues of gods and goddesses in ancient times. Paul had to overcome this attraction, because many people with whom he spoke had indeed experienced contact with their deities They had literally seen the god(desses; she had visited them, she had fulfilled their wishes, and they had been emotionally overwhelmed by her appearance.

In 2017, Flemish journalist Dimitri van Zeebroeck made a television series called *God Lives in Berchem* (Berchem is a borough of Antwerp, where I lived at the time). The series was a fascinating and cinematically beautiful documentary about the way religion is experienced in a modern city in all its diversity, but also in all its depths of experience. In one episode, a man talks about a figurine of Mary, the mother of Jesus, that sits on his mantelpiece, and to whom he prays regularly. One evening he sees her appear before him in the room. The man's testimony is overwhelming. He has really seen her; she has revealed herself to him. In a torrent of tears, he testifies that what he says is the whole and unadulterated truth. Such testimonies may be rare in society today, and although many may question them, this is how the world of human representation must have appeared in ancient times. And the attraction of images is still alive among us.

How was it possible for an individual in Paul's time, without support from friends and relatives, to make the massive leap from these very concrete and tangible emotional experiences to something as abstract as an invisible God? And a God you couldn't make an image of? And who only announced something as vague as a new kingdom? The strategy used by Paul aimed exactly at this material aspect of the statues: the images were only made of matter and made by men, so they could not have divine attributes. Sure, his strategy often did not work, but in several cases he will have succeeded, owing to his personality, dedication, humility, and passion. But a second hurdle had to be overcome: the belief that the executed criminal was Jesus and God.

It must have helped that the Roman rulers were unpopular and that their atrocities against the local population only aroused horror. The fact that Jesus was a victim of Roman atrocities must surely have aroused sympathy. But Paul's crucial argument was that after the execution, the same Jesus had risen from the dead—in other words, that he had conquered human mortality. Paul will have propagated this with vigor. He himself had encountered the risen Christ in the flesh! As a man of labor, Paul certainly seemed reliable and honest; as a craftsman, intelligent and well organized. Clearly he was a man with compassion and concern for the fate of others. This argument must have had a colossal appeal.

As human beings, we are all confronted with our finitude. Religions try to elevate us above this finitude. To hear that death had been conquered by someone, that this person delivered everyone from death and subsequently promised eternal life must have seemed to many a particularly enticing alternative to their daily sacrifices to the familiar images of the gods. And on top of that came a new kingdom, in which all of the current misery and injustice would be over, all through Jesus' sacrifice, through his death on the cross. The evil powers in the world had been overcome in one final battle. One no longer had to sacrifice to the gods, because everything was already settled; the salvation of mankind was on its way. The way to become part of this new kingdom, prepare for it and reap its benefits, was to convert to Christianity—straightaway.

A new religion

After Jesus' death, a conflict between his immediate followers and Paul was preprogrammed to happen. After all, the latter declared himself an apostle, although he had not been there at the time and had never met Jesus. He could not have known at all what had happened. But from his point of view, he didn't need to know. He didn't care, because he had received his message (and commission) directly from Christ himself. The beginning of his letter to the Galatians makes that perfectly clear:

> Paul, an apostle, (not of men, neither by man, but by Jesus Christ, and God the Father, who raised him from the dead) …
> (Gal. 1:1)

and

> But I certify you, brethren, that the Gospel which was preached of me is not after man. For I neither received it of man, neither was I taught it, but by the revelation of Jesus Christ.
> (Gal. 1:11-12)

Obviously such an attitude must have caused irritation among the real disciples. But there was more of such tension. In the second chapter of his letter to the Galatians, he mentions a conflict with Peter, whom he also publicly contradicts. There is specific information about this conflict in the Acts of the Apostles, which, as we know, was written by Luke, a supporter or follower of Paul. Chapters 15 and 21 of the letter explain how the conflict centered on the question of whether Gentiles who had converted to Christianity had to abide by Jewish commandments and laws. Conflict expanded into riots in Jerusalem, and Paul was taken prisoner by the Romans, partly for his own protection—otherwise he would surely have been killed by the Jewish mob.

Indeed, in the years 40 to 60, the local congregation of Jesus' followers in Jerusalem was Jewish through and through. Regarding Gentile converts, the prevailing opinion in this community was that God could not dissolve the covenant with the Jewish people because of some Gentiles. But that was exactly Paul's point, that Jesus' death on the cross and his resurrection had "set aside" Jewish law. According to Paul, the death of Jesus was the beginning of a new era; the time of redemption was near.

So there was already Christianity and an active Christian church in Jerusalem before Paul, and completely unrelated to him. After all, Paul did not meet Peter (or Cephas, his Aramaic name) until ten years after Jesus' death, and then it took another ten years for him to meet Peter and James again. At the same time, Paul himself was busy establishing and leading Christian communities everywhere. The point is not that these different communities coexisted, but that there were deep differences between Paul's vision of Christianity and that of Peter and James. The extent to which the positions differed is shown by the fact that Paul looked down disdainfully on his colleagues in Jerusalem:

But of these who seemed to be somewhat, (whatsoever they were, it maketh no matter to me: God accepteth no man's person) for they who seemed to be somewhat in conference

added nothing to me.
(Gal. 2:6)

In this extract, he is speaking of the brother of Jesus—who spent much of his life with Jesus. And here is his attack in the second letter to the Corinthians:

> For such are false apostles, deceitful workers, transforming themselves into the apostles of Christ. And no marvel; for Satan himself is transformed into an angel of light.
> (2 Cor. 11:13-14)

It is clear that Paul was not a man of compromise. His style is confrontational, with very clear positions that he defends with fire, not backing away from controversy. Therefore, even in his time there were fierce disagreements between supporters and opponents, between friends and enemies.

Interesting to note in this regard is the use of the word "gospel." In the New Testament it appears a total of 72 times, 60 of which come from Paul. And he refers not to the message of Jesus, but to *his* message, *his* vision! In this way he promotes himself to the thirteenth apostle, even considering himself a much more important apostle, because he has been chosen directly by Christ himself. He alone has received this revelation. He even sees himself as a kind of second Christ. He says this almost literally:

> For though ye have ten thousand instructors in Christ, yet have ye not many fathers: for in Christ Jesus I have begotten you through the Gospel. Wherefore I beseech you, be ye followers of me.
> (1 Cor. 4:15-16)

With this Christ, whom he invented, he feels completely at one.

But with Christ, not with Jesus. Not a single word of Jesus is quoted in any of Paul's writings! He uses the word "Christ" more than 150 times (in only 80 pages), and the word "Lord" more than 100 times as a reference to Christ. However, the name "Jesus" occurs only 11 times in his texts.

In considering all of this, it is important to remember that in the ancient world there was no separation between church and state. So the new order that Paul brought was a religious one, but at the same time a social and political one. And his political vision was fundamentally different from that of the Jerusalem group. But there is one historical fact that made his vision win: the destruction of Jerusalem by the Romans in 70, which brought the definitive end of the community of Christians in Jerusalem. Paul was dead by then, but with the disappearance of the Jewish-Christian community in Jerusalem, his vision now gradually took hold. Instead of Judaism, Christianity has now become universal:

> There is neither Jew nor Greek, here is neither bond nor free, here is neither male nor female; for ye are all one in Christ Jesus.
> (Gal. 3:28)

But wasn't Jesus' message already universal? Didn't he proclaim: "Love your neighbor as yourself"? That sounds a lot like the Universal Declaration of Human Rights—and that is how his words are interpreted today. But such an interpretation ignores the historical context of these words. Jesus did not mean that one must love all, but only the Jews. Biblical scholar Reza Aslan, like no other, draws attention to the fact that this maxim applied only to fellow Jews. For the Israelites, but also for the Christian community in Palestine in the first century CE, "neighbor" was synonymous with "fellow Jew" (Aslan 2013, p. 164). Jesus espoused the ethnocentric principle, as is evident from the message he gives to his followers:

> These twelve Jesus sent forth, and commanded them, saying, "Go not into the way of the Gentiles, and into any city of the Samaritans enter ye not: but go rather to the lost sheep of the house of Israel."
> (Matt. 10:5-6)

That we today nevertheless interpret the message "love your enemies" as universal is because the New Testament is steeped in Paul's view. The universal message of equality also seems to apply to the way Paul sees the position of women. But this is a complex story; I will explore that subject in a moment.

Jesus vs. Paul

In Matthew 19:16-22, the rich young man asks what he must do to gain eternal life. Jesus' answer is "Keep the (ten) commandments." But Paul claims that these commandments have been rendered meaningless by the crucifixion and resurrection of Jesus. The source for this is the Acts of the Apostles. There, Paul emerges as the true follower of Jesus. It has therefore sometimes been said that Christianity could be more accurately be described as "Paulism." Paul mentions almost nothing (except the Last Supper and the crucifixion) from the life of Jesus, and nowhere are the words of Jesus quoted. He even ignores things Jesus said, including that one must obey the Law of Moses. Not so, Paul! He even contradicts Jesus, for example: "For whosoever shall call upon the name of the Lord shall be saved" (Rom. 10:13). Compare this statement of Jesus himself, "Not every one that saith unto me, Lord, Lord, shall enter into the kingdom of heaven" (Matt. 7:21). In this way, Paul designs an entirely new kind of faith, different from what Jesus and from what the apostles proclaimed. First, there was a major problem in the apostles' proclamation of

Jesus' teaching, namely, the slanderous death of Jesus on the cross as a criminal. Remember what was said in Chapter 3 about how cognitive dissonance can be resolved? In Paul's case, this is done by creating a whole new Jesus: Ἰησοῦς χριστός (*Jesous Christos*), "Jesus the Anointed One," and the Messiah, as the Roman emperors adorned themselves with the title "Caesar."

The name Christ, however, is in complete contradiction to the person of the historical Jesus, who would have been shocked if he had been called the "Christ." But the success of Paul's creation can be seen from the fact that the later religion was called "Christianity" and not "Jesusism" or something like that. Jesus now becomes something divine, eternal. In the Jewish religion (in the Old Testament) and also for Jesus himself, this expression does not mean that he is a divine person, but that he is a mediator between God and man. So, the kings of Israel are referred to as the "Son of God" (see 2 Sam. 7:14). The literal "divine" meaning of the expression is not found in Mark (except in later additions), but appears for the first time in Luke 1:35. This is the so-called "Annunciation," not coincidentally, of course, since Luke is a follower of Paul.

Really nothing in other contemporary sources suggests such a view. Even in the *Book of Q*, which was perhaps written at about the same time as Paul's letters, there is no hint at all of such an "anointed" conception of Jesus. So Christ is an invention of Paul—an extremely successful one! Initially, this version of Paul's could not prevail, because the Christian community in Jerusalem kept the Law of Moses, while Paul found it unimportant. He even had to justify himself to James, Peter and John, and for this reason he traveled to Jerusalem (around the year 63). They looked upon him with suspicion and contempt, and even forced him to undergo a Jewish purification ritual in the temple.

But then comes the comeback: a surprising rehabilitation of Paul's ideas after the destruction of Jerusalem by the Romans.

The city was razed to the ground, so there was no longer a Christian community in Jerusalem. Many Christians were now non-Jews. Therefore, Paul's vision gradually eclipsed the Jewish vision of James, Peter and John. This entirely new religion was gradually detached from its Jewish roots. Throughout the Roman Empire, this new religion was now being embraced by various groups. Rome at this time was the largest city in the Western world, where a significant group of Christians now lived. In other words, Christianity became Roman instead of Jewish, and the two religions grew further and further apart.

I cannot stress this enough—shocking as this may sound, in spite of all that Christians have believed for over 2,000 years, Christianity in its official form has little, indeed *very* little, to do with what Jesus said and did. James Tabor (2012) succinctly summarizes the whole situation, so let me quote him in full:

> There was a version of "Christianity before Paul," affirmed by both Jesus and his original followers, with tenets and affirmations quite opposite to those of Paul. This is the lost and forgotten Christianity of James the brother of Jesus, leader of the movement following Jesus' death, and the Christianity of Peter and all the apostles. In other words, the message of Paul, which created Christianity as we know it, and the message of the historical Jesus, and his earliest followers, were not the same. In fact, they were sharply opposed to one another with little in common beyond the name Jesus itself.
>
> (Tabor 2012, p. xvi)

The position of women

As far as the position of women is concerned, one finds in Paul a remarkable mixture of a positive attitude and at the same time an imperious, patriarchal rejection of the role of women. One could even speak of a complete schizophrenia in his writings.

First of all, Paul had several female followers who were actively involved in spreading the good news. But thereafter, one finds blatantly misogynistic statements in his letters.

Throughout the ancient world, women were largely confined to their homes. They had to take care of the household, the birth and education of children, and the intimate care of their husbands. Jesus' followers seem to have departed from this pattern. A clear indication of this is found in Luke:

> and the twelve were with him, and certain women, which had been healed of evil spirits and infirmities, namely, Mary called Magdalene, out of whom went seven devils, and Joanna the wife of Chuza, Herod's steward, and Susanna, and many others which ministered unto him of their substance.
> (Luke 8:1-3)

It is clear from this passage that women played an important role in the environment of Jesus himself. In the earliest period after Jesus' death, about which we are informed by Paul's letters, Christian communities offered women the opportunity to escape their usual restrictive conditions by making their homes available for Eucharistic "meals" and prayers. In this way, women could transform their homes into public religious gatherings. The earliest documents and archaeological findings, for example at Dura-Europos, show that such religious gatherings took place mainly in private homes. As a result, women also acquired social prestige, and possibly political authority and leadership.

In Paul's letter to the Galatians, the egalitarian tenor of this early Christianity is already clear, as mentioned earlier, "Here is neither male nor female: for ye are all one in Christ Jesus" (Gal. 3:28). Paul also explicitly greets women in his letters, such as Priscilla, Julia, and Phoebe. The authentic letters show that women played a considerable role in the earliest Christian communities, as is evident in Paul's letter to the Romans:

> I commend unto you Phoebe our sister, which is a servant
> of the church which is at Cenchreae: that you receive her
> into the Lord, as becometh saints, and that ye assist her in
> whatsoever business she hath need of you; for she hath been
> a succourer of many, and of myself also. Greet Priscilla and
> Aquila my helpers in Christ Jesus; who have for my life laid
> down their own necks (...). Greet Mary, who bestowed much
> labor on us. (...) Greet Tryphena and Tryphosa who labor in
> the Lord. Salute the beloved Persis, which labored much in
> the Lord. (...) Salute Philologus, and Julia, Nereus and his
> sister (...).
> (Rom. 16:1-16)

Phoebe is even referred to by Paul as a "deaconess," someone who
helps found churches and provides support, perhaps including
financial help through fundraising. She is also referred to in the
letter as "overseer," in Greek προστάτις (*prostatis*), indicating
a wealthy and leadership position. All of these elements point
to a prominent role of women in the working life of the very
earliest Christian communities.

However, some of Paul's other expressions are diametrically
opposed to his praise of women as co-workers. One of the
clearest passages in this regard is found in the first letter to the
Christians of Corinth:

> Let your women keep silence in the churches: for it is not
> permitted unto them to speak; but they are commanded to
> be under obedience, as also saith the law. And if they will
> learn any thing, let them ask their husbands at home: for it is
> a shame for women to speak in the church.
> (1 Cor. 14:34-35)

This is shocking. It becomes even more shocking in another passage:

> For a man indeed ought not to cover his head, forasmuch as he is the image and glory of God: but the woman is the glory of the man. For the man is not of the woman, but the woman of the man. Neither was the man created for the woman, but the woman for the man.
> (1 Cor. 11:7-9)

All of this contrasts sharply with the praise for women elsewhere in his letters. And this is not a lapse, for it is not the only directive about the behavior and status of women. In the first letter to Timothy there is a similar admonition:

> Let the woman learn in silence with all subjection. But I suffer not a woman to teach, nor to usurp authority over the man, but to be in silence.
> (1 Tim. 2:11-12)

What Paul proclaimed in this regard was of great importance (and still is in religious circles) because he is the first to give explicit guidelines about the position of women in church communities.

However, although these passages come from Paul's authentic letters, there is disagreement among experts as to whether these passages were added later and therefore did not come from Paul himself. In any case, these directives contradict the other purely egalitarian passages in the letters. However the controversy is resolved among experts, these guidelines on the role of women were nonetheless obviously accepted by church authorities. Even after 2,000 years, women are still excluded from public functions within the Catholic Church as a direct consequence of the letters of Paul. But it has nothing at all to do with Jesus' proclamation of the good news.

Christianity? Paulism!

Paul, like Jesus, had an apocalyptic vision, a vision that the world was coming to an end, or rather, that a new era was in preparation. This view was based on the conviction that God was not in control of everything on earth, that God had given in to the evil forces that caused all the suffering and misery on earth. But the apocalyptic view also implied that God would soon destroy these evil forces with the help of people who would carry out his plan of salvation. So there was much in common with Jesus' vision. But that's where the similarity ends. Paul was a Pharisee, and according to the New Testament, Jesus was at odds with that sect. Last but not least, Paul came from a different country and spoke a different language. He did not like what Jesus had preached. The stubborn adherence to the Jewish law in particular was a thorn in Paul's side. And it was precisely this adherence which carried major negative consequences for joining the new religion. According to Jewish law, men had to be circumcised, the Sabbath had to be respected, and the regulations concerning kosher food had to be observed.

Let me be very clear: what Paul proclaimed has nothing—absolutely nothing—to do with Jesus' message any longer. How could it be otherwise? Not only did he never talk to or meet Jesus, but he also demonstrated reluctance to mention anything from Jesus' message. Everything Paul claims is based solely on his own vision, his own subjective experience. Only the image of the crucified and risen Christ has a place in this vision, not the living Jesus and what he preached, not even marginally. One can rightly ask oneself here:

Was Jesus a Christian?

Epilogue

The *Donatio Constantini*

It is the 30th of March in the year 315. These are turbulent times. The former emperor, Diocletian (244-311), had carried out the bloodiest persecution of Christians. But two years later, thanks to Emperor Constantine (280-337), tolerance toward Christians suddenly prevails in the Roman Empire. The emperor has just been miraculously cured of leprosy by Pope Sylvester I (†335), who recommended immersion in holy water. The emperor is so grateful that he gets himself baptized, and entrusts the pope with a very special gift: power over his empire!

This gift will become known to the world as the *Donatio Constantini* (Constantine's donation). In other words, Christianity, through the pope, now rules not only over the spiritual life of the faithful, but also has full power over earthly matters, including politics. For almost 1,000 years, the *Donatio Constantini* document will codify this power of the popes over Christian Europe. And it will be referred to and made use of regularly. Pope Hadrian I (772-795), for instance, invokes it to admonish Charlemagne in 778 that it is about time for him to make a donation to the Church, in the same way as his father, Pepin the Short (715-768), had done for the Papal States in 756.

In about 300 years, Christianity had grown from a small sect of Jesus followers to a world power, in which the head of the Church, thanks to the *Donatio Constantini*, exercised totalitarian power over the souls and bodies of its subjects. Only—the gift of Constantine never existed! It was a forgery from the eighth century, or "fake news" as one would say nowadays. This forged document was at the center of the struggle between secular and ecclesiastical power, between emperor and pope for more than 700 years. Moreover, it led to the Great Schism within Christianity. In 1054, Pope Leo IX, in a dispute with Michael Caerularius, patriarch of Constantinople, referred to the document at length to claim his monopoly over Christianity, with the result, however, that the Eastern Church (today's Orthodox churches) separated from Rome. However, there were doubts about the authenticity of the document, and in any case it was the source of a centuries-long bloody feud between church and state.

The fact that people thought critically about the so-called donation can be read in Dante's *Divine Comedy*. In the 19th canto, the pilgrims Dante and his guide, Virgil, enter the part of hell where popes also suffer eternal punishment. Their crime is simony: spiritual values are sold for material gain—so named after Simon the Magician, as recounted in the Acts of the Apostles:

And when Simon saw that through laying on of the apostles' hands the Holy Ghost was given, he offered them money, saying, "Give me also this power, that on whomsoever I lay hands, he may receive the Holy Ghost." But Peter said unto him, "Thy money perish with thee, because thou hast thought that the gift of God may be purchased with money." (Acts 8:18-20)

Dante accuses Constantine of having introduced simony into Christianity through his "gift":

Ahi, Costantin, di quanto mal fu matre,
    O Constantine, of how much mischief the mother,
non la tua conversion, ma quella dote
    not so much your conversion, but that gift,
che da te prese il primo ricco patre!
    by which you created the first rich father (the Pope)!
(*Inferno*, Canto XIX, 115-117)

Dante probably did not know the contents of the document, but considered it reprehensible, because the emperor simply could not submit, for he was supreme: the Augustus. Equally importantly, Dante considered it the origin of all simony in the Church. Like many others, Dante wanted to return to the original Christianity, and saw the papacy and ecclesiastical leadership as the source of decline from the original spirit of Christianity, and ultimately of its destruction through the abuse of power.

However, it took until 1440 before the deception came to light. For the first time, Italian philologist Lorenzo Valla subjected the text to a linguistic analysis. His critical method showed that the document could not possibly have been written by a contemporary of Constantine. He proved this through a meticulous analysis of the language used. The document contains terms that refer to the medieval system of feudality—which did not exist at the time of Constantine. In fact, the document mentions Constantinople as Constantine's capital, but the city was not called that at the time (it was called Byzantium). Valla's historical-critical analysis laid the foundation for the scientific method that Erasmus was able to use for his first critical edition of the New Testament. A few years later, Valla also showed that the so-called correspondence between Seneca and Paul was similarly forged, and that it dated from the fifth century.

This was not, however, as one would expect, the end of the story. The pope at the time, then Pius II, immediately accepted Valla's rejection of the *Donatio Constantini* as a forgery, but declared that it did not entail any change to papal power. After Valla's death, his work was largely forgotten—until Martin Luther revisited Valla's rejection of the *Donatio Constantini* with the intention of reforming the Church. Thereafter, Valla's work was immediately placed on the *Index Librorum Prohibitorum* (Index of Forbidden Books). Granted, over the following centuries, the Church gradually reversed its position and accepted Valla's arguments. But again that took more than a hundred years.

The *Donatio Constantini* shows in an amazing way how the ecclesiastical authorities disregard their own maxim regarding the search for truth as one of the highest priorities for the faithful. For centuries, church authorities have been guilty of fraud, with the sole aim of enriching themselves and increasing their power. The work of Valla (and of philologists after him) laid the foundation for a search for rational, not religious, truth — as argued for in this book. The long string of forgeries is all the worse, because the "good news" of the Gospels emphasizes reciprocity. One expects the same degree of honesty and openness from ecclesiastical authorities that they demand from their subjects, as is found in the Gospels: "And as ye would that men should do to you, do ye also to them likewise" (Luke 6:31).

Finally, Valla's discovery sheds light on individual responsibility. Neither those in power, nor tradition, should be the basis for one's actions, but rather one's own critical senses. No one has argued the relevance of this issue more passionately than Rens Bod. His 2013 book *A New History of the Humanities* is a crystal-clear argument affirming the value of the humanities, especially philology, to society as a whole. The book you have just read places itself in this humanistic tradition. It is intended to encourage the reader to think critically about the roots of our culture, as contained in the New Testament (and other fundamental texts), against mystifications and conspiracy theories, with respect for the valuable contribution that the humanities have made in shaping our society.

Of course, it is possible to shrug and wonder, what is it to me? Within a generation, the Christian world has turned itself into a materialistic society without much concern for its own history. But as was argued in the introduction to this book, the fascination with this faith and its founders has not disappeared. We may forget, but the bedrock on which Christianity grounded our culture will not disappear. However, without solid historical-critical knowledge one remains at the mercy of mystifications that have survived some 2,000 years, of fallacy and folklore, the refusal to fathom where we come from, and what happened on the way to the present. Those who indulge in present-day ignorance are easy prey for cynicism, conspiracy theories, despair—and an uprooted existence.

My book has placed Jesus' apocalyptic teachings in the context of his time, exposing ambiguities, inaccuracies, and even forgeries. Without this independent historical approach, the story is indeed "unbelievable." So keep believing—in criticism!

Appendix

The Case of Galileo: Religion and Science

Church leadership does not seem to keep up with the times. For example, in 1633 Galileo Galilei had to renounce his theories by order of the Inquisition (after threats of torture and burning at the stake). What were these theories about? Surprisingly, about things that no one has any doubt about today, namely that the earth revolves around the sun and not the sun around the earth and, moreover, that it rotates on its own axis, creating the optical illusion that the sun revolves around the earth. This was impossible, according to the Catholic Church, because the Bible clearly states the opposite. The issue, then, was the contrast between the geocentric and heliocentric worldviews. The former assumes that the earth is the center of the solar system, and the sun and the planets orbit the earth. The heliocentric worldview, which Galileo elaborated (following the Polish scholar Copernicus), demonstrated that the earth and the other planets orbit the sun, as we believe today and of which we are absolutely certain. But in Galileo's time, this was a major bone of contention. In this regard, the church authorities started from several biblical passages. Here are the most important ones:

- The sun also riseth, and the sun goeth down, and hasteth to his place where he arose. (Ecclesiastes 1:5)
- The world also is stablished, that it cannot be moved. (Psalm 93:1)
- Who laid the foundations of the earth, that it should not be removed for ever. (Psalm 104:5)
- The world also shall be stable, that it be not moved. (Chronicles 16:30)

The Church leadership considered all these passages as confirmation of the geocentric worldview. Curiously, they did not think to look at other passages that challenged this certainty, such as in the Book of Job:

- He (God) stretches out the north over the empty place, and hangeth the earth upon nothing. (Job 26:7)

But there was an even stronger argument for the ecclesiastical view. The Book of Joshua in the Old Testament tells how the Israelites clashed with their enemies. And in order to be able to kill them all, Joshua, the captain of the Israelites, prayed to God to make the sun stand still, so that it would not be dark and the enemies would not be able to escape. The text literally says:

And the sun stood still, and the moon stayed, until the people had avenged themselves upon their enemies. (…) So the sun stood still in the midst of heaven, and hasted not to go down a whole day.
(Joshua 10:13)

If God made the sun stand still, the Church argued, then this is clear evidence that the sun revolves around the earth and not vice versa, as Galileo claimed (based on minute observations). It is striking that all the Church's arguments come from the Old Testament, while Christianity actually relies exclusively on the New Testament. And in the whole New Testament, the question of the solar system is not mentioned anywhere. It can already be seen here that Christianity is indeed a hybrid religion, a mixture of Jewish religion with elements from the teachings of Jesus and the teachings of Paul.

For reasons of self-preservation, Galileo renounced his theories. Nevertheless, he was placed under house arrest for life, and his books were placed on the Index of Forbidden

Books. Believers were not allowed to read the books on this list under threat of eternal damnation in hell. The scientific work of Galileo remained on this list of forbidden books, even hundreds of years after there had been a complete consensus within the scientific community about the correctness of Galileo's theory. It was not until October 31, 1992 that the Vatican admitted its error, 359 years later! Will the Vatican accept the results of the critical scholarly research about the New Testament in 359 years? That will be then in the year 2378.

References

Adair, Aaron. *The Star of Bethlehem. A Skeptical View.* Jonathan M.S. Pearce, 2013.

Archer, Jeffrey (with Francis J. Moloney). *The Gospel According to Judas.* New York: St. Martin's Press, 2007. (In cooperation with *National Geographic.*)

Aristotle. *The Complete Works of Aristotle.* Vol II. Ed. Jonathan Barnes. Princeton, NJ: Princeton University Press, 1984.

Aslan, Reza. *Zealot. The Life and Times of Jesus of Nazareth.* London: The Westbourne Press, 2013.

Aune, David E. *The Blackwell Companion to the New Testament.* Wiley-Blackwell, 2010.

Bankl, Hans. *Woran sie wirklich starben. Krankheiten und Tod historischer Persönlichkeiten* (What they really died of. Diseases and death of historical figures). Wenen: Verlag Wilhelm Maudrich, 1989.

Bartlett, F.C. *Remembering. A Study in Experimental and Social Psychology.* Cambridge: Cambridge University Press, 1932 (reprinted 1995).

Ben-Yehuda, Nachman. *The Masada Myth: Collective Memory and Mythmaking in Israel.* Madison: University of Wisconsin Press, 1995.

Berlina, Alexandra. *Viktor Shklovsky. A Reader.* London: Bloomsbury, 2017.

Bod, Rens. *A New History of the Humanities.* Oxford University Press, 2013.

Branham, R.B. & M.-O. Goulet-Cazé. *The Cynics.* Berkeley: University of California Press, 1996.

Brontë, Charlotte. *Jane Eyre.* London: Wordsworth Editions, 1992 (orig. ed. 1847).

Brown, Dan. *The Da Vinci Code.* New York: Anchor Books, 2009.

Carrier, Richard. *Proving History: Bayes's Theorem and the Quest for the Historical Jesus*. Amherst, NY: Prometheus Books, 2012.

Chabris, Christopher & Daniel Simons. *The Invisible Gorilla and Other Ways Our Intuition Deceives Us*. London: Harper, 2010.

Chaniotis, Angelos. *Age of Conquests. The Greek World from Alexander to Hadrian (336 BC – AD 138)*. London: Profile Books, 2018.

Cohen, Paul A. *History and Popular Memory: The Power of Story in Moments of Crisis*. New York, NY: Columbia University Press, 2014.

Crombag, Hans. *Hervonden herinneringen en andere misverstanden* (Resurrected memories and other misunderstandings). Amsterdam: Contact, 1996.

Crossan, John Dominic. *The Historical Jesus: The Life of a Mediterranean Jewish Peasant*. San Francisco, CA: HarperSanFrancisco, 1994.

Crossan, John Dominic. *Jesus. A Revolutionary Biography*. San Francisco: HarperCollins, 1995.

Crossan, John Dominic and Jonathan L. Reed. *In Search of Paul: How Jesus's Apostle Opposed Rome's Empire with God's Kingdom*. San Francisco, CA: HarperSanFrancisco, 2004.

Darnton, Robert. *The Forbidden Best-Sellers of Pre-Revolutionary France*. New York: Norton, 1996.

Deschner, Karlheinz. *Kriminalgeschichte des Christentums* (Christianity's Criminal History). 10 vols. Reinbek: Rowohlt, 1986-2013.

Diogenes Laërtius. *Lives of the Eminent Philosophers*. Vol. II. Trans. R.D. Hicks. Cambridge, MA: Harvard University Press, 1991 (orig. ed. 1925).

Doherty, Earl. *Jesus: Neither God nor Man – The Case for a Mythical Jesus*. Ottawa: Age of Reason Publications, 2009.

Durant, Will. *Caesar and Christ*. New York: Simon & Schuster, 1944.

Durrell, Lawrence. *The Alexandra Quartet*. London: Faber & Faber, 1957-1960.

Eakin, Emily. So God's Really in the Details? *The New York Times*, May 11, 2002.

Edwards, W.D., W.J. Gabel and F.E. Hosmer. On the Physical Death of Jesus Christ. *Journal of the American Medical Association* 255 (11), 1986, pp. 1455-1463.

Ehrman, Bart D. *Lost Scriptures. Books that did not make it into the New Testament.* Oxford: Oxford University Press, 2003.

—. *Lost Christianities. The Battles for Scripture and the Faiths We Never Knew.* Oxford: Oxford University Press, 2005.

—. *The Lost Gospel of Judas Iscariot: And a New Look at Betrayer and Betrayed.* Oxford: Oxford University Press, 2006.

—. *Jesus, Interrupted. Revealing the Hidden Contradictions in the Bible (and why we don't know about them).* New York: HarperCollins, 2010.

—. *Forged: Writing in the Name of God – Why the Bible's Authors Are Not Who We Think They Are.* New York: Harper, 2011.

—. *Did Jesus Exist? The Historical Argument for Jesus of Nazareth.* New York: Harper, 2012.

—. *How Jesus Became God: The Exaltation of a Jewish Preacher from Galilee.* New York: HarperCollins, 2014.

—. *Jesus Before the Gospels: How the Earliest Christians Remembered, Changed, and Invented Their Stories of the Savior.* New York: HarperCollins, 2016.

—. *The Triumph of Christianity: How a Forbidden Religion Swept the World.* London: Oneworld Publications, 2018.

Ehrman, Bart D. and Zlatko Plese. *The Apocryphal Gospels: Texts and Translations.* Oxford: Oxford University Press, 2011.

Eisenman, Robert. *James the Brother of Jesus: The Key to Unlocking the Secrets of Early Christianity and the Dead Sea Scrolls.* New York: Viking Penguin, 1997.

Elias, Norbert. *The Civilizing Process. Sociogenetic and Psychogenetic Investigations.* Oxford: Blackwell, 2000 (orig. ed. 1939).

Elliott, J.K. *The Apocryphal New Testament.* New York: Oxford

University Press, 1993.

Festinger, L. *et al. When Prophecy Fails: A Social and Psychological Study of a Modern Group that Predicted the Destruction of the World*. University of Minnesota Press, 1956 (reprinted 2009).

Festinger, L. *A Theory of Cognitive Dissonance*. California: Stanford University Press, 1957.

Finnegan, Ruth. *Oral Poetry: Its Nature, Significance and Social Context*. Bloomington, IN: Indiana University Press, 1992.

Flavius Josephus. *The Jewish War*. Oxford: Oxford University Press, 2017.

Funk, Robert W. *The Poetics of Biblical Narrative*. Sonoma: Polebridge Press, 1988.

Gadamer, Hans-Georg. *Truth and Method*. London: Bloomsbury Academic, 2013 (orig. ed. 1960).

George, L. *Crimes of Perception: An Encyclopedia of Heresies and Heretics*. New York: Paragon House, 1995.

Goode, William J. *World Revolution and Family Patterns*. New York: Free Press, 1963.

Goody, Jack. *The Domestication of the Savage Mind*. Cambridge: Cambridge University Press, 1977.

Grant, Michael. *Jesus: An Historian's Review of the Gospels*. London: Rigel Publications, 2004.

Halbwachs, Maurice. *La mémoire collective* (Collective Memory). Paris: Presses Universitaires de France, 1950.

Harber, Kent D. and Dov J. Cohen. The Emotional Broadcaster Theory of Social Sharing. *Journal of Language and Social Psychology*, 2005. Doi: https://doi. org/10.1177/0261927X05281426

Havelock, Eric. *The Muse Learns to Write: Reflections on Orality and Literacy from Antiquity to the Present*. Yale University Press, 1988.

Heilen, Stephan. The Star of Bethlehem and Greco-Roman Astrology, Especially Astrological Geography, in: Peter D. Barthel and George H. van Kooten (eds.), *The Star of Bethlehem and the Magi. Interdisciplinary Perspectives from Experts on* the Ancient Near East, the Greco-Roman World, and Modern Astronomy. Leiden: Brill, 2015, pp. 297-357.

Hezser, Catherine. Jewish Literacy in Roman Palestine. Tübingen: Mohr-Siebeck, 2001.

Hibbert, Christopher. The French Revolution. London: Penguin, 1980.

Hock, Ronald F. The Social Context of Paul's Ministry: Tentmaking and Apostleship. Philadelphia: Fortress Press, 1980.

Hofstede, Geert. Culture's Consequences: Comparing Values, Behaviors, Institutions, and Organizations Across Nations. London: Sage Publications, 2003.

Hughes, David. The Star of Bethlehem: An Astronomer's Confirmation. Walker & Co., 1979.

Hume, David. An Inquiry Concerning Human Understanding. Oxford: Oxford University Press, 2008 (orig. ed. 1748).

Ibn-al-Muqaffa'. Kalilah and Dimnah: Fables of Virtue and Vice. New York: NYU Press, 2022.

Kant, Immanuel. Groundwork for the Metaphysics of Morals (Grundlegung zur Metaphysik der Sitten). Trans. and ed. Allen W. Wood. New Haven, CT: Yale University Press, 2002 (orig. ed. 1785).

Lord, Albert B. The Singer of Tales. Cambridge, MA: Harvard University Press, 1960 (reprinted 2019).

Lüdemann, Gerd. Paul: The Founder of Christianity. Amherst, NY: Prometheus Books, 2001.

Mack, Burton. The Lost Gospel. The Book of Q and Christian Origins. San Francisco: HarperCollins, 1993.

Mack, Burton. Who Wrote the New Testament? The Making of the Christian Myth. San Francisco: HarperCollins, 1995.

Maslen, Matthew and Piers D. Mitchell. Medical Theories on the Cause of Death in Crucifixion. Journal of the Royal Society of Medicine 99 (4), 2006, pp. 185-188.

Meier, John Paul. A Marginal Jew: Rethinking the Historical Jesus. New York: Doubleday, 1991 (3 vols).

Metzger, Bruce M. *The Canon of the New Testament: Its Origins, Development, and Significance.* Oxford: Clarendon Press, 1987.

Metzger, Bruce M. *A Textual Commentary on the Greek New Testament.* Peabody, MA: Hendrickson Publishers, 2005.

Mill, John Stuart. *On Liberty.* Harmondsworth: Penguin, 1981 (Ursprüngliche Ausgabe 1859).

Moltmann, Jürgen. *Der gekreuzigte Gott. Das Kreuz Christi als Grund und Kritik christlicher Theologie* (The crucified God. Christ's cross as basis and critique of Christian theology). Munich: Kaiser, 1972.

Nestle-Aland. *Novum Testamentum Graece.* Stuttgart: Deutsche Bibelgesellschaft, 2012.

Nikolajeva, Maria. *Aesthetic Approaches to Children's Literature. An Introduction.* The Scarecrow Press, 2005.

Nixey, Catherine. *The Darkening Age. The Christian Destruction of the Classical World.* London: Pan Books, 2017.

Nongbri, Brent. *God's Library: The Archaeology of the Earliest Christian Manuscripts.* New Haven, CT: Yale University Press, 2018.

Ong, Walter. *Orality and Literacy.* London: Routledge, 1982.

Opie, Iona and Peter Opie. *The Lore and Language of Schoolchildren.* Oxford: Oxford University Press, 1959.

Parry, Milman. *The Making of Homeric Verse. The Collected Papers of Milman Parry.* Oxford: Oxford University Press, 1988.

Peters, Edward. *Heresy and Authority in Medieval Europe.* University of Pennsylvania Press, 1980.

Price, Robert. *The Incredible Shrinking Son of Man.* Amherst, NY: Prometheus Books, 2003.

Pritchard, J.B. (Ed.). *Ancient Near Eastern Texts Relating to the Old Testament.* Princeton, NJ: Princeton University Press, 1950.

Qur'an. *The Study Quran: A new translation and Commentary.* Ed. Seyyed Hossein Nasr. New York: HarperCollins, 2015.

Repschinski, Boris. *Vier Bilder von Jesus. Die Evangelien – alt, doch aktuell* (Four Images of Jesus. The Gospels – old, but up to date). Würzburg: Echter, 2016.

Rodriguez, Rafael. *Oral Tradition and the New Testament (A Guide for the Perplexed)*. Bloomsbury Academic, 2013.

Rubin, David. *Memory in Oral Traditions: The Cognitive Psychology of Epic, Ballads, and Counting-out Rhymes*. Oxford: Oxford University Press, 1998.

Samuelsson, Gunnar. *Crucifixion in Antiquity: An Inquiry into the Background and Significance of the New Testament Terminology of Crucifixion*. Tübingen: Mohr Siebeck, 2013.

Saramago, José. *The Gospel According to Jesus Christ*. Vintage Classics, 1999.

Schaff, Philip. *The Didache: Teaching of the Twelve Apostles and the Epistle of Barnabas*. FV Editions, 2020.

Schröter, Jens. The Gospel of Mark. In Aune, 2010, pp. 272-295.

Skolnik, Fred. *Encyclopedia Judaica*. New York: Macmillan Reference USA, 2006.

Smallwood, E. Mary. *Legatio ad Gaium*. Leiden: Brill, 1961.

Spinoza, Benedictus. *Tractatus Theologico-Politicus*. Ed. Robert Willis. Andesite Press, 2015.

Stanzel, Franz. *Theorie des Erzählens* (Theory of Narrative). Stuttgart: UTB, 2008.

Tabor, James. *The Jesus Dynasty*. London: HarperCollins, 2006.

Tabor, James. *Paul and Jesus: How the Apostle Transformed Christianity*. New York: Simon and Schuster, 2012.

Thayer, Joseph & James Strong. *Thayer's Greek-English Lexicon of the New Testament: Coded with Strong's Concordance Numbers*. Hendrickson Publishers, 1995.

Theissen, Gerd and Annette Merz. *The Historical Jesus: A Comprehensive Guide*. Fortress Press, 1998.

Tóibín, Colm. The Testament of Mary. Harmondsworth: Penguin Books, 2012.

Tuson, Mark. *The Didache: A New Annotated Translation*. ISBN-13: 9798511036212.

Van Houten, Kees. *Bach en het getal* (Bach and numbers).

Zutphen: Walburg Pers, 1985.

Van Peer, Willie. The Measurement of Metre: Its Cognitive and Affective Functions. *Poetics* 19, 1990, 259-275.

Van Peer, Willie. Guest editor of the thematic issue on "foregrounding." *Language and Literature* 16, no. 2, 2007.

Van Peer, Willie. *Stylistics and Psychology. Investigations of Foregrounding*. London: Routledge, 2020.

Van Peer, Willie, Frank Hakemulder and Sonia Zyngier. *Scientific Methods for the Humanities*. Amsterdam/Philadelphia: John Benjamins, 2012.

Vansina, Jan M. *Oral Tradition as History*. Madison, WI: University of Wisconsin Press, 1985.

Wall, Barbara. *The Narrator's Voice. The Dilemma of Children's Fiction*. London: Palgrave Macmillan, 1990.

Wilson, James Q. *The Moral Sense*. New York: The Free Press, 1993.

Wright, N.T. *Paul: A Biography*. San Francisco: HarperOne, 2018.

Zerubavel, Yael. *Recovered Roots: Collective Memory and the Making of Israeli National Tradition*. Chicago, IL: University of Chicago Press, 1995.

Zugibe, Frederick T. *The Cross and the Shroud: A Medical Inquiry into the Crucifixion*. New York: Paragon House, 1988.

Zugibe, Frederick T. *The Crucifixion of Jesus: A Forensic Inquiry*. New York: M. Evans & Co., 2005.

ACADEMIC AND SPECIALIST

Iff Books publishes non-fiction. It aims to work with authors and titles
that augment our understanding of the human condition, society and
civilisation, and the world or universe in which we live.
If you have enjoyed this book, why not tell other readers by posting a
review on your preferred book site.
Recent bestsellers from Iff Books are:

Why Materialism Is Baloney
How true skeptics know there is no death and fathom answers
to life, the universe, and everything
Bernardo Kastrup
A hard-nosed, logical, and skeptic non-materialist metaphysics,
according to which the body is in mind, not mind in the body.
Paperback: 978-1-78279-362-5 ebook: 978-1-78279-361-8

The Fall
Steve Taylor
The Fall discusses human achievement versus the issues of war,
patriarchy and social inequality.
Paperback: 978-1-78535-804-3 ebook: 978-1-78535-805-0

Brief Peeks Beyond
Critical essays on metaphysics, neuroscience, free will,
skepticism and culture
Bernardo Kastrup
An incisive, original, compelling alternative to current mainstream
cultural views and assumptions.
Paperback: 978-1-78535-018-4 ebook: 978-1-78535-019-1

Framespotting
Changing how you look at things changes how
you see them
Laurence & Alison Matthews
A punchy, upbeat guide to framespotting. Spot deceptions and
hidden assumptions; swap growth for growing up. See and be free.
Paperback: 978-1-78279-689-3 ebook: 978-1-78279-822-4

Is There an Afterlife?
David Fontana
Is there an Afterlife? If so what is it like? How do Western ideas
of the afterlife compare with Eastern? David Fontana presents the
historical and contemporary evidence for survival of
physical death.
Paperback: 978-1-90381-690-5

Nothing Matters
a book about nothing
Ronald Green
Thinking about Nothing opens the world to everything by
illuminating new angles to old problems and stimulating new
ways of thinking.
Paperback: 978-1-84694-707-0 ebook: 978-1-78099-016-3

Panpsychism
The Philosophy of the Sensuous Cosmos
Peter Ells
Are free will and mind chimeras? This book, anti-materialistic but
respecting science, answers: No! Mind is foundational
to all existence.
Paperback: 978-1-84694-505-2 ebook: 978-1-78099-018-7

Punk Science
Inside the Mind of God
Manjir Samanta-Laughton
Many have experienced unexplainable phenomena; God, psychic
abilities, extraordinary healing and angelic encounters. Can
cutting-edge science actually explain phenomena
previously thought of as 'paranormal'?
Paperback: 978-1-90504-793-2

The Vagabond Spirit of Poetry
Edward Clarke
Spend time with the wisest poets of the modern age and of the
past, and let Edward Clarke remind you of the importance of
poetry in our industrialized world.
Paperback: 978-1-78279-370-0 ebook: 978-1-78279-369-4

Readers of ebooks can buy or view any of these bestsellers by
clicking on the live link in the title. Most titles are published in
paperback and as an ebook. Paperbacks are available in traditional
bookshops. Both print and ebook formats are available online.
Find more titles and sign up to our readers' newsletter at
http://www.johnhuntpublishing.com/non-fiction
Follow us on Facebook at
https://www.facebook.com/JHPNonFiction
and Twitter at https://twitter.com/JHPNonFiction